Teen-Centered Library Service

Recent titles in
Libraries Unlimited Professional Guides for Young Adult Librarians
C. Allen Nichols and Mary Anne Nichols, Series Editors

Classic Connections: Turning Teens on to Great Literature
Holly Koelling

Digital Inclusion, Teens, and Your Library: Exploring the Issues and Acting on Them
Lesley S. J. Farmer

Extreme Teens: Library Services to Nontraditional Young Adults
Sheila B. Anderson

A Passion for Print: Promoting Reading and Books to Teens
Kristine Mahood

The Teen-Centered Book Club: Readers into Leaders
Bonnie Kunzel and Constance Hardesty

Teen Programs with Punch: A Month-by-Month Guide
Valerie A. Ott

Serving Young Teens and 'Tweens
Sheila B. Anderson, Editor

The Guy-Friendly Teen Library: Serving Male Teens
Rollie Welch

Serving Urban Teens
Paula Brehm-Heeger

The Teen-Centered Writing Club: Bringing Teens and Words Together
Constance Hardesty

More Than MySpace: Teens, Librarians, and Social Networking
Robyn Lupa, Editor

Visual Media for Teens: Creating and Using a Teen-Centered Film Collection
Jane Halsall and R. William Edminster

TEEN-CENTERED LIBRARY SERVICE

❖ ❖ ❖

Putting Youth Participation into Practice

DIANE P. TUCCILLO

Libraries Unlimited Professional Guides for Young Adult Librarians
C. Allen Nichols and Mary Anne Nichols, Series Editors

Libraries Unlimited

An Imprint of ABC-CLIO, LLC

A B C ☰ C L I O

Santa Barbara, California • Denver, Colorado • Oxford, England

Library of Congress Cataloging-in-Publication Data

Tuccillo, Diane P., 1952-
  Teen-centered library service : putting youth participation into
practice / Diane P. Tuccillo.
    p. cm. — (Libraries Unlimited professional guides for young
adult librarians)
  Includes bibliographical references and index.
  ISBN 978-1-59158-765-1 (pbk. : alk. paper) 1. Libraries and
teenagers—United States. 2. Young adults' libraries—Activity
programs—United States. 3. Teenage volunteer workers in
libraries—United States. 4. Student library assistants—United States.
5. Young adults' libraries—United States—Case studies. 6. School
libraries—United States—Case studies. I. Title.
  Z718.5.T84   2010
  027.62'6—dc22   2009045692

14 13 12 11 10   1 2 3 4 5

This book is also available on the World Wide Web as an eBook.
Visit www.abc-clio.com for details.

ABC-CLIO, LLC
130 Cremona Drive, P.O. Box 1911
Santa Barbara, California 93116-1911

This book is printed on acid-free paper ∞
Manufactured in the United States of America

Copyright Acknowledgments
The following are registered trademarks of Search Institute:
    Search Institute®
    Developmental Assets®

Dedicated to the memory of my dear friend, James Cook (1953–2005), an exemplary teen services librarian from the Dayton Metro Library in Ohio, who loved, respected, and valued teenagers and delighted in connecting them with books, reading, and libraries.

CONTENTS

LIST OF FIGURES

SERIES FOREWORD

We firmly believe that teens should be provided equal access to library services, and that those services should be equal to those offered to other library customers. This series supports that belief. That is why we are so excited about *Teen-Centered Library Service.* Remembering that our focus should be on the teens, not on ourselves or our colleagues, is the most important aspect of what we do. If we lose sight of those teens, they will lose sight of us.

We are proud of our association with Libraries Unlimited, which continues to prove itself the premier publisher of books to help library staff serve teens. This series has succeeded because our authors know the needs of those library employees who work with young adults. Without exception, they have written useful and practical handbooks for library staff. In this volume, Diane Tuccillo adds her name to that list.

We hope you find this book, as well as our entire series, informative, providing you with valuable ideas as you serve teens, and that this work will further inspire you to do great things to make teens welcome in your library. If you have an idea for a title that could be added to our series or would like to submit a book proposal, please e-mail us at lu-books@lu.com. We'd love to hear from you.

Mary Anne Nichols
C. Allen Nichols

FOREWORD

In the first chapter of this book you will read about the swarming of New Jersey's Maplewood Memorial Library each afternoon by middle schoolers. After a while, library management recommended that closing the library's doors after school was out for the day was a prudent gesture that would prevent a potentially dangerous and out-of-control situation from occurring.

Fortunately for everyone involved, the community did *exactly* the right thing by *not* closing the library's doors to the young teens. Instead, they asked teens for input and offered an appealing variety of afterschool programs and activities that addressed the needs and interests of local teens, who simply needed something positive and relevant to do during the hours between school and dinner.

At one time I might have agreed that bolting the library's doors to keep unruly kids out made perfect sense. After all, the *real* taxpayers were being saved from having to mingle with teens who talk too much, move in packs, and can just be plain annoying. However, two events drastically changed the way I look at teens.

The first happened when I was living in Florida, a state that, in some locations, caters to retirees to the detriment of youth. Each year, as part of the summer teen recreation program, the county organized activities for teens, which had never before caused a ruckus. For one party, a beautiful city park on the shores of the Gulf of Mexico, surrounded by homes easily costing a couple of million dollars each, was chosen as the venue. The party was to be chaperoned and would end at 10:00 p.m. But the party never happened, because one individual living close by put a halt to the event on the grounds that it would disturb his sleep. It struck me at that time how unfair it was that one person, who could have worn a pair of earplugs for an hour or two—or gone to a movie—could deny teens this social event. I also remember feeling mildly annoyed that retirees would move into gated communities and immediately demand that any reminder of youth, such as basketball hoops, be taken down. However, at that time I did not speak up for teens. It would take another occurrence before I would be ready.

The second event that had a profound impact on me was the death of my son's girlfriend in 2001. Her death caused me to truly reflect and question my responsibility to advocate for all teens, especially those who had "issues" or were lost or overwhelmed by what was happening to them as a result of familial stress, divorce, and other problems that were largely out of their control.

A real "ah ha" moment came to me when I serendipitously encountered a fantastic body of research conducted by Dr. Emmy Werner and Ruth Smith that proved there is a quality called *resiliency* that protects at-risk children and teens (and even adults) from falling apart and losing ground in the face of life's difficulties.

Werner and Smith's Kauai Longitudinal Study followed a cohort of children born in 1955 for 40 years on the Hawaiian island of Kauai. They identified many protective factors that helped at-risk children and teens to overcome adversity and challenges, but a cluster of three factors stands out:

- above-average cognitive skills and a pleasing personality that causes others to respond favorably;

- affectionate and warm ties with adults who help the youth develop trust, autonomy, and initiative; and

- being able to rely on supportive organizations such as churches, youth groups, or schools.

Resilient children often remembered a supportive and encouraging teacher who made all the difference. Resilient children tended to read, to have hobbies and interests that their peers respected, and to volunteer to help others. When I read the results of this important research, it seemed to me that *librarians* were in the perfect place to promote resiliency. *We* promote reading. *We* are mentors, whether we realize it or not. *We* encourage hobbies and interests because we select books on these topics for patrons and develop related programming and activities.

We also provide teens with opportunities to develop social skills through involvement on the library's teen advisory board and other volunteer opportunities. It struck me that *we* could be vehicles to develop and nurture resiliency among teens. I realized that the library profession was not just about ordering books, cataloging, and keeping the shelves straight, but with teens in the mix, it was also about relationships.

Back in 2001, the concept of resiliency was not on the radar of most librarians. The need to create nurturing and resiliency-producing environments for this age group was often a hard sell for those librarians in need of their own strengthening as a result of slashed budgets, long working hours, and adult patrons who could be difficult at times. Almost a decade later, it is a whole new ball game regarding the proactive role of librarians to strengthen and promote resiliency in teens.

The Young Adult Library Services Association has especially promoted the concept that librarians who serve youth must understand and appreciate the uniqueness of teens. Both school and public librarians are embracing the concepts of resiliency and youth development. We are realizing the truth of the African proverb, "It takes a village to raise a child."

It is books such as this one that help librarians to go beyond the traditional to create libraries that work for and with teens. Besides the fact that it is just plain right to view ourselves as an important factor in teens' development, it is essential that libraries accept their community responsibility and accountability to our younger patrons. It is empowering to realize that we have a stake in America's future, as we in turn empower our teens.

Thank goodness I have found my voice. Whenever a door is cracked, I am more than willing to walk through the opening to share my message about our responsibility toward today's youth: That although our profession does a respectable job with children of storytime age, overall teens still do not get their fair share of library attention and resources. The way I see it, one day in the not-too-distant future, teens who have not been served well or have not had a say in the past will be old enough to vote "yea" or "nay" on library referendums for new buildings or budget increases. How can we count on teens, who grow up to be the adults of the future, to view their community libraries as deserving if their voice has been totally dismissed? By serving teens well and allowing them to be part of their libraries, we are ensuring a positive library future.

Another point is that a society is not built on its elders, but rather on its young people. It is a frightening possibility that the large number of baby boomers will use up their share of resources and more, thus leaving little for youth. We cannot allow adults to forget that a healthy America depends on empowering and positively developing our children and teenagers, not the older generations.

Through this book, the reader will learn about the programs and services that engage teens and will have them rushing to the library to participate in activities they enjoy. Librarians will be exposed to the foundational concepts for creating a teen-friendly library environment—resiliency, youth development, and youth participation. One of my favorite quotes is, "Like its politicians and its wars, society has the teenagers it deserves." If we "do not like" the teens we have, let us work together to produce the kind of teens we *do* want.

Diane Tuccillo's book shows librarians the way!

Dr. Jami L. Jones
East Carolina University
Greenville, North Carolina

ACKNOWLEDGMENTS

Any good work is the sum of its parts, and this book is no exception. Such an all-encompassing examination of youth participation in libraries would not be possible without the contributions of a wide variety of people working with teenagers in libraries today.

I offer my very special thanks to Lisa Bowen, Melanie Limbert-Callahan, Kathee Herbstreit, Gina Macaluso, Renée McGrath, Maureen Ambrosino, Kate DiPronio, Saleena Davidson, Tracey Briseño, Kimberly Paone, Alison O'Reilly, Rachel Wilson, Patrick Hughey, Jennifer Dillon, Denise Saia, Bob Nelson, Lindsey Dunn, Stephanie Robinson Borgman, Susan Chappell, Sally Roof, Lynn Bosso, Samantha Nicholson, Terry Domino, Tina Moschella, Lisa Elliott, Erin Schaarschmidt, Robyn Hammer-Clarey, Sandy Imperio, Martha Choate, Ernie Cox, Wendy Rowe, Kim Olson, Pat McCleary, Judy Macaluso, Eva Nottage, Jon Gilliom, Mary Ann Lewis, Joy Millam, Beth Gallaway, Nancy Devlin, Lisa Matte, Alleen Nilsen, Jane Folger, Sue-Ellen Jones, Liz Danforth, Giny McConathy, Lu Benke, Mary Moyer, Ariana De Leon, Joann Pompa, Valerie Nicholson, Kelly Johnson, and Spring Lea Henry for the e-mails, supporting documentation, teen quotes, and encouraging words that you sent me.

A special thanks to Jami Jones for writing her inspiring foreword on a subject near and dear to both our hearts.

Appreciation is extended to Kelly Hoppe, from Bowie High School, and the Bowie Unified School District in Texas, and to Barbara Sutton, from the San Diego County Library in California, for the use of their PowerPoint presentations.

I am grateful to Penny Markey, from the County of Los Angeles Public Library, for kindly allowing me to use and adapt the outline of teen participation models from *Teens: The Community Service Solution*.

Thanks to Jennifer Wharton, from the Matheson Memorial Library in Wisconsin, for her willingness to connect me to all the great PUBYAC listserv librarians who had shared information with her about teen participation ideas.

Special thanks to the current teens, and former library teens who are now adults, for sharing their insightful perspectives with me: Jenny Knatz, Nicole Nixen, Chelsea Cooper, Ashwini Dhokte, Lisa Yosevitz, Chirag Bansal, Tyler Rudolph, Samantha Salcedo, Kyle McCulley, Shaun Snead, Louisa Abiuso, Daniel Wozniak, Sarah Nagaratnam, Seetha Talluru, and Zachary Hillenbrand, plus the other teens who sent me heartfelt quotes that might not appear on these pages but whose words still inspired me as I wrote. Also, thanks to the teens in libraries everywhere who contribute their time, effort, and ideas to making libraries exciting and cool places to be for each other and for those people in, and sometimes even beyond, their communities.

Hats off to the ever-patient interlibrary loan staff at the Harmony Library branch of the Poudre River Public Library District in Fort Collins, Colorado, where I work, who secured every single one of the research materials I needed, obscure as some of those items might have been.

A huge thanks to my friend, author Victoria Hanley, who graciously read my chapters and gave me words of encouragement and extremely valuable feedback.

I can't even begin to say thank you to my wonderful husband, Mick, who was my computer guru and my confidante, and who good-naturedly tolerated way too many nights reading alone, watching cooking shows on television alone, or taking the dog for a walk alone while I worked away in my office.

I could not have done it without each and every one of you.

INTRODUCTION

It has been ten years since Elaine Meyers' groundbreaking *The Coolness Factor: Ten Libraries Listen to Youth* reported the results of the Readers Digest/Wallace initiative that studied positive youth development through libraries in conjunction with the Urban Libraries Council. In the article, teen feelings about their libraries being "not cool" were earnestly expressed and were taken to heart by the adults working with them. The solution, the teens said, was to ask them for their opinions and get them directly involved.[1]

Since that article was published, many libraries with little or no teen services have taken those admonitions to heart and changed their focus to make such services a priority. In addition, those libraries that were already providing teen services stepped up their efforts to improve them. An important element of this increased attention has been adding and building teen participatory opportunities on many levels in both school and public libraries.

But how do you begin these ventures if your library is moving forward with teen participation for the first time? How do you find and encourage the teens to participate and keep their activities relevant and engaging? What are the latest and the greatest workable ideas for getting teens involved? How do you empower teens to take leadership roles in their libraries and communities?

Surely you are asking yourself at least one or maybe all of these questions. In this book you will explore the current teen participation scene in both school and public libraries and find answers to these questions and more. My inspiration for sharing this information with you comes from a combination of my extensive personal experiences working with teens in libraries and traveling around the country giving workshops in libraries of all sizes.

After publishing my first book, *Library Teen Advisory Groups*, for Scarecrow Press in 2005, I began providing these workshops to teach library staff how to start, promote, expand, and develop teen advisory boards (TABs), an essential part of any strong teen services program. The workshops were called "A TAB Can Work for You, Too!" However, as the workshops progressed, I realized that many libraries were also looking for more generally all-encompassing teen participation ideas and opportunities, including and beyond TABs. To meet these needs, I developed a presentation called "Youth Participation in Your Library: Putting It into Practice." From these expanded workshops, the idea for this book was born.

The purpose of this book is to provide background and examples that will help you put effective youth participation into practice in *your* library. School and public librarians on the front lines working with teenagers will be the greatest beneficiaries of its information. However, library support staff and others who serve and work with teens in libraries in secondary ways will also discover helpful ideas and advice to get teens involved. In addition, managers and administrators will find much food for thought to assist them in making decisions and in providing support that encourages active teen contributions in their libraries.

In carefully organized chapters, you will find plenty to guide and hearten you, from the reasons we need to make teen participation in our libraries a priority, to examining historical perspectives on youth participation, to discovering successful and exciting ideas you can emulate. You will find a series of helpful examples from a wide variety of school and public libraries where active and diverse youth participation is already in gear. Samples of forms, flyers, and other materials are included so that you can adapt them to your library's needs. In addition, you'll find ways you can design, plan for, and evaluate your library's youth participation endeavors, plus useful resources for further help and information.

Perhaps best of all, this book offers a hearty dose of inspiration through careful research and through relevant individual experiences, quotes, and anecdotes shared by librarians and teens throughout the country, which illustrate points made and support the issues discussed. I hope all facets of this book increase your enthusiasm for actively incorporating teen contributions into your library picture.

Keep in mind as you are reading that truly effective teen services in libraries must grow, change, and evolve. As Kimberly Bolan aptly states about teen spaces in libraries (this also connects to the concept of employing youth participation): "Making libraries irresistible and integral to kids isn't impossible. It just takes some work…Start with an outline of your goals, and then gradually build a plan by doing your homework, seeking teen input, and getting buy-in from your administrators. . . . Dare to have a dream and make it happen."[2]

It is up to those of us who are on the front lines of library work with teens, in conjunction with other members of our library communities and our communities in general, to buy into the concept of youth involvement and sustain it with our policies and practices. It is important for us to guide teens and to value their input; listen to and act upon what they tell us; and learn about and try new methods that draw teens to books, reading, and libraries. When you encourage teens to become directly involved like this, you not only provide a way for them to connect with their libraries in the present, but you also help shape them into stronger, more self-assured adults who read and who will use and support their libraries in the future. This book makes a powerful case for why these things are so important and explains how to make them come to pass.

ENDNOTES

1. Meyers, Elaine. "The Coolness Factor: Ten Libraries Listen to Youth," *American Libraries* 30 (November 1999): 42–45.

2. Bolan, Kimberly. "Looks Like Teen Spirit: Libraries for Youth Are Changing—Thanks to Teen Input" *School Library Journal* 52 (November 1, 2006): 44.

1
❖ ❖ ❖

WHY TEEN LIBRARY PARTICIPATION IN THE FIRST PLACE?

Whether teens come from a challenging, low income background or are well-to-do yet shy and feel like outsiders, and every possible personal situation in-between, library participation can be a path to building self-esteem, channeling energy into positive outlets, and developing maturity. It can be a channel for teens to be resilient—to help overcome whatever odds they are facing and to build a stronger future from that foundation. All the while, they are likewise developing a deeper connection to books, reading, and their libraries.

If you are already in the trenches working with teens in libraries, the information in this chapter will reinforce what you may already know, enhance your interactions with teens, and give you some new ways of thinking about and advocating for them through your work. If you are an outsider looking in, perhaps a manager or administrator wondering why teen services is important at all, you will find good reasons here to lend your support and encourage youth participation to be part of your library picture.

UNDERSTANDING YOUTH AND THEIR ROLE IN THE COMMUNITY

First and foremost, how does effective library youth participation happen, and why? Let's start off by taking a look at teens.

Teens are at a very special stage in life, where they are not quite children and not yet adults. Hence, the seemingly contrary term "young adult" was coined to define them. For the most part, libraries aim their "teen" or "young adult" services at those in middle school or junior high through high school, or ages 12 to 18, give or take a year or two in either direction.

Adults who know and work with teenagers on a regular basis—teachers, parents, librarians, youth counselors, and others—may be very aware of the diverse characteristics of the dichotomous stage that occurs during this decade-long period of adolescence. However, knowing the elements exist and *understanding* the way they affect how teens grow and develop from childhood into adulthood may be two different things. *Understanding* is the vital component in knowing how to interact well with and inspire teens.

We've all heard the complaints from adults who say teens are troublesome; they are a bother; they want negative attention. Sometimes these complainers are our library colleagues. Often, adults like this, who say they "do not like" teens or are "afraid" of them (and there are many adults who feel this way!) simply lack understanding. They do not see the vital connection between how we meet the needs of teens in our communities and the behaviors we see exhibited by them.

Peter L. Benson and his colleagues from the Search Institute® did a 15-year study on how to mobilize public will, capacity, and commitment to encompass all young people in supportive, attentive, and caring communities to foster positive Developmental Assets®.[1] Some disquieting revelations from their research were that from birth to age 18, many youth do not have close associations with adults outside their own families, and that many spend considerable time each day without an adult present. They are not well known in their own neighborhoods and are ignored or unwelcome in public places, especially when in groups. They might find themselves targeted for well-meaning programs without any youth input, lacking safe places to congregate, and excluded from contributing to community efforts to address their needs.[2]

Considering these findings, which match the background details of many negative stories and situations we see regularly reflected in the media, it is not surprising that teens are often considered "troublemakers" or "nuisances" in our communities. Libraries are not immune to this thinking. However, there is no reason why libraries that view certain teen behaviors in a negative light cannot face the issue head on and turn it into a positive. Experience and research suggest that librarians can reverse negative behaviors and help teens make a successful journey from adolescence to adulthood by building trust, mutual understanding, and shared values among people and institutions.[3]

Turning Disquieting Revelations into Positives

One demonstration of turning a negative into a positive that made it into the news in 2007 was the situation at the Maplewood Memorial Library in New Jersey. When the Maplewood Middle School ended classes each weekday, some students came to the library nearby to study or read. However, other students would "fight, urinate on the bathroom floor, scrawl graffiti on the walls, talk back to librarians or refuse to leave when asked. One . . . threatened to burn down the branch library. Librarians call(ed) the police, sometimes twice a day."

The library reacted by declaring that its two buildings would close weekdays from 2:45 through 5:00 p.m. "until further notice." Its administrators and staff grew "frustrated by the middle schoolers' mix of pent-up energy, hormones and nascent independence" that seemed to be at the root of the problems.[4] This sounds like the "disquieting revelations" from the Search Institute research mentioned above, doesn't it?

Keep in mind that the situation in the Maplewood Memorial Library was and is not unique. Consider these other examples:

- An Ohio library banned those under age 14 if they were not accompanied by adults during afterschool hours.

- An Illinois library adopted a rule suspending library privileges for repeat offenders.

- Many libraries are adding security guards *specifically* for afterschool hours.

- A middle school in Louisiana that required daily permission slips for students to use the public library after school was threatened with a lawsuit by the American Civil Liberties Union.[5]

Benson notes that a solution to conflicts like these with young people rests on the shoulders of *all* a community's residents and institutions, not just families. They can comprise an effective foundation that supports, encourages, motivates, guides, and empowers young people through thousands of individual and group acts of caring and commitment. They are the ones who build relationships day by day that confirm to youth that they are known, valued, listened to, and connected.[6] The networks through which these bonds are made are called "social capital" by sociologists. Social capital is the glue that holds us together, and it shapes the way youth develop, view others in their communities, and relate to institutions—including libraries.[7]

As a fundamental part of social capital, libraries fill a special role as a valued community institution. They can make a difference and encourage positive change by helping teenagers take more ownership in the library. This is accomplished by getting them directly involved in library work and decision making and by creating an environment that is welcoming and affirming to young clients.[8]

With concepts like these in mind, Maplewood Memorial Library and its community embarked on solving its problem. Paul Kuehn, a Rutgers University alumnus, the director of Rutgers' Global Partnerships for Activism and Cross-Cultural Training (Global PACT), and a lifelong Maplewood resident, read the article about the library and its problems with the middle schoolers in *The New York Times.* He got in touch with Fred Profeta, Maplewood's mayor and a family friend, offered Global PACT's services, and brought a proposal to D. Michael Shafer, a Rutgers political science professor who founded Global PACT in 2002. Profeta responded: "We knew we were not reaching all the kids in our community and that some were falling between the cracks. We needed to figure out how to appeal to that missing group in order to engage them."[9]

Kuehn, Shafer, and Rutgers student-facilitators met in Maplewood with groups of about 50 middle and high school students and separately with adults, including parents, teachers, middle school and township officials, and local ministers. Participants described their community, identified its shortcomings, and talked about the lack of interesting, affordable afterschool activities. Global PACT reported its findings to the Maplewood Youth Task Force and *suggested after-school activities that the students could create and run themselves.*[10]

The italics indicate the importance in noting that youth participation was an ingredient in determining a solution. Allowing young adults to recommend and help run their activities empowers them and shows respect. It also ensures that they are going to have access to activities that really mean something to them, making acceptance and involvement more likely.

Inexpensive and timely ideas included increasing unstructured "hang out" opportunities for teens near the middle school, expanding high school peer-counseling services to middle school students, and developing local job and volunteer options for teens. A more ambitious future step would eventually establish a youth recreation center. Global PACT facilitators planned to return to Maplewood to train middle school staff and students in establishing and running their own activities, because Global PACT's aim is to provide community stakeholders and experts with the tools they need to make their community work better.[11]

The solution to the Maplewood delimma is exactly what Peter Benson and his Search Institute® colleagues advocated in their study and what many other experts who study adolescent behavior likewise encourage. Communities must come together to support their teens, in libraries as well as in other relevant organizations, facilities, institutions, and agencies.

THE TEENAGE BRAIN, FOSTERING RESILIENCY, AND POSITIVE YOUTH DEVELOPMENT

Clearly, it is vital for libraries to be connected to and considered an essential part of communities in working with and serving youth. We can't encourage teen involvement if we don't appreciate, empower, and respect young people. From a library perspective, we must aim to be sure that all adults who encounter teens in their library work, even indirectly, are aware of and understand the traits of adolescents and the important functions libraries can perform in their lives on a variety of levels. The more that library staff members comprehend adolescent developmental patterns and understand that we are part of the community foundation that supports and advocates for teens, the better they will be at successfully working with, guiding, and enjoying them rather than fearing or shying away from them. This is part of the idea behind the exciting teen summits to encourage youth and library staff input and involvement that you will learn about in chapter 8.

Hard-Wiring the Library Connection

In addition to discoveries about the ways teens are viewed and treated in our society, recent research into the workings of the adolescent brain have clarified and sometimes refuted past assumptions about the ways teens learn, grow, and perceive the world through the young adult years.

When we set out to enhance teens' library experiences to allow them personal appreciation of books, reading, and the library environment during this pivotal time, anticipating that such behavior will accompany them into adulthood, we are applying some of the basic concepts substantiated by this brain research.

On the Shoulders of the Whole Community: A Firsthand Look at the Maplewood Memorial Library Story

Prior to the threatened closing in 2007, the Maplewood Public Library had very active and well-attended teen programs and an enthusiastic 33-member teen advisory group. We also offered instant messaging reference service to teens and had good relationships with them. Unfortunately for the teens, we were the only free afterschool activity. They had nothing to do other than the programs we offered or to hang around town. Most of the parents in this community both work, so the kids needed some choices.

Fortunately, the library's protest catalyzed the rest of the community, after many years of trying to get their attention. A local church stepped in and offered an afterschool space, games, and snacks. Then the middle school contracted with an organization to open a free, afterschool program for middle schoolers. The Hub now offers games, snacks, sports, activities, and lots of room to really hang out. The library was given the funds to hire an afterschool security guard. She is great with teens and has developed good relationships with them, thus freeing up the staff to have more positive interactions with them. And the library never had to close its doors, for even a day.

Our mayor initiated a teen advisory board through a local organization called YouthNet. YouthNet, along with the library, is working hard to give the teens the opportunities for the recreation, letting off steam, being heard, job skills, and learning what they need and desire.

Despite the way the library was portrayed in the media, our staff members are youth-friendly and vigorously defend kids' rights to be here. It is just that when the number of kids gets to be so large, the library cannot function, no matter how good our intentions are. Most people in town avoided the library after school. For example, teens would knock over elderly patrons or small children in their haste to get in and out of the door, even though we always had a staff person at the door to meet, greet, and keep the peace. It was a situation that required the community to get together and come up with alternative solutions.

The library has also been trying to fund a new teen space—a space where they can be comfortable, have plenty of computers and video screens, and an adult mentor, our YA librarian, to help them. We are having trouble funding this, but hope it can still happen.

Our library staff members feel very deeply that teens need to be heard, that their needs are of primary importance, and that they deserve much more than they get. Perhaps seeing how we addressed this problem head-on will help other libraries see that the solution is to get teens engaged and involved.

I would like to add that of the many good things that arose from this difficult situation, the best thing was that we could finally hire a dedicated teen librarian. He has been able to spend time with the teens and has built great relationships with them, and you can see the exciting things that are going on in our library for teens by going to our Web site, www.maplewoodlibrary.org.teenprograms.html.[12]

Jane Folger
Youth Services Coordinator
Maplewood Memorial Library, New Jersey

Knowing more about why the concepts are valuable can strengthen and improve these efforts. It is essential for school and public librarians who work with teenagers to have at least a basic awareness of the current findings and to consider how to apply them to benefit their teen clientele. Luckily, there are many interesting and useful resources available to help us.

Barbara Strauch, the medical science and health editor at *The New York Times*, highlights some groundbreaking discoveries in her book, *The Primal Teen*: "The teenage brain, it's now becoming clear, is still very much a work in progress, a giant construction project. Millions of connections are being hooked up; millions more are swept away. Neurochemicals wash over the teenage brain, giving it a new paint job, a new look, a new chance at life. The teenage brain is raw, vulnerable. It's a brain that's still becoming what it will be."[13]

These immense transformations leave teens susceptible to negative influences while allowing them to be fertile ground for positive ones. Scientists have discovered that perceptions and behaviors that are reinforced during young adulthood become hard-wired into the brain as teens mature.[14] When positive, appealing elements are provided through library services for teens, a permanent connection to books, reading, and libraries will often accompany them into their later years.

Opportunities that allow teens to directly participate in and influence what happens in their libraries can develop an even stronger bond. This bond goes beyond books, reading, and enthusiastic library support. It reaches the hearts, minds, and personalities of the teenagers themselves, helping them to become upstanding and productive human beings, hard-wiring a connection that will be reflected in all facets of their lives. It is

Participation gives teens a feeling of ownership in their library, evidence of which I have seen at TAG meetings where the teens are involved in decorating and improving the library space. The time we spend together gives them a greater understanding of what a librarian does, which may pique career interest.[15]

Alison O'Reilly
Teen Services Librarian
Austin Public Library, Texas

exciting to realize that valuing reading and the library is an elemental part of the picture. Let's examine further how it happens.

The Value of Resiliency in Developing Positive-Minded Youth

One way both school and public libraries develop these values is by providing a special place where teens may experience *resiliency*. Resiliency is a concept based on the realization that some people are more able to sustain themselves in adverse conditions and situations than others. Its foundation is the highly regarded Kauai Longitudinal Research Study, mentioned in this book's foreword, which evaluated biological and psychological risk factors, stressful life events, and protective factors on all children born on the island of Kauai in 1955 from birth through maturity. The study revealed that the more positive internal and external factors the people possessed, the better able they were to surpass obstacles of adversity and successfully navigate adolescence to become resilient adults.[16]

This research is important because it demonstrates from another perspective how libraries can play a fundamental role in developing positive youth. Factors elemental to this role are reflected in the Library Ladder of Resiliency model, which illustrates how young people interact in achieving resiliency on "rungs" ranging from bottom to top.

The bottom rung, which serves as a foundation for the ladder, is mentoring and making connections. Like the supportive teachers who were instrumental presences in the lives of resilient children from the Kauai Study, school and public library administrators can build this rung by hiring well-trained media specialists, youth or teen librarians, or other appropriate library staff members who are talented in working with young people to serve their clientele. Simply having objective adults present who like teens, listen, and acknowledge their interests, and providing a special place to gather comfortably with other teens can get them engaged and enthusiastic about the library, reinforcing the strength of the rung.

The second rung is reading and its promotion. The Kauai Study reflects the fact that thriving adults are usually those who have developed effective reading skills. This makes sense when you consider that reading below grade level is often the precursor to a student dropping out of school. In addition, reading itself can be a way for teens to escape their cares and relax. It also allows them to develop an understanding and acceptance of their own problems and situations as well as those of their peers and others in their lives. Reading-oriented participation activities and access to carefully developed and maintained library collections for teens permit this reading "rung" to develop as a natural progression from the first rung.

Promoting decision-making and problem resolution skills by empowering teens and encouraging library involvement constitutes the third rung. Librarians can be instrumental in ensuring that opportunities to hone these skills are available. These opportunities may come in all shapes and forms, such as advisory groups, serving on library boards, or contributing to focus groups. The key is for librarians to guide teens while providing them with information and ideas as a starting point, allowing them to come up with feedback and solutions that are taken seriously and are put to good use.

Reaching the fourth rung of the ladder, we find ourselves at the one that encourages social skills. Teens are incredibly social beings who prize positive relationships, especially friendships. When teens interact socially not only with their adult advisor but also with other teens who have a like-minded affinity for books, reading, and libraries, they can develop a new social network that boosts their self-esteem and develops resiliency. Directly participating in library planning, programs, activities, and events with these fellow teens as a cohesive group enhances the stability of this rung.

The fifth rung is developing hobbies and interests. Libraries may serve as a resource for learning a variety of appealing pastimes while allowing teens to share their special interests with others. At our last teen advisory board meeting, the teen members discussed programs they want to plan and offer to their peers over the coming year. Ideas ranged from a macramé workshop to making decorated personal journals to a poetry slam to a Halloween costume contest, and more. After a creative writing program held this year, one of our rather quiet and shy teens told me that he came to the program because his friends were going, and that he was glad he went. He had no idea he liked to write creatively, as science and math were his main focus, and the program opened his eyes to a new personal dimension. Such opportunities to learn about and explore new hobbies and interests through library participation effectively top out the Library Ladder of Resiliency (see figure 1.1).[17]

TRAITS OF TEENAGERS, YESTERDAY AND TODAY

Understanding the traits of teenagers can help you directly tie in to positive, resiliency-enhancing behaviors that will benefit teens and your library, now and in the future. This section examines these traits and how they apply to the Library Ladder of Resiliency.

Amelia Munson, one of the pioneering young adult librarians at the New York Public Library during the first half of the twentieth century, was a visionary who understood and appreciated these traits. She knew and respected teens and advocated for them to have a place and a say in their libraries. In her book, *An Ample Field*, which was published in 1950, she encouraged other librarians to do the same and aptly described the five prominent traits of adolescents that clarified their social and emotional behaviors.[18] Readers of her book cannot help but be impressed by her foresight, wisdom, and the universal appeal of her advice.

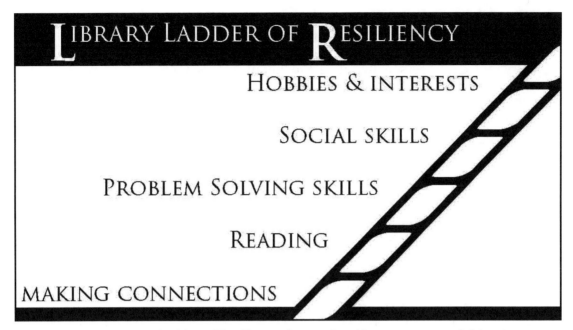

Figure 1.1. Library Ladder of Resiliency. *Source:* **Jami Jones at www.askdrjami.org; reprinted by permission of the author.**

As you take notice of these traits, think about the teens you know and work with in your library or in other parts of your community. You will see that the traits are evident in today's young adults, just as they were in adolescents in the past, emerging in the preteen years and still apparent in many younger college students. Though the importance and exhibition of the traits fluctuates as teenagers mature, basically they are

- awareness of one's self,

- uncertainty,

- hero worship,

- clannishness, and

- audacity of belief.

Librarians on the front lines of youth services, and others who work with and support teens in libraries, may benefit by realizing how these common traits can usher teens in a constructive direction up the Library Ladder of Resiliency through library-oriented youth participation projects that are created by and for them. Following are explanations of the traits and some ways we can specifically connect them to the youth participation experience. Concrete examples illustrate how each trait coincides with today's world of library youth participation and how the concept of resiliency may be enhanced.

Awareness of One's Self

As teens become conscious of themselves as individuals, with their own beliefs and viewpoints, their need for outlets of discussion and opportunities for self-expression becomes strong. With guidance from an understanding librarian, library youth participation can serve as a channel for these needs by allowing teens to create, plan, and run projects and events; encouraging them to take part in writing, book discussions, book reviewing, and other activities that promote communication and sharing personal thoughts; and requesting teen feedback, ideas, and opinions that are not just given lip service but are heeded. Most important, this guidance can bring books and reading to the forefront of their attention.

One of the vital results of developing one's identity in a library setting is that it affords an opportunity for teens to personally connect to literature. When teens have a vested interest in the written word, realizing that it holds a wealth of information and entertainment for them because they *want* to experience those things, not just because they "have to," it is quite an empowering personal discovery. They see that they, as individuals, can not only enjoy and absorb all that books have to offer, but can also share their thoughts and feelings about what they have read with their peers. They realize that their connection to literature is not limited to reading books, but is expanded to include discussing, sharing, and writing about them. Addressing the teen trait of awareness of oneself through library and literature involvement may solidify this positive behavior in the future and place teens firmly on all five of the resiliency ladder rungs.

Awareness of Oneself: Nicole's Story

Nicole was a member of the Young Adult Advisory Council (YAAC) at the City of Mesa Library in Arizona as a junior and senior in high school. She definitely found it a highlight of her teenage years, because participation deepened her appreciation for books, exposed her to new genres, and socialized the activity of reading.

As an only child, Nicole usually had to entertain herself when she was younger, and she found endless hours of entertainment through reading. However, as a teenager, reading began to fall by the wayside as she spent more time on other leisure activities such as listening to music and watching television. Although she often visited the library, it was to check out books for school projects. She began to develop the attitude that she read enough during the day for school activities and that her brain "needed a rest" from reading after school.

One day, something changed. During one of her routine visits to the library for school research, she happened to see a stack of papers sitting on a counter, which turned out to be the teen-produced *Open Shelf* newsletter. She began to read its book reviews. As she was reading them, she remembered why she had read so much in the past. Some of the stories described in the reviews sounded incredible.

Nicole immediately began looking for a few good pleasure-reading titles. For the next few weeks, she checked out more and more books for leisure. The more she read, the more she wanted to discuss some of those novels with her friends. However, conversations revolving around reading did not last very long, as her friends were more interested in discussing music and television. Nicole recognized that the reason she had not been reading very much was its lack of importance to her peers. As much as she enjoyed reading, she also now knew that she wanted to share this activity with others. She looked at the copy of *Open Shelf* she had picked up and realized that the reviews in it were written by other teens who were members of YAAC. She immediately knew this was something she wanted to join.

In YAAC, Nicole found a place where she could express her thoughts about the books she was reading. Although reading is often viewed as a solitary activity, for Nicole, YAAC turned reading into a social activity. It allowed her to share her love of reading with peers she would have never met. She met people from other schools and was exposed to a variety of authors and genres that she would not have read. She said that often, the best book discussions took place *after* the YAAC meetings, as many of the teen members would began their searches for a fresh round of books by seeking advice from one other.

Nicole found herself regularly contributing to the *Open Shelf* newsletter, the centerpiece of YAAC. During meetings, all the teens would enthusiastically relay information about their latest reads, and frequently discussions of one book would lead to discussions of other authors or topics. Every meeting exuded positive energy generated from finding a gem in the sea of books in the library or from critically evaluating a plot that could have been written better. *Open Shelf* allowed the teens to take the energy generated during the meetings and share it with teens all over their city. Some books were so good that Nicole said, "You just felt like running up to people to tell them to read them."

Other times, the teens came across books that they felt they needed to warn people to avoid. *Open Shelf* captured teens' passion for reading by allowing them to voice their appreciation for incredible books and their disappointment over not so stellar ones.

Nicole said that *Open Shelf* was responsible for renewing her interest in reading as a teen and that it sparked interest among some of her friends at school. Although none of her friends ever joined YAAC, they did begin reading *Open Shelf* after she showed them the reviews she had written. Over the two years that she was a member of YAAC, she noticed that some of her friends were reading more often. One even began coming to school early and reading novels until the school day began. Another friend asked her for suggestions because she realized that reading relaxed her. In turn, her friends were eager to discuss the novels they experienced.

When she started college, Nicole didn't have as much time for pleasure reading as before, but she tried to read as much as possible. She met other people who love reading as much as she does and has enjoyed many conversations about books. "I can honestly say that my involvement in YAAC as a teenager is responsible for my continued appreciation of reading as an adult. By turning my leisure reading into a social activity, YAAC instilled a sense of entertainment as well as critical thought into reading. The only regret I have about joining YAAC is that I did not join sooner!"[19]

Uncertainty

While teens are in that place between childhood and adulthood, they often feel torn between the two. It is a confusing and sometimes overwhelming stage. As David Walsh says in his exposé on adolescent behavior, "The transition from childhood to maturity is nothing short of a metamorphosis. Just as a caterpillar becomes a butterfly by living for a while cramped in a cocoon, kids must go through the awkwardness of adolescence to become fully grown up."[21]

Teen participation is incredibly beneficial to the teens, both those who participate and those who don't. The teens who participate get practice in brainstorming in a meeting setting. They routinely interact with me, my boss, and other adults who are involved in programs that we present. They get experience in the steps in planning something. They get to experience having their opinion valued and heard and I believe it makes them more aware of the power of their beliefs and opinions. They get to see the difference that they make to children, other teens, and in the community.[20]

Tracy Briseño
Library Assistant—Teen and Youth Services
Ames Public Library, Iowa

It is uncertainty that produces the "effect" of aloofness and obnoxiousness that teens might exhibit at times, and which frightens many adults in libraries and other settings. As Amelia Munson pointed out about teen behavior almost six decades ago, and still an appropriate observation, "Don't think young people today are not uncertain; that cocksure manner of theirs is only an attempt at concealment of insecurity, but it is an easily pierced defense."[22]

As discussed previously, when teens "act out" due to insecurity, restlessness, disrespect, or discomfort, often adults, in libraries and elsewhere, respond by creating reactionary rules to squelch the behavior and keep teens at bay. Special parameters may be set regarding where, when, and how teens may access the library. Situations like that which occurred at the Maplewood Memorial Library come to mind. Instead of welcoming them, teens might be discouraged from using the library at all, or only be allowed to use it on a limited basis. Encouraging teen participation might be the last thing considered in library settings where teens are a "problem." However, as those in Maplewood discovered, the trick is that *incorporating opportunities where teens can feel like they belong and can take part in the library is likely the most effective solution.*

In order for this to happen, librarians must gain knowledge of adolescence and learn ways to make the library inviting rather than discouraging. This starts with a combination of library administrators and managers supporting, funding, and advocating for solid teen library services, while ensuring skilled teen service specialists are hired in their library settings. As mentioned previously, you will see in chapter 8 that many libraries today are doing just that by providing "teen summits," "teen forums," and "teen workshops" to address the issues surrounding positive teen involvement and to inform library staff about teen wants, needs, and interests.

Teen specialists who know how to pleasantly address the trait of uncertainty and channel it for positive youth behavior and development are crucial. They help teens feel comfortable by showing that they respect and enjoy "both sides" of young people and are the most successful in attracting teens to the library and getting them to take part in youth participation endeavors. When teenagers work with adults who truly like them despite their "uncertain" demeanor, their defenses come down, they can "be themselves," and they can readily and comfortably participate.

As the Library Ladder of Resiliency reflects, the first or bottom rung, "mentoring and making connections," is the essential support for the remaining rungs, and accommodating this trait of uncertainty can initiate and develop comfortable connections between adults and teens. Librarians who openly accept the aspects of childhood still evident in teens, balanced with acknowledgment of the budding maturity they are experiencing, get the best results and create the strongest bonds with them.

Beyond Uncertainty: The Pima County Public Library Story

In 2007, the Young Adult Library Service Association's Sagebrush Award (www.ala.org/ala/yalsa/awardsandgrants/sagebrush.pdf), presented for an outstanding reading or literature program for young adults, was given to Joanna Peled at the Valencia Branch of the Tucson-Pima County Library in Arizona, now the Pima County Public Library. Peled won the honor for a project called "That's My Take."

The inspiration for "That's My Take" came when a group of lively teens needed a way to channel their energy in the library. Instead of telling them to leave, Peled challenged them with a peer reader advisory project. It grew from short written descriptions of their favorite books into a cooperative film project among the library, television station Tucson 12—the City Channel, and the Metropolitan Education Commission's Youth Advisory Council/Tucson Teen Congress. Six video trailers of contemporary and classic titles were produced, in both English and Spanish. Participating teens chose the books, wrote the scripts, created the storyboards, and performed.

The teens who participated in the original project developed higher self-esteem and self-confidence, learned work skills, and helped to reach fellow teens throughout the community with the message that books and reading can be fun. In addition, teens from around the country can view the dramatic book videos online, and some teens are even duplicating the project in their own libraries.[23]

To get more details about the project and to see the videos, check the library's Teen Zone Web site at www.library.pima.gov/teenzone/trailers. Learn more about creating teen book review podcasts and "book videos" in chapter 6.

Hero Worship

Teens involved in library youth participation projects in libraries, especially those who are part of teen library advisory boards, are usually readers who often discover author heroes in addition to the favorite movie, television, and musical stars with whom they identify. The intensity with which teens react to published authors can be just as exciting and memorable as their responses to a sports celebrity or the members of a popular rock band.

Last summer I attended a Stephenie Meyer author talk and book signing with a group of teens. Although I knew of Meyer's overwhelming popularity due to her series of vampire books, I was amazed to see over 500 teens packed into a high school auditorium in their free time, jumping to their feet while enthusiastically cheering and applauding Meyer's arrival on stage. This was teen hero worship at its prime, but not for a rock or movie star. It was for a "book star." If J. K. Rowling or Christopher Paolini made public appearances like this, many teens would also be exuberant about meeting their author heroes.

I have also seen stars in teen eyes when they have had the opportunity to see talented, popular, but less famous authors in their midst. When we took nine of our teen advisory group members to the annual Colorado Teen Literature Conference, every teen was excitedly anticipating going back to the library and checking out books by the authors he or she had met. The teens said they were looking forward to next year's conference already so they could meet new authors. Providing opportunities for teens to come in personal contact with the authors of the books they see on the library shelves and in bookstores through their library participation can truly nurture this trait of hero worship while promoting the value and excitement of reading.

In addition, consider this: There is another kind of hero worship librarians often underplay. Teens often look up to and admire their librarian advisors as objective adults who appreciate them, listen to them, have fun with them, share their interests, and encourage them to grow. The best advisors for library youth participation are those who understand teens, enjoy them, and encourage them to experience books, reading, and their libraries in ways with which individual teens connect best.

As Amelia Munson noted, various kinds of teen hero worship are important during adolescence as teenagers seek independence, laying the foundation for a future closer relationship with parents and other family members during adulthood. Librarians can play a vital role in nurturing this trait and fulfilling its purpose by giving teens opportunities to interact with their author heroes. They can also nurture it by being mentors, friends, good adult examples, and guiding lights for the teens they work with in libraries. Accommodating this trait helps to place teens on the first, second, and fourth rungs of the resiliency ladder.

Clannishness

The paradox of adolescence is that teens are discovering individuality at the same time they are looking for a place to belong with friends and others like themselves. Some teens indulge this trait in a negative fashion by joining gangs or other groups engaged in questionable behavior, just to experience this sense of belonging. Library youth participation activities provide a *positive* way for teens to experience this camaraderie and feel important as part of a group while catering to distinctive aspects of personality.

In relation to the trait of clannishness, the peer associations that occur through teen library participation cannot be underestimated, and they relate most strongly to the fourth rung on the resiliency ladder, "encouraging social skills." It is important for libraries to not only provide avenues for teens to interact on library oriented projects, but also to encourage fun times during which teenagers can laugh, make new friends, cheer each other on, and enjoy one another's company. In addition to making friends and developing a sense of belonging, teens may also learn to appreciate working with others who might be different from them.

Melanie Limbert-Callahan, teacher-librarian at Shepherd Junior High School in Arizona, says about the members of her school library teen participatory groups: "We have student council members to shy wallflowers, and popular to not-so-popular students. We have a mixture of ethnicities, and a range of intellectual abilities. We have several special education students. This teaches tolerance and acceptance of all."[24]

You'll learn more about Melanie's teens and their accomplishments in chapter 3.

Finding a New Clan: Larry's Story

One day a few years ago, while I was still working at the youth services reference desk at the City of Mesa Library, a man approached and said, "I am so glad you are still here. I need to tell you something. You saved my life."

When my heart stopped racing, my mind comprehended the identity of this man. My brain tunnel-visioned back 20 years, to when a young teen named Larry came to the library every day, without fail, as long as we were open. He hung around, talked to me and the other young adult librarians, chatted with his peers, and helped however he could in the Young Adult area. He cleaned records (we had records then, not CDs), helped set up for programs, and did other tasks as needed. He was a part of our Young Adult team—we expected Larry to be there and to assist however he could. He expected us to be there for him—to listen, to laugh, to be an integral part of his life. When he graduated from high school, we said a fond farewell and wished him the best in his future.

Now that future was staring me in the face. Larry said I saved his life. *We* saved his life—I and the other Young Adult librarians who were there for him, almost every day. But the part of this picture he didn't add was that he was instrumental in *saving his own life.* We simply provided the catalyst. The man who came to the library that day explained how he had built his life on the positive elements we had provided. He told me about his three children in California who are readers because he and his wife read to them and take them to the library on a regular basis. He described how they do not have a television in their house, but they do have lots and lots of books, and talk about books and reading every day.

Larry kept his eye on books and reading and libraries as important positive influences, and passed that wisdom on to his family. He told me that as a teenager, when he came to the library so frequently, he was really avoiding being drafted by a local gang. We knew about the gang and suspected the potential recruiting situation, but never said a word about it. We understood the choices Larry was making, and we were glad to be there for him.

Larry wanted—and received—something better that we librarians and the other teens who regularly came to the library were able to provide: a place to belong and to be respected. A place to be himself in a constructive and uplifting fashion. A place where he could pass on what he learned to the next generation. A place where resiliency reigned.

That is a striking and essential element of providing youth participation in libraries—the opportunity to transform negative clannishness into something positive.

Audacity of Belief

The general consensus among adults is that teens feel infallibility and a determination to do just about anything they set their minds to, usually believing nothing bad can happen to them and whatever they settle on, they can do. This long-held principle is not exactly true, as some research shows that teens are actually afraid of all kinds of things, such as their own and their parents' deaths, being injured, receiving bad grades, or being shunned by their peer group. Even peer pressure may actually be the result of teens choosing friends on purpose who behave as they want to behave.

Essentially, teens "sometimes don't recognize different options, and can often be forced into making poor decisions in situations that are both emotional and stressful. But contrary to how it often appears, teenagers do 'think,' using whatever skills and knowledge they possess at the time."[25] Sometimes, in their audacity of belief, teens simply make very poor decisions. However, just the opposite can also be true, when teens choose to take positive risks that turn out well.

Audacity of belief can also refer to teens' exploration and experimentation with ideas and belief systems—political, religious, social, and even scientific. What better place to explore ideas and other belief systems than the library? At the Niles Public Library District in Niles, Illinois (www.nileslibrary.org), they do just that. Teens participate in "Thursday Afternoon Fights," an ongoing teen participation program through which they can freely discuss hot topics and important social issues.[26]

Whether helping teens to make sensible decisions, allowing them to take positive risks, or aiding them in questioning their world so that they may develop into smart, perceptive adults, libraries can provide teens with involvement opportunities to enhance this trait, to teens' benefit and the benefit of their communities.

Even Smart Teens Can Take Dangerous Chances

We can all think of examples when teens might have exhibited this trait in a negative manner—when they might have experimented with drugs, driven dangerously, gotten caught up in a harmful social movement, or taken other potentially detrimental risks.

I remember a situation in which a high school senior, who was an honor student and regular library volunteer, took her parents' car and drove it hundreds of miles (when she was supposed to be at a friend's sleepover) to meet a boy she had connected with on the Internet. On the way, she flipped the car, totaled it, and ended up in the emergency room. Luckily, she had the prudence to put on her seatbelt before leaving, and with generally minor cuts and scrapes she was soon fine, physically. She was grounded until high school graduation, with few exceptions, one of which was volunteering at the library. The girl was extremely embarrassed and ashamed about what she had done and refused to talk about it. However, it seemed that she had learned a lesson, and she was anxious to move beyond her mistake.

What made an apparently smart, seemingly sensible young adult behave in such a thoughtless manner? She put herself in a position where she felt the need to make a decision, and she chose the wrong path. Besides being in a car accident, did she consider the prospects of meeting a strange person from the Internet? She did not. In her mind, "audacity of belief" led the way, and ultimately she learned the difficult lesson about how misguided she had been in thinking nothing could happen to her while taking such dangerous chances.

On the other hand, library youth participation can often channel this mindset in a *positive* way by empowering teens to apply this trait in innovative directions, allowing them to try unique library projects and activities that have the potential to make a difference. It permits teens to hone their decision-making and problem-solving skills, which is the third rung on the resiliency ladder.

Empowering Teens

Empowerment is about taking young people seriously, about believing that they have something to contribute to the community, and trusting that they want to do so. It is about adults sharing power *with* young people. It means that adults work *with* young people, not just *for* them, to fashion solutions to problems. Youth are empowered when the opportunities they are given to lead and participate in community life are real, when they are not taken over by adults if the young people's ideas seem naïve or inefficient.[27]

One of my favorite stories reflecting teen "audacity of belief" and allowing teens to be empowered took place in 2005 at the Maricopa County Library's George L. Campbell Branch in

Arizona. The teen members of the newly formed library advisory group decided they wanted to host a spring poetry slam. With their advisor's guidance, they learned how to plan and run a slam. Part of the preparations included selecting prizes for the winners of the competition. The teens thought that the coolest prizes would be a Border's bookstore gift certificate (to which their librarian advisor readily agreed), plus a box of Twinkies and a block of Velveeta (which caused their librarian advisor to shudder and take a deep breath as she remembered how important it is to allow teens to make decisions and take risks).

The prizes turned out to be a huge hit among their peers, and the teen advisory board members (and their advisor) were thrilled at that result. When the teens decided to do another poetry slam in the fall, they not only used the previous popular prizes, but added a can of Spam to the mix! Their librarian was glad she had entrusted and empowered them to take risks that paid off in a well-received program by and for the teens of her community.[28]

TO SUM UP

It is startling to recognize that development of the teenage brain continues for longer than a decade, during which time young adults are setting the stage for positive or negative behaviors and perspectives that will affect the rest of their lives. That awareness can help librarians to incorporate the most effective methods of reaching their teen clientele during those pivotal years by providing a special place where positive outcomes and resiliency can be met. As vital components of healthy communities that nurture, support, and encourage teens, it is important for all libraries serving young people to understand the beneficial roles they play from a variety of angles.

Acknowledging and accepting the general traits common to the teen personality goes hand-in-hand with that acquired knowledge. Librarians and others who work with teens can use the information as a springboard to stand up for teens, offering grounds for getting them directly involved and ensuring they have a voice. Not only does this comprehension assist in developing the most effective library youth participation programs, activities, and events, but it provides basic *justifications* for encouraging library youth participation endeavors in the first place. Library administrators and managers need to recognize the importance of such endeavors and carefully consider these justifications as they are funding, advocating for, and supporting library teen services.

Some essential rationales for offering youth participation opportunities include the fact that they provide a catalyst for teenagers to enter adulthood as readers, learners, and library supporters; they promote reading and the library by teen participants to their adolescent peers, who in turn will hopefully also partake in what the library has to offer; they proliferate library usage by helping teens to eventually pass on their love of books and libraries to their offspring; they uphold the concept of positive youth development in our communities; and they affirm the prospect of librarianship as a career option for young people.

The Long-standing Benefits of Involving Young People in Library Activities

Alleen Pace Nilsen teaches classes in young adult and children's literature in the English Department at Arizona State University and is a great believer in the importance of connecting teens and libraries. With Ken Donelson, she is the author of *Literature for Today's Young Adults,* 8th edition (Allyn & Bacon, 2008). She shares the following insights about the importance of teen library involvement:

On the first day of class in my children's and young adult literature classes, I usually ask students to tell about a favorite book or a favorite reading experience they have had. This is sort of a warm-up for their next assignment, which is to write a reading autobiography in which they relate what influenced them to become "readers." My ulterior motive is to get them to think about what worked for them, so that they can try to recreate similar experiences for the young people they will work with.

Every year at least three or four students mention some kind of special relationship with a library and/or a librarian. The events they talk about range from something as mundane as shelving books to helping the "little kids" during summer reading programs, and to something as unexpected as getting accidentally locked in the library one night. I have had a couple of students talk about helping to host a visiting author, and a few more talk about being on a teen advisory group where they helped librarians decide on which books to order and helped make recommendations to fellow students by contributing reviews to either a printed or online newsletter. I have also had a couple of boys mention helping with computer game nights.

Even university graduate students like to participate in library events. Our doctoral students in English Education are required to complete three internships, one related to research, another to teaching, and a third one to whatever they can come up with relating to books and young people. A few years back when the newly remodeled Phoenix Central Library opened, three of our doctoral students worked together to prepare an exhibit of archetypal characters as illustrated in Newbery Award books. They worked with the library's special collections and archives and hunted through antique stores and their own keepsakes so that they could make the displays more than just books. They also prepared a slide show and a take-home brochure, and were on hand to help out with at least some of the pre-scheduled school visits where busloads of students came in for tours of the new library, which included our students' presentation in the children's section.

Those who came on the field trips to the grand opening of the library have probably forgotten about the exhibit and the program, but the three doctoral students who worked together to make it all possible became good friends and colleagues who went on to work together in other projects, including a joint presentation at the National Council of Teachers of English annual conference.

One of the things I think of when I hear students happily reminiscing about their library activities is the theme song from television's *Cheers,* with its refrain about "a place where everyone knows your name." Kids need such places just as much as do adults, and with schools cutting back on extra curricular activities because so many kids have after-school jobs or due to economic downturns, it's more important than ever that libraries find ways to bring teens together on a regular basis so that they can not only learn each other's names but also get to know other kids through sharing their reading, library activity, and online experiences.

As proven by one of my students this year who surprised us all by saying that she met her husband in a teen book discussion group, there's hardly a better way to get acquainted and to build lasting friendships than through sharing reactions with other people who have also read the same book or have had positive library experiences in common.[29]

Want to Learn More?

Try these books written for teens that encourage resiliency, foster positive youth development, and promote the 40 Developmental Assets®. Add them to your teen collection to get and provide a more in-depth look at adolescent psychology and sociology:

Benson, Peter, et al. *What Teens Need to Succeed.* Minneapolis, MN: Free Spirit Publishing, 1998.

Covey, Sean. *The 7 Habits of Highly Successful Teens.* New York: Simon & Schuster, 1998.

———. *The 6 Most Important Decisions You'll Ever Make: A Guide for Teens.* New York: Fireside, 2006.

Jones, Jami. *Bouncing Back.* New York: Franklin Watts, 2007.

Weston, Carol. *For Teens Only: Quotes, Notes, and Advice You Can Use.* New York: HarperTrophy, 2003.

ENDNOTES

1. Peter L. Benson, *All Kids Are Our Kids,* 2nd ed. (San Francisco: Jossey-Bass, 2006), 3.
2. Benson, *All Kids Are Our Kids,* 11.
3. Jami Jones, "The Power of Partnerships: When Librarians Bring People Together, Everyone Wins," *School Library Journal* 51 (May 2005): 33.
4. Tina Kelley, "Lock the Library! Rowdy Students Are Taking Over," *New York Times,* January 7, 2007, www.nytimes.com/2007/01/02/nyregion/02library.html?_r=1&emc=eta1&oref=slogin (accessed May 11, 2008).
5. Kelley, "Lock the Library!"
6. Benson, *All Kids Are Our Kids,* 14.
7. Jones, "Power of Partnerships," 33.
8. Benson, *All Kids Are Our Kids,* 271)
9. Patricia Lamiell, "Rowdy Kids in the Library? Rutgers to the Rescue," *Rutgers FOCUS,* March 28, 2007, news.rutgers.edu/focus/issue.2007-03-28.0562364514/article.2007-03-28.0071486324/article_page_view (accessed May 11, 2008).
10. Lamiell, "Rowdy Kids in the Library?"
11. Lamiell, "Rowdy Kids in the Library?"
12. Jane Folger, e-mail message to author, June 25, 2008.
13. Barbara Strauch, *The Primal Teen: What the New Discoveries about the Teenage Brain Tell Us about Our Kids* (New York; Doubleday, 2003), 8.
14. Jennifer Burek Pierce, *Sex, Brains, and Video Games: A Librarian's Guide to Teens in the Twenty-first Century* (Chicago: American Library Association, 2008), 32.
15. Allison O'Reilly, e-mail message to author, July 15, 2008.
16. Jami L. Jones, "Resiliency High: A Blueprint for Resiliency-Based Education," *Ask Dr. Jami,* www.askdrjami.org/pdf/resiliency_high.pdf (accessed April 11, 2008).
17. Jami Jones, "Libraries as Resiliency Havens for Children and Youth," in *Resiliency in Action: Practical Ideas for Overcoming Risks and Building Strengths,* ed. Nan Henderson, 103–4 (Ojai, CA: Resiliency in Action, 2007).
18. Amelia Munson, *An Ample Field* (Chicago: American Library Association, 1950), 7–8.
19. Nicole Nixen, e-mail message to author, June 2, 2008.
20. Tracy Briseño, e-mail message to author, July 28, 2008.

21. David Walsh, *Why Do They Act That Way?* (New York: Free Press, 2004), 14.

22. Munson, *Ample Field* , 8.

23. Young Adult Library Services Association, *2007 YALSA/Sagebrush Award for a Young Adult Reading or Literature Program* (American Library Association), www.ala.org/ala/yalsa/newsandeventsb/sagebrush.cfm (accessed September 17, 2009).

24. Melanie Limbert-Callahan, e-mail message to author, February 21, 2008.

25. Strauch, *Primal Teen*, 90–91.

26. Tracey Firestone and Kate Wolicki, comps. "Thursday Afternoon Fights: Most Valuable Discussion Program," *Voice of Youth Advocates* 29 (October 2006): 306–7.

27. Yvonne Pearson, Kristin Johnstad, and James Conway. *More Than Just a Place to Go: How Developmental Assets Can Strengthen Your Youth Program* (Minneapolis, MN: Search Institute, 2004), 39.

28. Diane P. Tuccillo, "Successful Teen Advisory Groups: Teen Driven . . . with Guidance and a Helping Hand," *Voice of Youth Advocates e-VOYA* (December 2005), pdfs.voya.com/VO/YA2/VOYA200512SuccessfulTeens.pdf (accessed September 17, 2009).

29. Alleen Pace Nilsen, e-mail message to author, June 15, 2008.

2

We've Come a Long Way: History of Youth Participation in School and Public Libraries

We can't know where we are going until we recognize where we have been. That's why it is important for us to learn about and understand the roots of teen library services and the growth and development of teen library participation. If you think that teen participation in libraries is a fairly new concept, you might be surprised to learn that advocates for giving teens a place and a say in their library programs, services, collections, and activities have been around for quite some time.

In this chapter, you will learn about several advocates for youth participation in past library settings who laid the groundwork for teen involvement in libraries today. Better yet, you will discover some interesting philosophical perspectives on the roles of teens in libraries today.

LOOKING BACK: THE ROOTS OF TEEN LIBRARY PARTICIPATION

Although libraries through the ages have a long and illustrious history, libraries as we currently think of them were not always part of our culture. The multifaceted libraries that comprised the foundations of our present-day system did not begin until the mid-nineteenth century. Those libraries were not particularly youth friendly, and it was not until the latter part of that century that real attention began to be paid to libraries serving young people.

Librarians at that time were extremely wary of what children and teenagers were reading and felt that much of the material they selected was detrimental. Early libraries for youth were located in schools. In general, it took decades before teenage patrons were allowed full use of library facilities, found diversity and relevance in library collections for their age group, and were given respectful inclusion in library volunteerism and other avenues of youth participation. However, there were some early exceptions that foreshadowed the growing attitudes and efforts we see today in encouraging and empowering teens to be an active part of their libraries.

In the early to mid-1900s, a number of libraries and librarians strongly advocated for services that focused on teenage library users. Some of the best known were on the East Coast and in the Midwest, located in major cities such as Boston, New York, Cleveland, and Baltimore. Libraries in neighboring communities were often influenced by what they saw happening in these major cities. Because of this proximity, we can trace some of the earliest young adult departments and services to libraries located near these cities.

A Personal Perspective

As a child and teen in the 1960s, I grew up near one of these cities—New York—using a community library that had a young adult department. The Rutherford Free Public Library, six miles from New York City and the Hudson River in New Jersey, also offered a separate card for each age level that the library served: child, young adult, and adult. Having such a tiered system of public library cards to restrict access was common throughout the country and lasted for yet another decade or so after I left young adulthood.

This age level system can be traced back to at least the 1930s, when Clarence E. Sherman, a librarian from the Providence Public Library in Rhode Island, addressed the National Council of Teachers of English convention to explain it in 1938. In discussing teenagers and their use of the library, he advocated public library cards delineating ages of maturity. At the same time, however, he highly encouraged special library spaces designated for teenagers: "Every central library and each branch library should have a young people's alcove or a section of shelving for youth to which they can turn with confidence . . . a young people's library to serve young folks of the middle and late teens, both in and out of school . . . [they] would be infinitely better off in a reading-room of their own."[1]

School libraries, by their very nature, were already providing unique services for teenage students in their schools, a few with direct student input and involvement. Sherman's enthusiastic recommendation for communities to allocate further special spaces particularly for teenagers in public libraries was a definite step in the right direction. Although any library can offer opportunities for teens to become involved, the best ones are those that recognize the importance of a designated teen space that connects participatory activities to that space.

Teens, Library Cards, and Library Spaces

At that point in teen library services history, the good news was that special teen spaces were being encouraged in public libraries. The bad news was the recommendation that teenagers be restricted from full library access. At the library of my youth, these suggestions were followed. Despite lack of access to the adult collection, my library had a Young Adult Room created for teenagers and a Young Adult Librarian to serve us.

When I was in sixth grade I traded my Children's card for a Young Adult library card because I was in "advanced reading," I had to get forms signed by my reading teacher and my mother so that I could get that card. I treasured it and was thrilled that as a sixth grader I could freely enter and use the Young Adult Room, which was normally only available to junior and senior high school students. However, I was still not permitted in the Adult section. It was in the YA Room that I got to know Mrs. Marguerite McLaughlin, the Young Adult Librarian.

Mrs. McLaughlin recommended books to me that I loved, and I came to highly respect the special position she held of working with teenagers and books and reading. Interestingly, the first professional librarian position I ever had was as Young Adult Librarian at the Rutherford Free Public Library after Marguerite retired, while I attended Rutgers to get my MLS. This experience brought me full circle and gave me lots of food for thought about how teen services evolved and its place in the library world.

What, No Teen Outreach or Participation?

One thing my memories bring to mind is that although careful attention was paid in my library to the young adult collection and teen reader advisory, there was no outreach to teens in the community, and few teen participation opportunities were offered. Occasionally there might be a Girl Scout project in which teens read picture books for a storytime to young children. In addition, teenagers were hired to work after school as pages and shelvers. For the most part, though, teens did not play an active role in our library, nor were they encouraged to do so.

When I asked about this imbalance, I was told that such outreach to teens was not necessary. However, as I studied for my library science degree at Rutgers, I learned how badly our library was behind the times in this respect. I was determined that active teen participation and outreach would be a fundamental part of my future library work. I could envision a richer library of my youth had teens been truly involved.

Luckily, the richer place I imagined has become a reality. Times have greatly changed at the Rutherford Free Public Library. Little by little, YA librarians were able to add teen programming and services. The library now has lots of teen activities, a lively MySpace presence, and a teen advisory group (www.rutherfordlibrary.org). It is exciting that teens in Rutherford have a special teen space and collection, and they are also connected to and involved in their library.

I offer this personal example because, unlike the Rutherford Public Library, there are still many libraries today that have not yet bought into the concept of providing teen services. I am amazed to see requests on listservs and blogs for guidance from school and public libraries seeking to provide any sort of teen services for the very first time. There are also plenty seeking to improve the basic services they already have through teen participation. It is always promising when they reach out to do so.

My story explains a part of young adult library services history that directly connects to the current recognition, development, and value of teen library participation. Exploring further will enlighten and inspire you to add or improve teen services in your library with teen involvement that suits your library setting. You will find examples of such involvement intertwined throughout the illustrious library history discussed below, followed by information and advice to help you bring them to life in your library.

BEYOND "CHILDREN AND DOGS NOT ADMITTED"

Looking back at the last two centuries, we can see that teen participation in libraries started out slowly and has grown to be an important ingredient of contemporary teen library services. Its roots lie in the creation and expansion of libraries, a growing focus on reading and education for youth, and the contributions of library advocates for teens. As you scrutinize this history, consider the cumulative influences that brought library teen services and teen library participation to its present level.

Let's start at the beginning. Throughout the nineteenth century, widespread illiteracy persisted in Europe. It was in America that developing a learned population to support the political and religious foundations of society became important, and the concept of providing libraries for young readers was eventually born.[2]

I say "eventually" because youth library services did not happen overnight. Well before they were even imagined, Benjamin Franklin started the first semblance of a public library in

America when he suggested to adult members of a middle-class social and literary club in Philadelphia that they should share books with each other. This led to the creation of the Philadelphia Library Company in 1731, a subscription library that served as an example for the fashioning of future libraries.[3]

Soon public libraries began forming in schools in New York, New England, and the Midwest, basically using parts of school buildings to house them.[4] However, the concept of these early libraries was not to encourage use by youth. Rather, they were founded for those who had *graduated* from the schools so they could embark upon higher education independently. As a matter of fact, some libraries even had signs declaring, "Children and dogs not admitted." Those under age 14 were not allowed. In addition, adults could not check out books for home use and were expected to read and use reference materials in-house, at the library facilities themselves.[5]

Early Influences in Encouraging Youth Services in Libraries

In the late 1800s school and public libraries began transformations that would incorporate reading and services for youth, which would eventually develop into our contemporary library services. However, it was a long and tedious evolution. Early influences for offering library youth services were social reformers who saw a need for urban youth to find wholesome alternatives to street life, the existence of tightening child labor laws, the imposition of laws surrounding educational requirements, and the emergence of youth who had increased ability and leisure time to read.[6]

Another step forward was Melvil Dewey's recommendation in 1896 that the National Education Association form a Library Department. This department would include and promote libraries as a fundamental element of the education process, as important as the regular classroom. As a result of Dewey's recommendation, public libraries were placed in high schools in Ohio, New Jersey, New York, and elsewhere. In 1916, high school libraries were standardized across the United States, and their numbers steadily grew until the Great Depression.[7]

In the early years of U.S. libraries, there was little opportunity for teens to have a say in them and to become personally involved. However, there were some notable exceptions. The dedicated librarians who saw the need for and promoted initial library youth participation experiences thankfully also took the time to share their perspectives. As you read about their ideas and experiences, consider the positive aspects relayed about working with teens at that level, which reflect similar involvement today.

A Library Teen Participation Experiment Gone Right

Carrie E. Tucker Dracass was the librarian at the Englewood High School in Chicago in 1911. When the high school was remodeled and a new library was added, she realized what a difficult task it would be to get it reorganized. She proposed an "experiment" that was put into action: Students from the school would be enlisted to help. Thirty-eight volunteer students were enrolled and received instruction on the operation of a well-run library. Some of the teen volunteers completed their service time during the regular school day and some during afterschool hours.[8]

When she developed the student library volunteer program, Ms. Dracass offered reasons why it would benefit the youth. She said that participating students would come in close contact with quality literature while learning vocational skills that might help them pay their way through college or encourage them to enter the library field itself. She highlighted the social advantages of promoting "civic usefulness in making the small library of utmost possible value to its community," and "training in meeting people whom one is to serve." She added that this volunteer program afforded "a solution of a present-day problem—how to teach a subject essential to the welfare of a community through practical application in the community life." The students in the program were given much responsibility and were often left in charge of the entire library when she was busy in the classroom. Many of them moved on to library careers after completing high school.[9]

This early library youth participation "experiment" shares the elements of resiliency, empowerment, and community engagement described in chapter 1, which you will see demonstrated in upcoming sections and chapters. Ms. Dracass not only presented her "experiment" in a positive light that projects today's concept of "positive youth development," but in addition, as an evaluative measure, she collected quotes describing the reactions and responses of the actual teen participants. After you read the following excerpts from the quotes, keep them in mind as you read further quotes from contemporary teens in other parts of this book. You will notice that the comments made by teens in 1911 are not so different from those made by teens in the twenty-first century:

> "The work that I have done has made me like to read more solid books, for being among books so much I naturally look over more of them than I otherwise would."

> "Knowing these things has helped me to tell other poor souls that have come into the library how to obtain the information that they have looked for in vain and to help the younger boys and girls select suitable reading."

> "It has made me do many things that I never thought that I could do. . . . One soon discovers that things worth doing are worth doing well."

> "Responsibility was put upon me—something that I never had before—and . . . in finding information for others, I was learning *some few things* for myself."

> "It has given me a broader and more sympathetic feeling for people as a whole and a strong desire to be of use and help to others."

> "Most, or in any case, half of the people who use the library now are Freshmen and Sophomores, while . . . [before the volunteer class] most of the Freshmen did not know such a place existed."

> "It has imbued me with the library spirit and I intend to educate myself for a librarian."

Ms. Dracass sums up the value of her "experiment" with great words of wisdom that connect to the concepts of developing positive youth assets and fostering resiliency: "The shaping of personal activity by experience is education. Thus, while assisting in managing one great department of the school for the common good, the community interest, the pupils are developing their own physical, moral, and intellectual activities."[10]

The positive youth development concepts we talk about and put into practice today essentially echo past discoveries like this one about teen involvement in libraries.

Enlisting Students as Library Assistants

In 1915, Emma J. Breck, from the University High School in Oakland, California, presented a paper before the National Council of Teachers of English (NCTE) defining the principles of an efficient high school library. At the conclusion of her presentation, the NCTE approved the plan and vowed to give it the utmost publicity through special committees and the group's educational association liaisons.

The paper explained Ms. Breck's perspectives on positively connecting teenagers with books and reading for pleasure, not just for school work, and including the value of interesting magazines; seeking support for the library by principals, school boards, teachers, and the community at large; keeping the library open at every available hour of the school day;

designing inviting and comfortable library spaces for student *use*, not for *show*; hiring well-trained librarians with personalities suitable for work with teenagers; and enlisting students as library assistants. All of these elements are found in well-run school libraries and public library teen services departments today.

Notice that "enlisting student assistants" is an important part of the picture. Ms. Breck viewed such service as essential, saying, "No social service in the school community quicker develops responsibility and a sense of proprietorship than this. These student assistants . . . may well be given some school credit in return for reliable and efficient service."[11]

Consider how this perspective relates directly to the teen service-learning connection we might promote to volunteers in many of our modern libraries.

A Junior High Teen Advisory Group: "Library Service"

Years after NCTE approved the "efficient high school" proposal of Ms. Breck, another school librarian likewise appreciated young adult contributions to library operations. Her name was Marion Lovis, and she worked at Hutchins Junior High School in Detroit, Michigan. In 1924 she described what she felt were characteristics of an outstanding junior high library setting. Her description included not only providing a rich array of well-selected, useful, and appealing books, magazines, and visual materials, but also teaching pupils to use the library to best advantage. She stressed student spirit and service, "the social facts that consideration of others, fair play, and co-operation bring about the best and happiest conditions in which to live," and "although we have become accustomed to think of the library in terms of its use in carrying out the purposes of the curriculum, it may have a social function of as great importance in carrying out the fundamental purposes of the junior high itself."[12]

In this spirit, Hutchins Junior High School offered of one of the earliest "library teen advisory groups." Called "Library Service," it comprised one student from each homeroom elected as a representative "librarian." Members met after school on alternate Mondays. A chairman, secretary, and representative for each grade were elected, and these students became the "executive committee." The "executive committee" would hold weekly meetings, make recommendations to the school librarian, and make decisions on how to handle the worst overdue book offenders.

Duties of the entire "Library Service" group were to improve the library in every possible way; to be the liaisons between the library and the homerooms; to make all library announcements; and to follow up on overdue books in the homerooms. Members who wished—and there were many—would also be regularly scheduled for work in the library: "They are at the age when they love to be in charge of something…and the spirit of helpfulness and responsibility which this little body of workers brings into the library is beyond calculation, since it spreads throughout the school."[13]

Ms. Lovis explained that she often had more helpers than work, and she had many "unofficial helpers" in addition to the "Library Service" members. To what did she attribute this popularity? Each young adult who provided volunteer assistance got to wear a special button that said "Library Service" on it! Those who wore the buttons were "very strict and energetic custodians of the library and its welfare."[14]

As I think about those teens in 1924 wearing their "Library Service" buttons, I cannot help but envision many of today's teens wearing their special library volunteer, summer reading assistant, or teen advisory group T-shirts, proudly advertising their library participation in a similar way.

Finally, Ms Lovis explained what she perceived as "a legitimate contribution . . . the library may make to the school as a social, as well as a reference, center." She shared examples of teens using the library for other purposes, such as for meetings and events of the Book Explorers Club or the Cartoon Club.[15] Flash forward, and likewise you might envision a Manga Club being held in and run by teens in a contemporary twenty-first-century school or public library.

The Importance of Library Involvement at an Early Age

Such concentration on youth participation was not limited to libraries in the United States. In 1924 in Paris, some American women began a very successful youth library modeled after the American public library. It was called l'Heure Joyeuse and offered children and young teenagers an appealing book collection, storytime and book discussion programs, and an opportunity to participate in daily library operations.[16]

Later, in 1957, Blanche Janecek, the high school librarian of the Laboratory School, University of Chicago, described teen participation in her library, which she explained had already been in practice for 50 years. That is quite a track record! Like the other librarians documenting their young adult participation in the earlier part of the century, she was a true believer in active student assistance. In her library's case, however, it was *paid* student help, combined with volunteers and students working off fines. She did not find that the experiences diminished because some students received payment and some did not. Interestingly, you will later learn about similar teen library involvement opportunities that exist today—also with pay.

Overall, Ms. Janecek said, "Students tell us that they benefit from the intellectual stimulation, from the satisfaction of doing something constructive, from the social opportunities afforded by becoming acquainted with the entire school population, and from the work experience which will help them get jobs later in college. Many students, because of these experiences, have considered the field of librarianship as a profession. . . . Whether students use a school library or a public library, favorable exposure is important. Young people are deprived of much, educationally, if they cannot start library experiences at an early age."[17]

Indications that this is true are documented in Barbara Will Razzano's 1982 study on youth library habits. Razzano examined library use by young people prior to age 18 and discovered a direct correlation between active adult library usage and support, and regular library visits and associations when those same adults were children and/or teenagers.[18]

As libraries developed throughout the last century, the seeds of the youth participation concept were planted via the efforts of these and other librarian pioneers who believed strongly in it. Although the model was extremely new, it was one for which positive evidence and support were gradually surfacing. Slowly but steadily, it has grown from its roots at Englewood High School, University High School, Hutchins Junior High, l'Heure Joyeuse, and others like them. Once the seeds germinated, careful nurturing through time allowed them to flourish.

Professional Associations That Promote Youth Services in Libraries

While early school and public libraries were developing and honing the facilities housing library collections for teenagers, recommending and creating policies and procedures for most effectively working with this age group, and introducing the idea of teen library involvement, the professional organizations devoted to supporting their work with young people in libraries were founded and were evolving. In general, the histories of the major national professional groups that support this work today—the National Education Association (NEA), the National Council of Teachers of English (NCTE), the International Reading Association (IRA), the American Association of School Librarians (AASL), and the Young Adult Library Services Association (YALSA)—parallel the development of youth services in libraries and the years during which these services grew in the United States.

The direct correlation between the expansion of these organizations and the growth of today's library youth services and participation is interesting. Obtaining tools and information to provide the best, most insightful, and well-rounded teen services and teen participatory opportunities available can be achieved by connecting with and keeping abreast of the offerings of these major organizations. Membership and professional participation in associations suitable to a particular librarian's work setting is a valuable connection. You'll read more about how these organizations contribute to teen participation in chapter 8.

BRINGING IT ALL TOGETHER: LINKING IDEAS, ACTIONS, AND YOUTH-SERVING GROUPS

Libraries are not the only places where attention to teen participation has been and is being paid. The increased involvement of teens in libraries today can be linked to ideas about teen involvement by those practiced in other organizations, agencies, and associations that also work with and for teens. Let's see how those early, related influences helped to inspire an attitude of appreciation for later teen library participation.

National Youth Administration

At the government level, one of the first organizations that promoted youth activity and involvement was the National Youth Administration (NYA). Although it was divided into national regions, it operated independently at state levels, and young men and women in the programs lived in camps, dormitories, or other residential centers. NYA was established in 1935 under the New Deal movement to provide work training and paid job opportunities for youth ages 16 to 25 along with courses in reading, writing, mathematics, self-improvement, citizenship, vocational guidance, and more. In addition, NYA offered opportunities to learn and participate in athletics, hobbies, drama, games, music, and dance. The program only lasted eight years, but though it would be decades before any other program legislating specific youth concerns would materialize through the U.S. government, NYA set the stage.[19]

National Commission on Resources for Youth: Defining Youth Participation

The successor to NYA was the National Commission on Resources for Youth, which initiated national movements promoting youth voice, youth participation, and community youth development. Founded in 1967, the commission was a U.S. federal program designed to indentify, research, promote, and sustain youth involvement opportunities nationwide. Meetings and studies were part of the process, and youth involvement in schools and communities grew considerably through its existence until the mid-1980s.

The focus on libraries was a particularly notable aspect of the commission, because for the first time teen library participation was openly recognized as a valid arena in the overall picture of active youth involvement. Besides defining and encouraging participation targeting youth on a variety of levels, the commission provided expert knowledge and resources to support ongoing activities long after its closure.[20] Much of the definitive and universal advice and information that appeared in its numerous publications on youth participation from that time constitutes a body of still-valuable and impressive resources.

As a guiding light to the overall mission of those publications, the National Commission on Resources for Youth developed an apt and broadly accepted description of what outstanding youth participation means:

> Involving youth in responsible, challenging action that meets genuine needs, with opportunities for planning and/or decision making affecting others in an activity whose impact or consequence is extended to others. . . . Other desirable features of youth participation are provisions for critical reflection on the participatory activity and the opportunity for group effort toward a common goal.[21]

Considering that definition, think back to the sections above about young adults participating in their libraries during various decades of the 1900s. You can see that those early school and youth librarians really understood what effective youth participation was all about, why it was important, and how to make it happen. When you fast-forward to the present in the upcoming chapters, you will see remarkable examples that illustrate these principles nowadays. You will also discover ways that you can effectively evaluate the youth participation opportunities you provide.

Responding to *A Nation at Risk*

In 1983, around the time that the National Commission on Resources for Youth ended, the U.S. Department of Education's National Commission on Excellence in Education conducted a study on the state of American education. Because the final report portrayed a formal education system that had deteriorated to a dangerous degree, it was titled *A Nation at Risk*.[22]

As a response to this dire report, the Department of Education's Center for Libraries and Education Improvement, Office of Educational Research and Improvement, organized a meeting of leaders from the library and information science community to develop a project called "Libraries and a Learning Society." A series of seminars, issue papers, and lively debate resulted in the publication of an important document, *Alliance for Excellence: Librarians Respond to* A Nation at Risk.[23]

Like the community interaction described in chapter 1 to encourage youth participation in libraries and elsewhere, this document reflected the same basic premise: that alliances among educators, parents, other citizens, and librarians are necessary to develop and nurture a Learning Society.[24] Although library youth participation was not addressed per se, a large part of the recommendations in the document included improvements to and heightened respect for school library media centers and public libraries. The many positive changes these would accomplish would serve to support the concept of youth involvement.

The Young Adult Services Division (YASD) of the American Library Association (ALA) also responded eloquently to *A Nation at Risk*. YASD passed a resolution stressing the role that librarians working in schools and public libraries have in the personal and educational growth of young adults. A direct mailing to school librarians in conjunction with the resolution immediately gained YASD 150 new members in 1986.[25]

The White House Conferences on Libraries and Information Services

The first White House conference was held in 1909, called by President Theodore Roosevelt. He used his influence to organize conferences that would address issues of importance to the people and that would conclude in real results.

The health and welfare of children was the focus of the initial conference and conferences that took place during every decade through the 1970s. In 1960, the conference was called the White House Conference on Children and Youth and aimed "to promote opportunities for children and youth to realize their full potential for a creative life in freedom and dignity."[26] In 1971, a White House Conference on Youth was held that focused on the need for equal educational opportunity, relevant educational systems, and student participation in educational governance. It also addressed the problems facing exceptional students, the problems facing high school dropouts, and the need to provide teachers with better preparation.[27] In a show of support for the youth needs and issues being addressed, YASD sent delegates to both the 1960 and 1971 conferences, and for the one in 1960 published and distributed an advocacy document called *Youth in a Changing World*.[28]

In 1980 the White House Conference on Children and Youth changed its name to the White House Conference on Families to expand its focus on family issues. Additional long-term conferences were the White House Conferences on Aging, held from 1961 through 1995.

Besides these conferences on children, families, and aging, others addressed drug abuse, the economy, education, nutrition, civil rights, disabled people, highway safety, and libraries. All of these conferences gave government and community leaders, interested citizens, and experts on the topic at hand a chance to discuss, review, evaluate, and develop recommendations, which would hopefully achieve the real results that President Roosevelt intended.[29]

Two White House Conferences on Library and Information Services were held, in 1979 and 1991. The first was called by President Jimmy Carter; the second was called under President Ronald Reagan and convened under the administration of President George H. W. Bush.

Reinforcing the Center for the Book

In relation to youth services, the 1979 conference resulted in a much more influential Library of Congress. The Center for the Book, which had existed since 1977, was part of this strengthened influence, which moved the center forward as a national leader in book, reading, and library promotion, with some projects designated for at-risk youth. Later, First Lady Barbara Bush took the literacy efforts of the Center for the Book under her wing and helped to spread the family literacy concept, connecting it with libraries nationwide.[30]

One of the exciting literacy promotions of the Center for the Book is the "One Book, One Community" project (www.loc.gov/loc/lcib/0601/cfb.html), which has grown greatly in popularity through the years. This project was the innovation of book guru Nancy Pearl, who began the "If All Seattle Read the Same Book" project in Washington State in 1998 with funding from the Lila Wallace Readers Digest fund and several local sponsors. Since then the concept has expanded throughout the country, and at the 2004 ALA Midwinter Conference, librarians from 54 communities in 23 states attended a preconference on training to become a "One Book" programmer.[31]

In relation to youth participation in libraries, the One Book concept is important because it too can be a trigger for teen involvement. Teen One Book projects have been held in a number of communities, and school libraries are joining in with One School reading programs. Teens can be directly part of such programs, as they help to select titles, promote the reading of the titles, and help to run programs related to the reading.

Developing the Concept of Youth Participation through YALSA

Another important aspect of the 1979 White House Conference on Library and Information Services was a resolution that youth be appointed as voting members on library boards. The idea was that youth should have a say in the library and information services provided for them. In agreement with the resolution, YASD established its ad hoc Youth Participation in Library Decision-Making Committee in 1981.[32]

Although the concept of including teenagers as voting members on library boards is reasonable and deserves the consideration it is given in chapter 8 of this book, the committee eventually reassessed its *primary* focus on this cause. As a result of study and discussion, the committee realized that its work should be to encourage youth participation in libraries on a much broader scale. In essence, it meant "giving young adults real control and responsibility for developing and carrying out projects that meet carefully identified, significant needs," and "letting young adults set the priorities and serve their own interests, rather than manipulating them into activities that the librarian sees as useful or appropriate." This called for allowing, with guidance, "a shift in emphasis and a more open, experimental attitude on the part of the library."[33]

After the YASD Board of Directors approved this change in focus, it revised the charge of the Youth Participation in Library Decision-Making Committee and endorsed the production of a handbook that would serve to explain the notion of youth participation, provide some examples, and give basic guidelines for achieving similar results. Hence, the *Youth Participation in School and Public Libraries* handbook was conceived and was published in 1983. Four years later, at the ALA Midwinter Conference in 1987, the ad hoc Youth Participation in Library Decision-Making Committee became the standing YASD Youth Participation Committee, which still exists today in the YASD's counterpart, the Young Adult Library Services Association (YALSA).

Since that time, the committee's charge has been, "To establish guidelines and/or procedures to involve young adults in the decision-making process which directly affects their access to information and library service at local, state, and national levels; and to provide continuing education and public professional awareness of youth participation."[34]

In 1991 YASD published a companion guide, *Youth Participation in Libraries: A Training Manual*, which provided a specific instructional model for investigating the value of youth participation and actually seeing it through. The interesting thing about this guide was its profession that the ideas and exercises it offered were appropriate both for teenagers *and* adults, independently or working together.[35] In chapter 8, you will learn how some libraries are expanding on this concept today.

In 1996 YALSA updated the information in the first two manuals and combined valuable information from both into a new volume, *Youth Participation in School and Public Libraries: It Works*. Although this publication, and the two manuals previously described, are now all dated and out of print, they set an example for planning, developing, and training for library youth participation in the twenty-first century.

The 1991 White House Conference on Library and Information Services

The 1991 White House Conference on Library and Information Services was truly a foundation of support for youth participation in libraries. A huge influence on the outcome of this conference was the YASD Board of Directors' and Legislative Committee's development of information packets and the YASD Legislative Committee's assistance in writing a paper, "Kids Need Libraries: School and Public Libraries Preparing the Youth of Today for the World of Tomorrow," which offered a framework for discussing issues pertaining to the advancement of library services to young people in the United States.[36]

The fact that 20 young people ages 13 to 18 were an integral part of the state delegations and conference proceedings demonstrated a support for and encouragement of teen library involvement. In addition to intense lobbying efforts by YASD members, other youth divisions, and youth advocates, the teens' presence was instrumental in the passage of the Omnibus Youth Literacy through Libraries initiative. This initiative made detailed recommendations for school libraries, public library children's and young adult services, and a partnership with libraries for youth title.[37]

In 2002 First Lady Laura Bush coordinated a White House Conference on School Libraries. However, encouraging active student participation in running and promoting their libraries was not included in the presentations and discussions at this conference.[38]

Public Libraries as Partners in Youth Development

A groundbreaking initiative in 1998 was the DeWitt Wallace-Reader's Digest "Public Libraries as Partners in Youth Development," brought to fruition as a joint effort of the Urban Libraries Council and participating libraries throughout the country. The creation and fulfillment of this initiative were instrumental in defining, testing, supporting, and advocating for the concept of youth participation in libraries. The culminating documentation describing and encouraging such youth involvement is fascinating and provides excellent evidence to justify any library youth participation activities. You can find information about online and in-print documentation at the Urban Libraries Council Web site (www.urbanlibraries.org).

MOVING AHEAD

Teen services and active teen participation in libraries took a great step forward during the decade following the 1991 White House Conference. Many libraries in the United States, as well as throughout the world, began to pay closer attention to welcoming active teen services and teen spaces in their libraries. However, there is more work to be done. There are still libraries that do not offer teen services at all, let alone youth participation opportunities. A large number of school libraries need to get students directly involved in library activities and promotion. And there are many libraries that have a great need to improve and expand whatever teen library opportunities they are providing. Perhaps, after two decades, it is time to propose and convene a new White House Conference on Library and Information Services with contemporary youth involvement included as a focal point.

From the rich groundwork that has been established by dedicated librarians and active youth-serving organizations in the past, we can move forward on the path they have prepared for us. We need to bring substantial library youth participation advocacy, support, and action into the future. Ultimately, this will benefit present-day teens and those from the next generations, much as it did for the enthusiastic, involved teenagers you read about from long ago. Read on, and explore ways *you* can help to make it all happen.

Read More about It!

Interested in learning more about the history of library teen services and youth participation in libraries? Try these enlightening resources:

Bernier, Anthony, et al., comp. *Two Hundred Years of Young Adult Library Services History: A Chronology.* Voice of Youth Advocates e-VOYA, pdfs.voya.com/VO/YA2/VOYA200708chronology_long.pdf (accessed September 16, 2009). A work in progress that is updated as new information is gathered, this resource is an excellent overview of the roots of teen services in libraries.

Campbell, Patty. *Two Pioneers of Young Adult Library Services.* Lanham, MD: Scarecrow, 1998. Learn more about Mabel Williams, Margaret Edwards, and other notable figures in early young adult services and how their influence is reflected in the way we serve teens in libraries today.

Donelson, Kenneth L., and Alleen Pace Nilsen. *Literature for Today's Young Adults.* 8th ed. Boston: Allyn & Bacon, 2008. The second chapter, "A Brief History of Young Adult Literature," includes very interesting facts and perspectives on the development of school and public libraries.

Edwards, Margaret A. *The Fair Garden and the Swarm of Beasts: The Library and the Young Adult.* Chicago: American Library Association, 2002. This classic by the young adult library services icon includes valuable history and background information about getting teenagers involved in their school and public libraries.

Herald, Diana Tixier, and Diane P. Monnier. "The Beasts Have Arrived: The Blooming of Youth Participation in the Young Adult Library Services Association," *Voice of Youth Advocates* (June 2007): 116–19. Written to celebrate the fiftieth anniversary of YALSA, this article is an interesting and comprehensive look back at the association's ongoing efforts to advocate for and develop youth participation in and through libraries.

Rogers, JoAnn V., ed. *Libraries and Young Adults: Media, Services, and Librarianship.* Littleton, CO: Libraries Unlimited, 1979. Linking historical roots to a state-of-the-art overview of the world of young adult librarianship, this guide serves as an in-depth picture of that fundamentally important period in teen service history.

Walter, Virginia A., and Elaine Meyers. *Teens & Libraries: Getting It Right.* Chicago: American Library Association, 2003. Read the chapter "Where We Came From" to learn more about the history of library teen services.

ENDNOTES

1. Clarence E. Sherman, "The Program of the Public Library for American Youth," *English Journal* 27 (January, 1938): 16–17.

2. Fred Lerner, *Libraries through the Ages* (New York: Continuum, 1999), 108.

3. Alleen Pace Nilsen and Kenneth L. Donelson, *Literature for Today's Young Adults*, 7th ed. (Boston: Allyn & Bacon, 2005), 55.

4. Nilsen and Donelson, *Literature for Today's Young Adults*, 55.

5. Lerner, *Libraries through the Ages*, 108.

6. Lerner, *Libraries through the Ages*, 108–9.

7. Nilsen and Donelson, *Literature for Today's Young Adults*, 63–64.

8. Carrie E. Tucker Dracass, "An Experiment in Library Training in the High School," *English Journal* 1 (April 1912): 221.

9. Dracass, "Experiment in Library Training," 222–25.

10. Dracass, "Experiment in Library Training," 227–31.

11. Emma J. Breck, "The Efficient High-School Library," *English Journal* 5 (January 1916): 10–19.

12. Marion Lovis, "The Library in the Junior High School," *English Journal* 13 (November 1924): 654–57.

13. Lovis, "Library in the Junior High School," 657–58.

14. Lovis, "Library in the Junior High School," 658.

15. Lovis, "Library in the Junior High School," 659.

16. Lerner, *Libraries through the Ages* , 110.

17. Blanche Janecek, "The Library, the Pulse of the School," *The School Review* 65 (Winter 1957): 487.

18. Barbara Will Razzano, "Creating the Library Habit," *Library Journal* 110 (February 15, 1985): 111–14.

19. Tally D. Fugate, *National Youth Administration* (Oklahoma Historical Society's Encyclopedia of Oklahoma History & Culture, 2007), digital.library.okstate.edu/encyclopedia/entries/N/NA014.html (accessed September 16, 2009).

20. "National Commission on Resources for Youth," *Wikipedia, the Free Encyclopedia,* en.wikipedia.org/wiki/National_Commission_on_Resources_for_Youth (accessed August 9, 2007).

21. National Commission on Resources for Youth. *An Introductory Manual on Youth Participation for Program Administrators* (Washington, DC: U.S. Department of Health, Education, and Welfare, 1976), 4.

22. United States Department of Education, Office of Educational Research and Improvement, Center for Libraries and Education Improvement, "Introduction," in *Alliance for Excellence: Librarians Respond to A Nation at Risk: Recommendations and Strategies from Libraries and the Learning Society* (Washington, DC: U.S. Government Printing Office, 1984), iii.

23. U.S. Department of Education, "Introduction," v.

24. U.S. Department of Education, *Alliance for Excellence*, 4.

25. Jane R. Fine, *YASD: A Narrative History from 1976 to 1992* (Young Adult Library Services Association, American Library Association, n.d.), www.ala.org/ala/mgrps/divs/yalsa/aboutyalsa/yasdanarrative.cfm (accessed September 22, 2009).

26. U.S. Department of Health, Education, and Welfare, Social and Rehabilitation Service, U.S. Children's Bureau, *The Story of the White House Conference on Children and Youth.* (Washington, DC: U.S. Government Printing Office, 1967), 1.

27. White House Conference on Youth, *Advisory Task Force Report to the White House Conference on Youth* (Washington, DC: n.p., 1971).

28. Carol Starr, *Brief History of the Young Adult Services Division* (Young Adult Library Services Association, American Library Association, n.d.), www.ala.org/ala/yalsa/aboutyalsa/briefhistory.cfm (accessed April 10, 2008).

29. Virginia H. Mathews, *Libraries, Citizens & Advocacy: The Lasting Effects of Two White House Conferences on Library and Information Services.* (Washington, DC: White House Conference on Library and Information Taskforce, 2004), 1–4.

30. Mathews, *Libraries, Citizens & Advocacy*, 5–6.

31. John Y. Cole, *One Book Projects Grow in Popularity* (Library of Congress, 2006), www.loc.gov/loc/lcib/0601/cfb.html (accessed September 20, 2009).

32. Ellen Lippmann et al. *Youth Participation in School and Public Libraries.* (Boston: National Commission on Resources for Youth, 1983), 1.

33. Lippmann et al., *Youth Participation*, 2.

34. Young Adult Library Services Association, *About YALSA: Youth Participation Committee Description*, American Library Association, www.ala.org/ala/yalsa/aboutyalsab/youthparticipation.cfm (accessed August 4, 2007).

35. Youth Participation Committee, Young Adult Services Division, *Youth Participation in Libraries: A Training Manual.* (Chicago: American Library Association, 1991). 3.

36. Fine, *YASD*.

37. Mathews, *Libraries, Citizens & Advocacy*, 9.

38. *White House Conference on School Libraries Proceedings* (Washington, DC: Institute of Museum and Library Services, 2002), www.imls.gov/news/events/whitehouse.shtm (accesssed September 17, 2009).

3

Ways Teens Can Participate: Teen Advisory Boards, Teen Volunteers, and Library Aides in School and Public Libraries

It is enlightening to explore the wide variety of teen participation opportunities available in libraries today. In the next chapters, you will be doing just that. You will learn about exciting programs, activities, and events that teens in your library might emulate.

These teen-oriented activities reflect the philosophical base of library teen services and the library youth involvement history we have investigated in the previous chapters. Through exploring the program and activity descriptions, you will discover a legacy of workable and successful ideas that reinforce a commitment to incorporating library teen involvement. Consider those that would be the best fit for your library setting as you make plans to improve or activate such participation.

FOUNDATIONS OF TEEN INVOLVEMENT

Teen advisory boards and organized groups of teen library volunteers are usually the foundation of any youth participation events, activities, programs, and services in school and public libraries. Therefore, we begin our exploration of teen involvement with these two kinds of groups. You will see, as we expand to other facets of successful participation, how teens active at this level are truly at its heart.

Teen Advisory Boards

Teen advisory boards (TABs) in libraries come in all sizes and can be organized in a variety of ways. No matter what a group is called—and you'll notice that names vary from simple and straightforward to extremely creative and unique—the teens who belong to yours can become the lifeblood of your school or public library.

One of the most important things to remember about TABs is that, in most library settings, these kinds of groups are not offered as "programs" per se. For the most part, teens who are participating in them are serving as *volunteers* who will help to provide program*s* for fellow teens, offer advice to their librarians, and give assistance in a wide variety of ways as needed. In school libraries, groups like this are usually considered extracurricular activities or are offered as ways to earn academic or service-learning credits. TAB members in public libraries may likewise earn service-learning or other volunteer hours through their participation.

Being aware of and promoting the differences between "program" and "volunteer group" can be instrumental in gaining support for your TAB and its activities. For example, when budget cuts occur, and programs must be downsized or eliminated, keeping your TAB in its proper category of "volunteer group" rather than "program" might be the variable that helps to save it. On the other hand, when funding is available to be allocated, you will have a good argument for providing money to pay for TAB meeting expenses in addition to the programs your teens wish to plan and run through your TAB.

In a public library, another good reason to ensure that your TAB is considered a volunteer group is that you might be able to enlist members and keep track of them in cooperation with your library's volunteer coordinator, if you have one. Whether you have such a coordinator or not, you will still want to make sure your TAB members are officially enrolled, with signed parental or guardian permission, so that they are covered under your library's volunteer insurance policy.

The Santa Cruz Public Libraries in California (www.santacruzpl.org/) require all volunteers—teens, adults, and even court-appointed community service workers—to complete a Friends of the Library volunteer application. Teens complete a Young Friends of the Library version (see figure 3.1). The teens are then covered under the library system's Friends liability insurance.[1] This might be another approach for your library to consider, if it currently does not have a system in place for insuring your teen TAB members and other teen library volunteers via town or city volunteer coverage.

Remember, providing liability insurance of some kind is a *very important step* that many libraries fail to take for their volunteers. Consider that if you are doing a program and a teen accidentally gets hurt, your library could be legally responsible. Insurance usually covers that liability for official library volunteers of any age. You will want to consult with the person in charge of your volunteers and/or your administrators to prepare the proper forms and follow approved procedures for making this happen.

What Kind of TAB Format?

If you have just one library in your town, or if you work in a school library, you might think that the choice you have for a teen advisory group format is easy: one group, one library. However, even that format might have sensible variations. If you work in a multi-library system, you have even more options for setting up and running your TAB.

In the next sections you will discover that there can be several format choices, as well as important considerations to keep in mind for each. You might even realize that the right format for your group is something completely new, based on the kinds of TAB arrangements described in the following library examples.

green

Young Friends Volunteer Application

Name_____ Phone_____

Address_____ Date of Birth_____

City_____ State_____ Zip_____

In case of emergency, please contact:
Name_____**Relationship** _____

Phone_____Address_____

Describe the special talents, hobbies or skills you would like to use as a

volunteer:_____

_____

Which library branch would you prefer? Please number your first three choices.
_____Aptos　　　　　_____Capitola　　　　　_____Garfield Park
_____Boulder Creek　　_____Central　　　　　_____La Selva Beach
_____Branciforte　　　_____Felton　　　　　_____Live Oak
　　　　　　　　　　　　　　　　　　　　　　_____Scotts Valley

What days and what times would you like to volunteer?
_____Monday　　　_____Tuesday　　　_____Wednesday
_____Thursday　　_____Friday　　　_____Saturday
_____Sunday (Central only)

Do you speak or understand a language other than English?_____

The following is a list of typical volunteer opportunities. Please check your preferences.

_____Make signs, posters and other artwork　　_____Clean books
_____Help with KIDS ONLY BOOKSALE　　　　_____Clean shelves
_____Set up/clean up for special programs　　　_____Shelve books
_____Prepare new paperbacks to be checked out　_____Help with SUMMER READING
_____Prepare craft materials for story time or preschool craft program

Signature_____ **Date**_____

Staff supervisor_____	Branch_____
Volunteer will work with_____	Day(s) and time(s) _____
Volunteer is completing community service requirements ____Yes ____No Hours required: _____	
Volunteer is available during summer vacation only ____Yes ____No	

Friends of the Santa Cruz Public Libraries, Inc.
P. O. Box 8472, 224 Church St., Santa Cruz, CA 95061 (831) 420-5790　　　　2/08

Figure 3.1. Santa Cruz Public Library, Young Friends Application

OCEAN COUNTY LIBRARY, NEW JERSEY: TABS IN INDIVIDUAL BRANCHES. The first option might be for a library system to have a TAB at each library location. That means there will be several TABs, each with its individual mission and flavor, depending on the teen participants and the community in which each branch is located. The benefits of doing a TAB this way are that teens do not have to travel far to get to meetings, because they are held in their neighborhood libraries, and a deeper sense of camaraderie develops when teens work with the same group and advisor at the same place on a regular basis. This option requires a teen services staff person or someone else willing and able to work with teens at each branch location, unless such staff member is able to travel among various branches.

The Ocean County Library (theoceancountylibrary.org/) in New Jersey has 19 library branches. In most of the branches, there are individual TAB groups. Each group has its own meeting times and plans its own events. However, all groups in the library system use the name "TAB," and the teens get the same T-shirts as part of their participation. A variation on this format might be to allow each TAB group to have its own name and its own T-shirt design. (See figure 3.2.)

A helpful goal each year for libraries using this system might be to occasionally get the members of a TAB from one branch together with the members from another branch, for a project, a joint meeting, or just socially. This way the teens get to know one another as they work from various locations on the overall library mission for teen services. The Ocean County Library System takes this one step further by holding a TAB Forum each year (more about this in chapter 8). This is a way for the TAB groups not only to get together socially, but to project and plan for the library system's future programs and teen services.[2]

POUDRE RIVER PUBLIC LIBRARY DISTRICT, FORT COLLINS, COLORADO: ONE TAB ROTATES MEETING LOCATIONS. Another TAB option for a library system is to have one TAB and have meetings rotate among branches. This works best in a city where there is a good public transportation system and there are only a few branches.

Here is a potential idea to check out: In Fort Collins, Colorado, there is city bus service provided by Transfort. A wonderful aspect of Transfort is that persons under 18 years old may travel for free at any time, to any stop! If you have local bus service that charges children and teenagers to travel, you might want to check into the possibility of negotiating such free transportation. Even if your community is not able to provide totally free bus service to youth for most of the year, you might discover that it can at least be arranged for the summer months when students are out of school and they need to be able to get to library events. Another option might be to negotiate a reduced rate for teens.

The Poudre River Public Library District (www.poudrelibraries.org), where I work, has three library branches, and we rotate our Interesting Reader Society TAB meetings equally among them. Because Fort Collins is not overwhelmingly large, parents or the teens themselves who are able can drive to meetings, or teens can take the bus or ride their bikes. This works out well in our community, and we usually have a good turnout for our meetings at each location.

SANTA CRUZ PUBLIC LIBRARY, CALIFORNIA: TWO KINDS OF TABS. The Santa Cruz Public Library has yet another system: two teen advisory groups. One is their Teen Advisory Council (TAC), which was established in 1996 and operates from a single location—the library system's young adult branch. The other is their Advisory Council of Teens (ACT), started in 2008, which includes members from its 10 library branches.

ACT meetings rotate among the library system's three centralized braches. Working together and separately, depending on the activity, TAC and ACT members help with outreach events such as a Teen Job Fair and the Friends of the Library Book Sales; record stories for the children's Dial-A-Story project; make material recommendations for the teen collection; and review and recommend titles for the teen Web page.[3] (See figure 3.3, p. 39.)

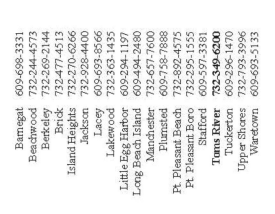

TAB TEENS SPEAK OUT

"The Teen Advisory Board gives teens something positive to do and to look forward to"

"Dude, who knew the library was so fun? There's all kinds of cool stuff to do here"

"I enjoy volunteering at the library. I give up a couple hours that would otherwise be spent in front of the TV. It makes me feel good to give back to my community"

"I got to design a poster about teen problems. It was awesome"

"TAB is a good opportunity for community involvement as well as a beneficial life experience"

"I started coming for the people and video games and stuff, but now I come because it's way cooler than my house"

Barnegat	609-698-3331
Beachwood	732-244-4573
Berkeley	732-269-2144
Brick	732-477-4513
Island Heights	732-270-6266
Jackson	732-928-4400
Lacey	609-693-8566
Lakewood	732-363-1435
Little Egg Harbor	609-294-1197
Long Beach Island	609-494-2480
Manchester	732-657-7600
Plumsted	609-758-7888
Pt. Pleasant Beach	732-892-4575
Pt. Pleasant Boro	732-295-1555
Stafford	609-597-3381
Toms River	**732-349-6200**
Tuckerton	609-296-1470
Upper Shores	732-793-3996
Waretown	609-693-5133

The Ocean County Library Teen Services Dept.
101 Washington Street Toms River, NJ 08753

OCEAN COUNTY LIBRARY TEEN ADVISORY BOARD
www.theoceancountylibrary.org

Figure 3.2. Ocean County Library, TAB Application Brochure

Ocean County Library
Teen Advisory Board Application

Name _____

Street Address _____

City _____ ST _____ Zip _____

Home Phone _____

Cell Phone _____

Teen Cell Phone _____

Email _____

School _____

Grade _____

Age _____ Date of Birth _____

May we contact you by text message?   Y   N

Shirt Size   S   M   L   XL   XXL
                    (circle one)

I hereby grant my permission for my child/charge to participate in the Teen Advisory Board (TAB) Volunteer Program at the Ocean County Library and any subsequent volunteer programs.

Parent or Guardian Signature

X _____

Check Us Out Online!

 Theoceancountylibrary.org/ teens/teens.htm

 Myspace.com/oclteen

 Facebook.com search "od teen"

How can I join?

Complete and return this application to your local branch of the Ocean County Library system. We'll do the rest.

No TAB at your branch?

Be a pioneer and start one! Contact the teen librarian at your branch to get started.

TAB Activities
Movie Events, Book Clubs, Anime Events, Open Mic Poetry Events, Graphic Novel/Manga Advisors, Teen Book Reviewers, Teen Focus Groups Advising on Teen Spaces, Fundraisers, Read-A-Thons, Gaming Tournaments, Author Events **& More!**

Who can join?
Teens in grades 7-12, from any school district in Ocean County, are eligible to join TAB.

What will teens do on the TAB?
Help the library stay current with teen trends and hot topics. Advise the library on collectons, programs and services. Suggest, plan, execute and attend programs. Connect with TAB's from other library branches. Publicize and promote programs.

Why should I join?
Make new friends and have fun while building teamwork and leadership skills. Earn community service hours which make a REAL difference in your community and get a free TAB t-shirt.

When does TAB meet?
TAB meetings and events vary in schedule. Ask a teen librarian at your local branch to see what's going on near you.

Figure 3.2. Ocean County Library, TAB Application Brochure (Cont.)

Figure 3.3. Santa Cruz Public Library, ACT Sign

AUSTIN PUBLIC LIBRARY, AUSTIN, TEXAS: ROTATE TAB BETWEEN PUBLIC LIBRARY AND SCHOOLS. The Teen Advisory Group (TAG) at the Southeast Branch of the Austin Public Library (www.ci.austin.tx.us/library/) was launched in 2006 and is still evolving. An interesting aspect of this TAG is where and when meetings are held. Most other public library teen advisory groups hold their meetings at the library itself, or one of its branches, usually once or twice a month. During the fall of 2008, librarians from the Southeast Branch began to hold TAG meetings in the local high school library, where many teens hang out during their lunch periods.[4]

Bringing some TAG meetings to the schools, in addition to holding some at the public library, is a unique joint venture that allows more flexibility for teens who wish to participate. Some of the meetings come to *them*, rather than having the teens come to the library for all of the meetings. Keep that idea in mind in case this option might work well in *your* community.

Meeting Time and Space

This mention of place and time brings up an important point. Although staggering meetings between the public and high school libraries works for this branch, how often and where meetings are held in any library or library system depends on a variety of factors. You should consider the schedule of a group's adult advisor, as well as the schedules of the teens who are or who will be involved. You also need to think about a comfortable and accessible meeting place.

Most libraries have a room or auditorium that can be reserved for TAB meetings. However, many small libraries do not have a meeting room. If this describes your library, you know finding a meeting place can be a real challenge, but it is one that is not insurmountable. If there is a nearby school, church, organization, or agency that might be willing to let the teens meet in one of their meeting facilities, you could try that as an option. The idea is to get the teens into the library as much as possible, but if there is no meeting room, at least they will have a place to plan, discuss, and interact. However, any programming or volunteer activities your teens develop and participate in should take place in the library building itself.

Another idea is to meet outside if there is a patio or picnic area available, although you would need a backup for inclement weather. You might also consider meeting in the library itself during off hours. Perhaps your library or one of its branches closes at 6:00 p.m. on Thursday evenings, or doesn't open until noon on Saturday. You could get permission to hold your meetings in the library before or after opening. Don't let the need for creative meeting space prevent you from starting and running a TAB!

Some TAB groups meet each month on the same day and at the same time. Some stagger the meetings so that one is held on one day and the next meeting is held on another. For example, one meeting might be held on a Saturday afternoon at 2:00 p.m., and the next meeting on a Thursday night at 7:00 p.m. In a branch system setting with one teen group, meetings rotating among branch locations have to be carefully scheduled and announced. Special activities, events, and training could require additional meetings or meetings of subgroups.

Talk over group needs, interests, and limitations with your teens, and let them know the perimeters of your schedule as you likewise learn about theirs, so that you can come up with meeting times and places that suit as many participants as possible. Your teens will probably come up with some good thoughts about scheduling meetings as well, so enlist their help.

SOUTH BRUNSWICK PUBLIC LIBRARY, SOUTH BRUNSWICK, NEW JERSEY: TWO-TIERED TABs. Another inspiring example of teen advisory board participation comes from the South Brunswick Public Library (www.sbpl.info). Its Youth Advisory Council (YAC) has approximately 35 to 45 members at any given meeting, with about 90 on the e-mail roster. In a township of fewer than 40,000 people, those numbers are impressive.

In a unique approach to how teen participation opportunities are offered, YAC is only the first teen advisory board level at the South Brunswick Public Library. In direct response to the teens asking for more responsibility and more opportunities to take charge, their attuned and dedicated advisor, Saleena Davidson, created an additional leadership group in 2006 called the Teen Special Forces (TSF), which the teens themselves named. It is a smaller group than YAC, with no more than 30 members, and all must fulfill certain requirements for admission as decided by the teens themselves. This includes 30 hours volunteering in the library, plus being recommended by a current member of the group *or* submitting letters of recommendation from respected community members.

TSF members are expected to create programs from start to finish with minimal input from Saleena. They also serve as teen trainers for other volunteers and have special membership cards that permit them to be in staff areas unsupervised. This privilege gives them telephone, desk, and computer access when needed for programming or support work.

YAC and TSF participation allows the teens to feel that they are truly a part of the library. A great deal of extraordinary programming has resulted from the efforts of these groups, both before and after the formation of TSF. For example, the teens created an original murder mystery dinner theater production. In 2005 they brought to life the idea of a town festival that they could help run, and it has been continuing successfully since then. As a matter of fact, it became so large that Saleena and the teens agreed to move the program under the auspices of the Children's Department.

The YAC and TSF teens also conceived and planned a program called "A Celebration of Art and Diversity," which highlighted performing and creative art from a variety of ethnicities and was so popular it has been repeated.[5] You'll notice as you read through the upcoming library examples in this book how many are art and performance oriented. These are definitely outstanding targets for successful teen participation programming, and you'll find out more about them in the following chapter.

If you have a large number of teens who wish to be involved in your library, like those at the South Brunswick Public Library, with some seeking a chance to be more empowered than others, you might want to consider a two-tiered advisory group arrangement for them. This library demonstrates that it can be done very well.

Teen Volunteers

Another popular method to incorporate library teen participation is to offer a regular teen volunteer program. These "programs" are ongoing opportunities for teens to be scheduled for specific times and targeted job duties, such as running and staffing children's and/or teens' summer reading programs, helping to shelve books, or providing craft programs for young children. Be aware that, like TABs, the term "program" is being used here in the context of a *volunteer opportunity*, not a short-term event or activity that would define a standard library "program" to which the general teen population would be invited.

Teens usually fill out an application to be volunteers, and many libraries require an orientation process and signed parental or guardian agreement stating that the responsible adult giving approval will support his or her teen's commitment. This means the adult understands that transportation will be provided and that the teen has permission to spend the time allocated to fulfilling his or her volunteer duties. Again, enrolling teen volunteers on the official library vol- unteer roster ensures that the teens are covered by library insurance when on duty.

You will see many positive examples of library teen volunteers throughout the coming chapters, plus a closer look at how to get teens involved in the first place in chapter 9.

Many of my teens use their YAC hours towards National Honor Society requirements, but many have also found friends and a safe haven here . . . sort of a second home with another "mom" to talk to. They seem to enjoy the power of controlling their own programming as well.

As for those who don't participate as volunteers, they still get to come to the programs, and reap the benefits, so to speak, of the labors of their fellows.[6]

Saleena Davidson
YA/Reference Librarian
South Brunswick Public Library, New Jersey

I've been a member of YAC for the last two years, and a member of TSF for about a year and a half. Anyone from middle schoolers to high schoolers can come and snack on food while bouncing around ideas for new programs or clubs, or ways to organize the teen volunteers themselves.

TSF has nomination-based entry. We make the final decisions on many teen activities, and then execute them. TSF plans the details of teen events, like what games to have, what movies to watch, or how to go about organizing everything, and then sets them in action with the help of other volunteers. Some of our current and upcoming teen-planned events include a Top Model contest, a Lock-In at the library, a Dance Dance Revolution tournament, and making crafts.

TSF meetings come directly after YAC meetings. YAC is kind of like the brainstorm to TSF's final draft. The meetings occur on the first Saturday of every month. Saleena hopes to expand both the YAC and TSF groups in the next few years since many of the current members have graduated.

I personally really enjoy both YAC and TSF meetings. YAC is much louder and vigorous, people talking at all times either in response to a question or just with each other. TSF is more subdued, although no less productive. Being a relatively quiet person, I sometimes have trouble getting out ideas in overwhelming environments. I never feel that way in YAC or TSF. The atmosphere is so laid back and inviting, maybe just because of my familiarity with the library and the people there, but it's definitely comfortable.[7]

Ashwini Dhokte
South Brunswick Public Library, New Jersey

Teens have personal reasons why they want to volunteer, and that can be either to make new friends or to earn hours for service learning. Many teens want to be part of something that helps their community and is interesting to do. Volunteering helps teens understand commitment and dedication, and helps teach job skills and pride in doing a good job.

Motivating teens is not hard when you let them have some control. Building a teen volunteer program that promotes respect and understanding instills a connection to service that can be the beginning of a lifelong commitment. Through teens communicating to other teens, the collective voice is heard and information is shared, loud and clear.[8]

Kathee Herbstreit
Volunteer Coordinator
City of Mesa Library, Arizona

Library Pals

At the Poudre River Public Library District, there are two young adult volunteer programs, one potentially leading to the other. Both foster a high level of youth participation and consciously aim to keep youth actively engaged in their library beyond the teen years. You have already been introduced to the Interesting Reader Society. Now, find out more about the other way that teens can get involved in this library system.

Fifty to sixty-five "Library Pals" volunteers who have completed grades 5 through 8 are recruited every summer via flyers, press releases, and school newsletter. The majority of these Library Pals are stationed at the Main Library with the others serving at the remaining two library branches. Applicants who were not able to get into the program the year before because it was full when they applied or because their application was submitted after the deadline are targeted to apply the following year.

Giny McConathy, the Children's Services library assistant in charge of the Library Pals program, says, "The library intentionally beats the bushes for kids whose parents might not have supported or pushed their son or daughter's participation the previous year." She stresses that the library focuses on recruiting disadvantaged young people who might not have the parental support and encouragement that other teens in the community do, and who really would benefit from participating in the program, by letting them know they are truly needed.[9]

Of course, *any* interested tween or teen from the community is highly encouraged to apply and participate—including those whose parents *are* particularly supportive—but the special effort to get *disadvantaged* youth involved may bring some young people into the library fold who might otherwise have never known about the library and what it has to offer.

REACHING OUT TO DISADVANTAGED YOUTH VOLUNTEERS. The Poudre River Public Library District is on the right track with its outreach efforts to recruit disadvantaged youth volunteers, according to the 2007 report based on the publication *Youth Volunteering and Civic Engagement Survey*, from the Corporation for National and Community Service, the first major national study of teen volunteering in more than a decade. This study gathered information on the volunteering habits and civic attitudes of youth between the ages of 12 and 18 and documented a difference in volunteer behavior among youth from differing economic backgrounds. Youth considered disadvantaged came from families that had incomes less than or equal to 200 percent of the 2005 federal poverty level guidelines. Based on this formula, 22 percent of all survey respondents were considered disadvantaged. Further analysis revealed that this population was significantly more likely to be black or African American, Hispanic or Latino, or born outside of the United States. They were also less likely than youth from nondisadvantaged circumstances to do well academically or have one or both parents with at least some college education.[10]

The results of the study indicated the following:

• A "class gap" exists in teenage volunteering. The volunteer rate of youth from disadvantaged circumstances (DAC) is 16 percentage points lower than the rate for other youth.

• Although youth from DAC are less likely to volunteer than other youth, when they *do* volunteer, *they do so with the same level of intensity*.

• Teachers play a key role in motivating youth from DAC to volunteer. Regardless of their economic circumstances, youth are most likely to volunteer because they are asked, and when they are asked, a teacher is the most likely person to make the request. Both public and school librarians may connect with teachers who can help recruit teens who would benefit most from their library volunteer activities. Librarians may also ask, and from my observations and experience, my guess is that when we do, we get just as much positive response as teachers do from the teens with whom we connect.

• DAC youths who volunteer demonstrate more positive civic attitudes than those who don't.

• A high percentage of DAC teen volunteers plan to graduate from a four-year college.

• Youth from DAC who volunteer have a high rate of continual volunteerism and are more likely than other youth to be motivated to gain skills.

• Youth from DAC are less likely than other youth to experience "pathways" to civic engagement unless they are invited and encouraged.

• Religious organizations and spiritual beliefs play a key role in volunteering among youth from DAC. You might contact some of your local youth ministers to see if they can recommend teens for involvement in your library.

• Volunteering among youth from DAC correlates with parental education levels. A majority of DAC youth volunteers have at least one parent who has attended college.[11]

The expectation is that the findings of this study will help community organizations, including libraries, gain greater insight into the importance of positive youth volunteering experiences. The aim is to close the gap between youth from disadvantaged and nondisadvantaged circumstances who volunteer, and particularly to engage more youth in disadvantaged circumstances to partake in volunteer service. This can be accomplished by ensuring that positive participatory opportunities are offered, they are well publicized, and libraries encourage special invitations to youth who might not be aware of opportunities or whose parents might not encourage participation. Recruiting teens from disadvantaged conditions will instill a constructive perception of libraries in them and offer a positive place for them to belong, in many of the ways described in chapter 1.

TEENS WITH DIFFERENT ABILITIES HAVE A PLACE, TOO. At the Poudre River Public Library District, special needs youth are also encouraged to be Library Pals when they are capable. Giny McConathy believes it is important to include teens who are "differently abled" whenever possible and to help them find a niche as library volunteers where they will feel successful and involved. She says that many teens with special needs can fill a role to benefit the library, and she seeks out opportunities for them. She has worked with hearing impaired teens, a little person, a developmentally disabled youth, and one with autism-like Asperger syndrome. It has sometimes been a stretch to provide opportunities for these teens as Library Pals, but Giny says that the task of donning the mascot costume has been a boon. If teens are extremely shy or can't speak well, wearing a costume to delight little children at a special event allows them to be helpful and successful. Another undertaking for differently abled youth might be to hand out bookmarks or other materials.

Having differently abled teens involved in library youth participation activities comes with additional requirements, not just patience and flexibility. The teens must be able to work with the library staff and other Library Pals independent of any parental assistance. Sometimes a nervous parent hovers nearby, hanging around the library during the two hours his or her son or daughter works a shift. But Giny notes that even parents of *non*-special needs volunteers sometimes do this. As long as such parents keep their distance, do not interfere, and leave the job of supervising and monitoring Library Pals to the staff, there is not a problem with parents remaining on the premises.

No matter the circumstances of teens who enter the volunteer program, it is vital for *all* of them to feel connected to the library and to develop a sense of teamwork and camaraderie. Giny says, "Library Pals need to feel like they are on the 'staff side of life.' They need to truly consider themselves library staff members. They also need to feel that their work is vital, whether it is shelving books or providing a storytime. Part of the training the teens receive is developing a variety of skills. Not every teen wants to be a star, but some teens do, and some fit into every 'comfort zone' in between. It is important to find the right teens to fill all the valued roles available."[12]

School Teen Advisory Clubs and Library Aides

Quite a few library-oriented people are surprised to learn that, like their public library counterparts, school libraries can and do have formal and informal teen advisory groups and other teen participation opportunities of various kinds. These groups and activities usually differ from but can complement the more common and better known "library aide" programs, which have their roots in some of the earliest secondary school libraries that were discussed in chapter 2. Both kinds of teen participation opportunities in school libraries are experiencing interesting and innovative changes these days. Sometimes they are even getting involved in partnerships with public libraries.

In the following sections you will learn how a selected sample of these school libraries benefit the teens, their schools, and even their communities through their youth participation endeavors. If you work in a school library, or partner with one, think about how you might incorporate the ideas reflected in the following examples in your own city or town.

Cedar Valley Middle School Library, Austin, Texas

At the Cedar Valley Middle School (schools.roundrockisd.org/cedarvalley), amazing things happen through the school library, simply because it has an official TAB. It all begins at the start of each school year, when Librarian Kate DiPronio calls an informational meeting for any students interested in joining the group. At the meeting, returning TAB members share information about what they do and how meetings are conducted. At the end, Kate sends around a sign-in sheet; she then sees who follows up by attending subsequent meetings.

TAB meets every other Friday during the school year to plan programs. The teens decide what they would like to do and how to plan and run each event. Kate serves as facilitator and guide only, ensuring the teens' ideas will unfold the way they wish.

Approximately 20 teens per year are involved in TAB in some capacity, with 10–12 being very active. Almost all of the students who belong to TAB are girls, but the teens who take part in the programs they provide are a good mix of each gender. At their programs last year, a low of 60 students and a high of 140 students participated in individual activities and events.

TAB plans and runs all "early release day" programs, which are on six days during the school year when the school dismisses students at 1:30 p.m. to allow for teacher in-service time. Program topics have included a game day, getting ready for summer fun with karaoke, a "Death by Chocolate" program, holiday crafts, and Halloween events.

TAB members involved in fund-raising run all aspects of the school library's book fair except for money collection. They organize set up, provide security, conduct promotional activities, and handle take down. They also do fund-raising called Mocha Madness, for which they make mochas and sell them for $1 before school.

TAB is instrumental in promoting the library to the school community. Members make signs for the hallways and are very vocal in spreading the word about what the library has to offer. TAB also promotes the library by producing public service announcements, recorded on video and shown over the schoolwide television system. In addition, members make READ posters using software from the American Library Association to promote reading among their peers.[13]

As you can see, the TAB at Cedar Valley Middle School is one inspiring example of what a *school* teen advisory group can be. Read on . . . .

Corona del Sol High School Library, Tempe, Arizona

At Corona del Sol High School (www.tuhsd.k12.az.us/CDS), teen members of the Friends of the Library (FOTL) Club plan monthly themes to encourage reading, promote the school library, and do much, much more.

FOTL Club is a group of about 12 enthusiastic students, and though their numbers are small, the positive effects of their work are extremely widespread. The group is well-rounded, consisting of regular students, honor students, and special needs students of both genders. FOTL members learn how to run meetings, manage time, fund-raise, and contribute creatively.

Members of the FOTL Club meet each Monday in the library right after school and must complete 20 hours of community service to earn a certificate of participation at the end of the school year. Projects and activities are developed by the teens through brainstorming and group consensus.

The FOTL Club functions under the auspices of the Friends of Libraries USA (www.folusa.org), and membership is open to any Corona del Sol High School student. Announcements of meetings are made to encourage all Corona students to come and join the group. FOTL Club members create new T-shirt designs every year to advertise the group and to promote reading. The back design encompasses the word "READ" in the languages offered at Corona del Sol as well as in the languages represented by their school's current English Language Learner students.

As a matter of fact, like Corona del Sol, any school library or public library young adult department that wishes to start a Teen Friends of the Library group may register as a member of FOLUSA (www.folusa.org/resources/html-versions/fact-sheet-5.php) for $50 per year.

An important note: FOLUSA encourages member groups to have dues. On the Web page that gives guidelines for starting a Teen Group, it even specifies: "Set dues, even if very low—it increases the importance of the group." Because of this recommendation, the FOTL Club *does* have dues of $5.00 a year. The money goes toward paying for the end-of-the-year banquet. However, libraries should consider whether, if such dues proved to be a hardship for any student who wishes to participate, they would have to make exceptions and special arrangements. This goes for any school and public libraries that want to operate their teen advisory boards under FOLUSA.

The FOTL Club members are involved in a wide variety of activities. They perform community service for their school, school library, local public libraries, and outside community. Each April the Club buys two school copies of the title selected for Arizona's "One Book. One Goal. One Month" program. The group publicizes upcoming events offered at the nearby Chandler Public Library's Sunset Branch and those offered at the Tempe Public Library. The club members also help decorate the school library's display cases and bulletin boards, and they make recommendations for books that they would like to see in the collection.

The philosophy of the FOTL Club members is that by working together they will leave the world a little better than the way they found it. This means providing service beyond the school library's boundaries, which leads members to do work with young children and to also do outreach fund-raising. You'll read more about these aspects of the group later in this chapter and in chapter 7.[14]

Corona del Sol FOTL Club Teens Speak Out[15]

We encourage our fellow students to make full use of library facilities by beautifying our school library and promoting reading through exciting contests and other activities that students and teachers alike can participate in.

Sarah Nagaratnam

I enjoy socializing with other members, being useful in doing more community service, and maintaining the library with fun, changing themes using posters, cartoon characters, and words.

Seetha Talluru

I feel as if I am indeed a "Friend of the Library." Along with the other members of the club, I work to make the library a better place, a more stimulating environment. Yet I also serve the school in that I encourage others to make use of this resource.

Whitney Brodersen

We help organize the shelves from time to time, so that other students can find the books they're looking for in the right place.

Zachary Hillenbrand

Shepherd Junior High School Library, Mesa, Arizona

The Shepherd Junior High school library in Mesa, Arizona (www.mpsaz.org/shepherd), serves a student body of 1,250 and has two active student library participation groups. Teacher-Librarian Melanie Limbert-Callahan said, "The most amazing fact regarding both groups is the diversity in them. An assortment of students from varying backgrounds are members. By participating in these groups, students learn responsibility, social skills, tolerance, and team work. Others benefit from the teen involvement because when they enter the library they see it as a 'student friendly' environment. They feel welcomed and accepted. They can also ask peers for recommendations."16 The following sections explain how all this is accomplished.

OFF THE SHELF BOOK CLUB. The first Shepherd Junior High library group is the Off the Shelf (OTS) Book Club. They meet once a week, and in 2008 there were 45 members, three-quarters girls and a quarter boys. Their mission is to develop activities to bring other students into the library. They invent and sponsor contests, feature books and make displays, paint posters, sponsor afterschool and/or lunchtime activities, and more. Their accomplishments are interesting and varied and could easily be duplicated by other groups.

In November, during National Games Week, students came to the library during lunch to play a variety of games, including Jeopardy, Yahtzee, Monopoly, cards, and others. One afternoon, students even stayed and played games until 5:00 p.m. This activity was a huge success, in part because of the great promotion by OTS members, who painted posters that hung in the halls to advertise the event. They even had a Monopoly game display with the history of the game highlighted. An original 1930s game, along with several variations of Monopoly, such as the *Star Wars*, *Simpsons*, and Coke versions, made the display interesting and colorful. In addition, the students made daily announcements on the PA system, and Melanie Limbert-Callahan submitted the information for the school television bulletin board.

This is just one of the many activities that OTS has sponsored. Others include some centered on weekly or monthly themes, such as Teen Read Week, Banned Book Week, and even "Appreciate a Dragon! Week." A Murder Mystery event the group created was called "The Pharaoh's Curse." Book Club members were all part of the drama surrounding fictional attempts to murder a high school prom queen. Students came after school to solve the mystery, enjoy treats, and have a great time.

Whenever OTS sponsors activities like these, whether it is the Murder Mystery event, game activities, or Dr. Seuss "Read Across America" events, participation is open to all students, which gets more teens involved. Contests, special activities, author visits, or celebrations are promoted during student and video announcements. OTS members paint posters to hang around the school and the library, make fliers, and visit homeroom classes.

They help to plan, run, and promote book fairs, which you'll read more about elsewhere in this chapter. Melanie also does classroom booktalks during which she promotes events. The school marquee and parent newsletters are additional sources of publicity.

Another component of the Book Club is its support of reading. The members help prepare for author visits by giving booktalks, painting posters advertising the events, and welcoming the authors. They even add a greeting of "Welcome . . . , author of . . ." to the school marquee. One advantage of club membership is that teens get to attend every author event and meet and pose in a group photo with each author, after which Melanie immediately prints the photo and has the author sign it. The photographs are then hung on the library's Author Wall.

A further Book Club responsibility is to suggest materials for the library. For books added to the collection, the members produce a quarterly publication that rates titles and summarizes story lines. They also make review cards, which are placed in the pockets of the books. In addition, some members periodically read ARCs and give Melanie feedback about the title's appropriateness for their library. Members who serve in this latter capacity are a limited group that has strong parental support for the activity.

Membership in OTS Book Club is advertised just like all the other school clubs, in the student handbook. Students also promote it during announcements, inviting everyone to attend with a "We hope to see you there!" message, and through video announcements that publicize all meeting dates and times. Sometimes members hang informational posters in the halls, and the school newspaper and the parent newsletter also promote the club.[17]

MEDIA SQUAD. Shepherd Junior High Library doesn't stop there. Its second active school library group is called the Media Squad. These students work in the library before and after school and/or during lunchtime. Their participation is strictly voluntary. However, students must still complete an application form to join (see figure 3.4, p. 48).

Once Melanie receives an application, she checks on the student's school performance. Next, students are interviewed about why and when they want to work in the library, and they are given a list of potential tasks to be performed. A pledge statement rounds out the application. Students who are approved must complete a training session, which lasts about a week.

Each year, Melanie has more than 30 students in Media Squad, 15–18 each semester, equally divided between girls and boys. Because the group is so popular and there are limited positions, she has had to turn away many others and direct them to the OTS Book Club instead. Having another group or activity for interested students to join instead of completely turning them away is important in encouraging, rather than discouraging, teen participation.

Media Squad members check books in and out, dust, clean, shelve, man the desk, and help fellow students find materials. They keep time cards of their service. A perk of being on the Media Squad is getting a first chance to check out new books from the library. There are also pizza parties at the end of each semester to celebrate a job well done.

One or more Media Squad contests are continually in full swing, each one addressing unique interests, to entice students to the library. They include Drawing Contests (for the artistic), "First Line" contests (for avid readers), "Famous Quotes" contests (teaches Internet use), trivia contests, and "Identify the Teacher" contests. There are also activities like "Vote for Your Favorite Book" and "Sound Off." Sound Off is a wall on which students may respond to a question or idea, like a graffiti wall.

To encourage Media Squad participation, students advertise the group during student and video announcements, as they do for the OTS Book Club. Students might also see other students working and inquire about how to apply.

Shepherd Media Squad Application

Thanks for your interest in being part of the Shepherd Media Squad. As a Media Squad member you may be asked to perform the following tasks:

- Check books in and/or out at the counter
- Put books in alphabetical order
- Reshelf books, magazines, etc.
- Dust computers or book shelves
- Make posters or signs
- Clean library tables

To be a part of the Media Squad you must have grades of C's or higher and have good moral character.

Name _____ Grade_____

Why do you want to work in the library? _____
_____
_____

When do you want to work in the library?   (Check all that apply)
☐ Before School   ☐ After School
☐ During A Lunch   ☐ During B Lunch   ☐ During C Lunch

How often do you want to work in the library?
☐ Every day   ☐ Mondays   ☐ Tuesdays   ☐ Wednesdays   ☐ Thursdays ☐ Fridays

I promise to be responsible, honest, and cheerful when working in the library. I will follow all the rules and perform my duties carefully and conscientiously.
Applicant's Signature _____

Grade Check _____
Principal's Approval _____

Figure 3.4. Shepherd Junior High, Media Squad Application

Melanie says, "I think the Book Club is outstanding. Members are so creative and innovative. That's why we won the Scholastic contests. Overall, I empower my students in both groups. I can't imagine not having access to their talents, energy, and innovation to help me. I know that many of my fellow librarians don't like to hand over responsibility to the students like I do. They fear that mistakes will be made. I don't share this concern. We all make mistakes!"[18]

As discussed previously, respecting and empowering teens is a vital component in fostering successful teen library participation. The Shepherd Junior High School Library serves as an inspiring example of a library at which students truly feel they have a place to belong, where they are trusted, where they are welcomed and praised, and that will permanently instill a love of libraries, books, and reading.

Bowie High School Library, Bowie, Texas

As you can see from the Media Squad example, one of the most effective ways to get teens involved in their school library is to offer some sort of student library aide program. Most of these programs not only allow teens to gain worthwhile library experience and to support their library, but they also might be given school credit for completing their service. This is especially important in a high school setting. Like other library participation experiences in which teens get service learning or other credit, being a library aide is a legitimate way to get teens involved. It also proves to be a big help to many short-handed school librarians.

At Bowie High School in Bowie, Texas (hs.bowieisd.net/?rn=9737668), librarian Kelly Hoppe has a library aide program in which seniors and the occasional junior may participate. Each student earns a half credit for each semester of service. The students perform a wide variety of tasks, including processing and shelving books, doing inventory, helping with the book fair, and anything else that is needed.

Generally, there are seven aides a semester, one per period, but occasionally there are two aides per period. Usually the aides are evenly divided between males and females. In this school library, there is no need to promote the library aide opportunity, because word of mouth is very effective, and students actually come to Kelly and ask to be aides. The guidance counselor schedules the interested students and asks them to consult with Kelly to make sure that being an aide is a good fit for both parties.

Kelly conducts a training process that library aides must complete before they begin their duties. In chapter 9 you'll find complete details on how she conducts this training and the expectations of the teen participants.

Because of the Bowie High School student library aide program, many students who might not normally go to the library come by just because they want to visit one of the library aides. Kelly does not have a problem with this as long as the students are not loud, and the aide still completes his or her duties.[19] What better way to get other students using the library and possibly being involved later on? Being flexible goes a long way when working with teenagers.

MEMORABLE MOMENTS REFLECT RESILIENCY. Students at Bowie High School who are official library aides learn customer service skills that can help them in the workforce when they graduate, especially if they are looking for an entry level position in a public or academic library. They also supply plenty of memorable moments that are proof of the resiliency-oriented differences this experience makes in their lives. Kelly has described some of those differences:

- One of the most responsible aides Kelly ever had was a teenage mother, who was a self-starter and with whom Kelly had the unusual experience of discussing child-rearing issues.

- A zealous Army Reserve recruit returned from basic training and demonstrated in Kelly's office the variety of push-ups he had learned. Enjoying funny moments together can be an important part of youth participation too, making an important connection between teens and the adults they look up to.

- A boy who was struggling with personal issues was adept at sewing and made a pillow in home economics, which he left in the school library—a pillow Kelly will always keep as a reminder of him.

- A homeless teen took care of hygiene needs at school, was very polite, and was determined to survive and graduate. Part of that experience was serving as a school library aide in Kelly's program. She said that he was one of those teens you want to take home and save, and the only thing she could really do for him was to pay for part of his graduation regalia, without his knowledge. When he returned for a visit two years later, obviously happy and doing well, Kelly knew she and her library had made a positive impact on his life.[20]

Don't many of these modern school library programs sound similar to aide programs from times long past? However, I bet those earlier librarians rarely, if ever, had to deal with issues such as teen pregnancy and homelessness—not because they didn't exist, but because such situations were minimal and were kept under wraps. Still, those librarians knew how important such programs were for the general development of the teens with whom they worked. School librarians today, like Kelly, know how important they remain in reinforcing positive youth development and asserting resiliency in a more open and accepting environment, and perhaps even providing a lifeline.

If your school library does not offer a library aide program, you might want to propose one, get it approved, and see it through. It is an extremely effective way of connecting teens to their library and encouraging their peers to come to the library as well. The bonus is that you will get some well-needed and appreciated assistance you might not have had otherwise!

An Important Note

Whether you are working in a school or public library, when teens have problems or issues for which they need help, they may confide in you. Of course, you might listen and objectively provide information and referral sources, but keep in mind that *librarians are not counselors or therapists*. It is important to remember that when a teen is in a predicament that requires advice or professional judgment, you should seek out the recommendations of your supervisor, administrator, or guidance counselor and not attempt to solve the problem yourself, tempting as it may be to do so.

PEER READER ADVISORY ACTIVITIES

It is exciting to serve on professional association committees for which you receive galley books or advanced reading copies (ARCs), or to ship an abundance of ARCs distributed by publishers back to your library after a conference. If you are like me, you share these ARCs with the teens who frequent your school or public library.

Often a teen becomes enamored with a certain title, and it won't come back. When you ask about it, the response is usually that the teen read it and shared it with a friend, who shared it with a friend, and so on. Soon the book is being passed around so much that no one knows anymore who actually has it! You might not get your galley book back, but you are probably thrilled that another book has struck a chord with teens and is being so well read because they are letting one another know about it. That was my first inkling of the popularity among teens of Stephenie Meyer's book *Twilight*, when it was just an ARC.

How word of mouth perpetuates the popularity of hot new books is one small, positive example of how teens connect to literature and reading on their own. Encouraging such connections is an utmost priority in any school or young adult library setting. We work hard to provide top-notch collections that fit our budgets and to promote the materials in those collections. Book displays, booktalks, reading lists, and other techniques are employed by librarians to inspire teens to read. However, as you can see from the ARC example, one of the most important and powerful ways teens get hooked up with the books they don't know they want is through *peer reader advisory*. Teens who participate in your library can be an instrumental force in promoting books to their fellow teens. Let's explore some other unique ideas that enhance this important element of youth participation.

First Reads Club and TAG Picks

At the Ames Public Library in Iowa (www.ames.lib.ia.us), TAG members get to try new teen-oriented ARCs first. The library has also established a First Reads Club for TAG members, who get to browse through the brand new young adult books before they hit the shelves, provided there are no preexisting holds on them.

If a TAG member chooses to read one of the brand new books, he or she may put a sticker in it saying "First Read by (Name)." TAG members also get to have "TAG Picks." They may select books that they have particularly enjoyed from any part of the youth or adult library collection and add a sticker on the outside saying "(Name's) TAG Picks." These books are prominently displayed in the teen space, called the APL Zone.[21] This is an easily replicated, effective peer reader advisory activity.

Book Blurbs and Thought Bubbles

Samantha Nicholson's job in Youth Services at the Middlefield Public Library (www.geauga.lib.oh.us/GCPL/libinfo/Middlefield/MIinfo.htm) is part-time, so she frequently depends on the help she gets from her teen volunteers. You will be learning more about her "drop in" volunteer program in chapter 5, but one special volunteer deserves mention here. That's because he is directly involved in peer reader advisory.

Samantha has a long counter on which to display books that have been pulled off the shelves in the teen area. Occasionally there is a theme to the books she chooses, and sometimes she picks a mixture of genres. No matter the focus of the regularly changing displays, she creates bookmarks that try to capture the allure of each title in one or two sentences, similar to the enticement of a movie trailer. The bookmarks stick out of the books so teens who are browsing can read them and decide quickly if the books sound interesting. It's a great way to introduce teens to titles that they otherwise may have overlooked.

A teen volunteer who enjoys and is skilled at writing sometimes helps Samantha with the "Book Blurbs" project. He was not interested in the other volunteer opportunities available, so she decided to put his writing skills to work in promoting books to other teens. Samantha asked him to choose appealing books and write blurbs about them. The young man appreciated her enthusiasm for his writing, and he is now helping his peers select some interesting titles. Samantha enjoys the way that writing book blurbs can encourage teens like this one to use their creativity, intelligence, and writing skills to promote literacy.[22]

This idea works well with an individual volunteer, as in the above example, and it could also be readily duplicated with any TAG or teen volunteer group. Teens might be asked to come to the library individually or in teams to pull good titles they have read and to prepare "Book Blurb" bookmarks for them. They might set up book displays so that fellow teens would be able to peruse the descriptions and select titles they would enjoy. Bookmarks may be as simple or as fancy as you are able to make them, and you may decide whether teen readers will keep the bookmarks that come in the books they check out or you will collect and reuse them.

Shari Brown of the City of Mesa Library in Arizona used the idea to make "book thought bubbles." Make, laminate, and cut out the little thought bubbles and stick them to books on a display by using two-sided tape. The thought bubbles might say, "Read me! I am full of excitement and adventure," "Have a box of tissues handy . . . I am a tearjerker," or "Don't judge a book by its cover. . . . I am fun!" Your teen volunteers will have a great time selecting the books and preparing imaginative and humorous thought bubbles.

Brainstorm with your teens (you'll learn more about this technique in chapter 9) about other ideas to inspire fellow teens to read. They might like to designate a wall or bulletin board as a place where teens may post their reactions to books on colored index cards, perhaps using different colors for different genres. They might set out a binder with blank pages at the desk where teens sign in for summer reading prizes, and ask teen readers to write down their favorite book of the month with a short review on a blank peel-back name tag. The tags may then be placed in the notebook so that other teens are able to read peer reactions and get recommendations. Your teens might also be interested in becoming involved with more sophisticated kinds of book reviewing, which you will read about in the next chapter.

Both school and public libraries will find these simple ideas effective ways for teens to "sponsor" good peer reader advisory endeavors. Why not give them a try?

Hosting Visiting Authors

At Stapley Junior High in Mesa, Arizona (www.mpsaz.org/stapley), the members of the Stapley Library Advisory Club (SLAC) get to read ARCs, recommend books for library purchase, run contests for their schoolmates, construct bulletin boards and displays, and be the first to read new books as they are acquired.

One additional job that they have is truly exciting. The SLACers (pronounced "slack-ers"), as they are affectionately called, get to meet and host visiting authors at their school. The highlight of their author visit schedule was hosting Stephenie Meyer, for which 250 copies of *Twilight* were sold, at the point when her highly successful writing career for teens was just being launched, and after which it began to be completely cool for teens in the school to be carrying around a 512-page book![23]

In 2008 the SLACers hosted Jon Lewis and Derek Benz, authors of The Grey Griffin series from Scholastic Books. Librarian Lisa Bowen said, "You'd have thought they were movie stars! The SLAC'rs made signs welcoming our guests and got front row seats for their presentation. Jon and Derek were overwhelmed by their intelligent questions and reading experiences. Jon even commented on the SLACers in his Amazon blog." The SLACers also enjoyed visits from Janette Rallison and Obert Skye. All the authors they met have been impressed by their knowledge and enthusiasm.[24]

If your teens are eager to host visiting authors, too, do what you can to support their interest. Find out if there are any local authors who write young adult books who might be willing to come to your library. Contact publishers to see if there might be a way to arrange an author visit. You might consider doing it as a school/public library cooperative venture. If any sort of library, reading, or literary conference is going to take place in or near your community, find out if authors who will be visiting for it might be interested in arranging a "detour" before or after to visit with your teens.

Sometimes a publisher will support an author visit free of charge, or for a nominal fee, depending on the circumstances. It is worth asking. Local authors will often give their hometown school or library a break from what is normally charged for presentations. Pooling resources with other libraries is often a good way to arrange funding. With enough foresight and planning, you might even apply for grants to pay for author visits. Your teens might also be willing to do some fund-raising to get a special author to come to their library.

Be sure your teens are in on every level of the author visit, from the planning, to the publicity, to the hosting. It will be a teen participation event they and their peers will savor.

TEEN BOOK DISCUSSION GROUPS

If you think back to chapter 1, you will recall the "traits of teenagers" that Amelia Munson so aptly described. Awareness of oneself was the first trait explained. When it comes to books, reading, and teenagers, there are few better opportunities for teens to express their individuality and singular voice than through book discussions. When teens select the books and conduct the discussions themselves, the results may be even more in tune with a goal of promoting self-discovery while simultaneously encouraging respect for the perspectives of peers.

Last spring, one of the teen members of our Interesting Reader Society at the Poudre River Public Library District selected *The Princess Bride* for one of our Teen-to-Teen Book Discussion programs (see figure 3.5, p. 54). Teens who signed up received a paperback copy of the book to keep and enjoyed refreshments during the discussion. The seven girls who participated had a fabulous time. The teen book discussion leader planned excellent questions and also provided an opportunity for her peers to make up their own to pose to the group. She even brought along a tiara for each girl to wear while posing her own question. The girls were so animated and engaged in the discussion that they didn't even realize that the ending time for the program had arrived, and they all said they wished it could continue longer. Though the size of the group was small, the results were outstanding. And really, if you think about it, isn't a small yet animated book discussion group the ideal?

Then there is the opposite end of the spectrum: large and multifaceted discussions of a variety of books and subjects. Many TAB groups enjoy these kinds of discussions at their meetings, and special discussion groups such as the Mock Newbery and Printz ones, discussed next, also fit the mold.

Resources for Effective Teen Book Discussions

The following resources may help you and your teens put together a meaningful teen book discussion:

Dickerson, Constance. *Teen Book Discussion Groups at the Library*. New York: Neal-Schuman, 2004.

Hennepin County Library. *Discussion Guides—Teen Books*. www.hclib.org/pub/bookspace/ BookListAction.cfm?list_num=469 (accessed September 19, 2009). A helpful guide created by librarians.

Kunzel, Bonnie, and Constance Hardesty. *The Teen-Centered Book Club: Readers into Leaders*. Westport, CT: Libraries Unlimited, 2006.

Talk It Up! www.multcolib.org/talk/ (accessed September 19, 2009). This is a great online source to start planning a book group for children and teenagers.

Teenreads.com. *Book Clubs and Reading Guides*. www.teenreads.com/clubs/ accessed September 19, 2009). Find online advice on starting a book club and selecting good titles for discussion.

Figure 3.5. Teen-to-Teen Book Discussion Flyer

Wake County Public Libraries' Mock Newbery and Printz Discussion Groups

In some libraries or groups of libraries, mock Newbery Award and Printz Award book discussions among the *adult* library staff members are common. What about among *teen* readers? When planned and organized well, mock discussions for them can also be an interesting, enlightening, and fulfilling participatory activity.

Numerous books considered for the Newbery Award and all of the books considered for the Printz Award are those aimed at the young adult age group. Many teens in middle school, junior high, or high school enjoy evaluating the prospective book choices for these awards when a program is offered for them at their local libraries.

At the Wake County Public Libraries in North Carolina (www.wakegov.com/libraries/default.htm), teens get that opportunity. The library provides nationally recognized "mock" Newbery and Printz book award clubs, which have been and can be an inspiration to other libraries wishing to embark on similar "mock" award programs. These clubs are based on the American Library Association's annual Newbery Award and Michael L. Printz Award committees. The Wake County book clubs give young adults a chance to pick what they believe are the most distinguished works published for teens during a given year and to compare their choices with the "official" ones made by the ALA committees.

The teen members of the clubs are very involved and dedicated. They meet every other week and weed down all the prospective titles to the "winner" and "honor" books. The teens don't stop there, either. They have bookmarks that label titles in the collection with a "teen choice" designation as a passive readers' advisory technique. In this way, club book award deliberation efforts extend to their peers, who discover the book recommendations through the club members' bookmarks.[25]

Mock Newbery Book Club

In 1998 librarian Teresa Brantley founded the Mock Newbery Book Club while she was serving on the ALA Newbery Award Committee. The club is open to middle school and older young adult readers, who consider the quality of books published by American authors for ages 14 and younger. The club meets every other week from April through the following January to discuss the titles members are reading.

The Mock Newbery Book Club is popular. The library always has more teens interested than can be accommodated, simply through word of mouth about the program. One way the library has accommodated the additional interest is by adding a blog, through which a more widespread group of young adults may share their opinions.

Typically, there are 20 to 25 members each year, a third new and the remainder continuing, with an even numbers of boys and girls. For each teen participant, a signed permission slip must be on record confirming parental awareness that his or her child will be reading books that may extend to an age 14 reading and interest level. The form also covers parental photo and blog permissions.

Book Club members are told that they must be willing to read all genres and that they are making a commitment to continue throughout the year. Four times per year, the Book Club has a Library Lock-In until 10:00 p.m. for the teens to hone their Short List.

Advisor Martha Choate says that she considers her role to be a supplier of new titles as well as a leader in questioning the teens about what they have read. She has added the group to publisher mailing lists and arranged networking opportunities with other mock Newbery groups online. Club members receive ARCs of books published during the current year from publishers and a local bookstore, and the library tries its best to purchase new titles as soon as possible. One of the enticements of this program is that teens may read books before the general public is able to read them. To supplement this interest, teens also visit authors at local bookstores, as well as inviting them to speak at their meetings.

Group discussions consist of passing around one to three copies of each title and sharing opinions about what was read. During this process, the teens develop their own short list and nominations for the Mock Newbery Award and Honors. To get to this point, Book Club members practice their discussion skills, which is one of the many benefits of participation. At each meeting the teens put into words how they feel about each book. They are encouraged to describe the characters and writing styles and to compare them with other titles currently being read. At the beginning of each year the club members learn that when describing a book, "good" is a "four-letter word" that is not descriptive enough for discussion purposes. They must be clear and complete as they work hard to convince each other what the "most distinguished" book is. As they go through the process of reading and discussing more than 200 titles each year, "best book" opinions change.

At first only a few members read consistently. However, as time passes and the teens see each other getting more involved, reading steps up. The best part is that all the Mock Newbery members see the library as a safe place for expression about what they read. Martha says the librarians have received letters and e-mails from parents expounding on the growth of sons and daughters who have developed a deeper love of reading and of reading in a variety of genres, as well as an ability to debate their point of view in a logical way.

In addition to their own discussions, Mock Newbery Book Club members constantly suggest books that other young teens might want to read. Members have produced 18 Kid-to-Kid reading lists in various genres and for various age ranges that are available in the countywide public libraries. These lists may help to fulfill a school assignment or assist a reader in finding something new to read for fun. The Wake County Public Libraries' mission statement includes a part that says, "To promote the love of reading." Mock Newbery Book Club participants definitely help to do that!

Whether it is a new branch of their library system, a school, or another public library that wants to start a Mock Newbery Book Club of its own, Martha finds many how-to inquiries about their inspiring program coming her way. She adds, "It is so exciting to work with these kids and to see their enthusiasm for reading!"[26]

Mock Printz Book Club

There is also a Mock Printz Book Club, in its tenth year, at the Eva Perry Library of the Wake County Public Libraries. It complements the Mock Newbery group, and teens ages 14 to 19, or in ninth to twelfth grades, are eligible. Interested teens fill out a sheet with contact information, and their advisor, Valerie Nicholson, communicates with them by e-mail. Older teens may also participate during the summer before they officially become college students.

In 2000, after the first Michael L. Printz Award was given to *Monster* by Walter Dean Myers, Lynn Kerr started the Eva Perry Mock Printz Book Club to accommodate teens who were in high school but did not want to leave the very popular Eva Perry Mock Newbery Book Club. Their Mock Printz Book Club filled a niche for the older teens and became the first of its kind in the nation. Although Lynn Kerr and Helen Yamamoto, who assisted, have since transferred to other libraries, Valerie Nicholson continues to coordinate the group.

The Book Club meets from April to January, every other Sunday. Each teen signs up to bring snacks and drinks to a specific meeting. The teens are not required to attend every meeting or to read a certain number of books. However, they do attempt to read as many new YA books as possible and to share their views of them, so that the club as a whole is able to review the majority of books.

The teen participants in the Eva Perry Mock Printz Book Club follow some straightforward rules. The first is to refrain from criticizing another book club member because of a difference of opinion. The next is that all opinions are valid. Last, each teen must remember to keep quiet while another person is presenting. At the same time, the club's approach is very flexible, as Valerie encourages *any* teen participation activities to be.

Despite occasional scheduling conflicts with such commitments as being in band or a play, or having a job, the teens continue reading because Book Club books are kept in Valerie's office, where they are easily accessible. Any time the library is open, they may return and check out books from the private Printz collection. To keep the collection manageable, the teens automatically remove books from the reading collection if the book receives three bad reviews. In addition, Wake County Public Library has set up a blog for the Mock Printz Book Club to share their opinions. This is another way that teens who cannot come to the regular meetings can keep up with the discussions.

In January the teens have final discussions and vote on the books they feel deserve the Printz Award and any Honors. This vote takes place *before* the actual Printz Award winners are revealed. To provide some closure after the announcements, club members meet for "Discussion and Dessert" to talk about and compare the actual winners to those they selected.

The Mock Printz Book Club receives lots of publicity. Every year in March there is a big display in the library about the Book Club and its winners. Bookmarks, which serve as invitations to sign up for the following year's book club, are placed in the showcased books. However, most new members join because of word of mouth. Valerie describes the Book Club to new teens who like to read and invites them to participate. Current members likewise invite other teens. In addition, the Book Club is advertised in the teen events section of the Wake County Library flyer and on the library's Web site.

As a finale, the teens dress up formally for Dr. Cris Crissman's Book Awards Ceremony on a live Internet webcam in February. With the YA literature graduate students at North Carolina State University, the teens discuss their Mock Printz choices and respond to questions from a worldwide audience. The teens also announce additional winners they have selected in categories such as "Best Male/Female Protagonist," "Best Villain," and "Best Male/Female Supporting Character." After the show, the teens socialize and eat pizza.

To keep active and be exposed to new experiences, the Mock Printz Book Club members also participate in as many invitational opportunities as possible, such as attending local author signings or going together to movies based on YA literature. They have enjoyed special honors, like being treated to dinner with author Neal Shusterman, whose book, *Unwind*, had just been chosen as the club's Mock Printz winner; having an article published about them in *Voice of Youth Advocates* (*VOYA*) magazine; and being the subject of a library science graduate research paper. They have made special appearances at the Wake County Employee Day festivities, which included discussing their favorite books for the county YA librarians, who wanted to know about new books with teen appeal. The Book Club members were even invited to attend the Charlotte-Mecklenburg Virtual Literary Festival for Teens on Second Life/Teen Grid, where they were asked to fill in for a missing presenter by sharing information about their Mock Printz winners and the workings of their club.

There are even more benefits to being part of the Mock Printz Book Club. Besides teens having access to many books in galley format, a copy of every newly published YA book that the library orders is placed on hold so the teens get first dibs on those in high demand. All overdue fines on book club books are erased, and teens receive one hour of community service for each book read. Library reading lists and recommendations for new teen titles are based on the Book Club's opinions. Each teen in the club is also given six plastic-covered, T-shaped poster board markers with "*TEEN CHOICE*" on one side and his or her first name or nickname on the other side. The teens place the markers in their favorite books. Their *Choice Books* are checked out faster and more frequently than other YA books, with parents and teens alike depending on the Teen Choice selections. Finally, the teens are encouraged to list the prestigious Eva Perry Mock Printz Book Club and YALSA's Teens' Top Ten/YA Galley project, in which they also participate, on their college applications under "extracurricular activities."

Valerie says, "I am truly grateful for the feedback that I get from these dynamic teens. It is so important that they realize the difference they make in my life, at Wake County Public

Library, and in the world of YA literature. Every January, after their winners are selected, I make a toast to the teens of the Eva Perry Mock Printz Book Club to let them know how special they are. I love when they come back from college to see me at the library and tell me that the Book Club was such a fantastic time in their lives. I consider the Eva Perry Mock Printz Book Club to be a unique opportunity for teens who have a passion for reading."[27] Perhaps you will be inspired to try a similar book club at your library.

Next Chapter Book Club

At the Thousand Oaks Grant R. Brimhall Library (www.toaks.org/library), there is a unique teen reading club opportunity. Cosponsored by the Friends of the Library and the Kiwanis Club of Thousand Oaks, the Next Chapter Book Club is available for teens with developmental disabilities. Its seven members meet at the library for an hour weekly to read and discuss adapted versions of classics. Just as in any teen book club, the teens take pleasure in snacks and conversation. For additional enjoyment, the group engages in supplemental activities such as trying on period clothing and keeping a library scrapbook of their activities.

Two adult volunteer facilitators guide the reading, discussion, and activities and encourage other interested teens to sign up. A club like this allows teens with special needs to be involved with reading and their library in a way that matches their abilities, like some of the Library Pals discussed previously in this chapter. Keep in mind that, after being trained, even teens who are not developmentally disabled could get involved, serving as volunteers to assist their peers in the reading club.[28]

COLLECTION DEVELOPMENT AND MAINTENANCE PROJECTS

Building and maintaining a teen library collection can be challenging. You want to make sure you have a wide variety of types of materials and subjects that are of high appeal to teens, plus those interesting items that might have appeal for the special teen reader. However, you don't want shelf sitters, and you want to make sure everything is in the best condition it can be. You also want to make sure the items you need to retain are in the proper place and in good order, with items suitable for display placed in attention-getting areas.

As they do at the Wake County Public Libraries, solicit input from teens on what should be in their collections. At TAB meetings, they may peruse catalogs and reading lists, make notations on the latest items that should be purchased to attract teen library users, and warn you about what to avoid. They might also clue you in on missing items and holes that need filling in the teen collection.

At our Interesting Reader Society (IRS) teen advisory group meetings, we pass around sheets on which the teens may list any items they would like to see in the collection. We also ask teens who are regular library users but who are not in IRS to write down any items they would like to see added to the collection. These valuable tools are kept handy when doing collection development.

As you know, collection maintenance takes much time and effort. When you take the trouble to analyze, revamp, and display your teen collection, you want to be sure it is the best it can be. Getting teen input can help tremendously in ensuring that your collection weeding, replacement, updating, displaying, and shelf-reading projects are done in the most effective manner to satisfy teens' needs and interests. The teens who help you do this will have a sense of pride and accomplishment when they see a well-rounded, well-used collection because of *their* efforts.

A Teen Weeding Project

Selecting and promoting books is one thing. But you might be wondering, how do you get teens on board for a *weeding* project? Librarian Kimberly Paone at the Elizabeth Public Library in New Jersey (www.elizpl.org) has the answer. She works closely with her teen advisory council (TAC) to make the process streamlined and effective. She starts by making sure her teens know how important the task is to the library, equal in value with more enjoyable aspects of collection development. Here's how the process works at her library.

Members of the TAC are invited to come in at an agreed-upon date and time, usually a Saturday morning or a mid-week evening when things are quiet. Teens are given a short list of general questions to think about as they make their way through the part of the YA collection to which they have been assigned, with the size of each assignment correlating with how many teens show up for a given project date.

When the teens begin their YA collection weeding project, they are asked to consider the answers to the following questions for each book:

- Is the book in bad condition? Are the pages/cover ripped or missing? Are there yellowed pages, or is there writing, highlighting, or other markings on the pages? So that teens make sensible choices, Kimberly usually shares examples of which kinds of condition problems are acceptable and which are not. She shows the teens which items they will keep for a while and which are dumpster-worthy.

- Has the book circulated in the past three years? Teens at this library can check the inside back cover to find out. Once they do, they need to determine how many times each item has actually been checked out. Another method would be to confirm circulations against a printout.

- Is the cover outdated, boring, or very ugly? Sometimes a book's cover affects the way it is received by teens browsing the library and may be the reason a book might not be checked out for a long period of time.

Kimberly asks the teens to consider each question when looking at each book in their assigned section. If they deem the book to have condition problems, see that the book has not circulated much or at all in three years, or has a bad cover, they put the book on a cart. They are given scrap paper and asked to make a brief note on each book they pull, stating why it was pulled and whether they think it should be recycled and replaced or just removed and recycled.

Obviously, after the carts are turned in at the end of the event, Kimberly has to go through them book by book to read the teens' notes and make a final determination on what stays, what goes, and what needs to be reordered. Nevertheless, having the teens do those first steps is a great help. Usually the teens who attend are avid readers and library users, and they find gems that they'd never seen before among the weeded books. Most leave the event with a sense of accomplishment *and* a large stack of books to check out! Interestingly, this indicates that those shelf sitters might indeed be the very books teens don't know that they want, and just the right books to feature on a reading list, book display, or during a booktalk presentation.[29]

Summer Collection Maintenance Helpers

Sometimes teen collection maintenance projects take teens beyond the teen collection. At the Lake Jackson Public Library in Lake Jackson, Texas (bcls.lib.tx.us/branches/lak/lakejackson.asp), at least 20 student aides help Children's Librarian Susan Chappell during the summer reading program by signing up the participants and giving them their prizes as they complete their reading logs. Each teen is scheduled to work two hours a week. However, about the middle of July things start to slow down a little, and the teens begin other projects, dealing with collection maintenance.

This is a smart way to utilize teens who are already on hand helping at the library at a time when there are usually no educational conflicts. By giving the teens additional projects that are time intensive and for which they can do a great deal of the groundwork, a vital task can be accomplished in a quick and efficient manner. For example, one summer the student aides examined every easy reader and picture book the library owned for condition. The procedure, similar to that used by the teens at the Elizabeth Public Library, went like this:

- The teens filled the top of a book truck with a row of books and opened each one. Those that were in acceptable condition, the teens reshelved.

- Books that appeared to have problems were placed on the bottom shelf for Susan to peruse.

- To assist even further, the teens divided the problem books into stacks comprising those they felt needed simple repairs, which a library clerk would then do, and those needing to be withdrawn and/or replaced.

- After each book truck was done, they pulled the next batch of books from the shelves and started another round.

Susan says, "The teens were a great help. This is something so large I would never have been able to do it myself. Even with the teens' efforts, it took about a month to complete the project."

A previous summer project for the teens was looking up the easy reader books to see if they were on the "Accelerated Reader" list. Those that were on the list received a stamp on the inside of the cover and a notation of the reading level and point value. This was done to give participating children and parents an easier way to find the titles.

When the library switched to its current checkout system, it allowed the librarians to print out circulation lists that the aides could use to weed and improve the rest of the children's collection. They would straighten a row ahead of Susan, and working in pairs, they would set the books listed in *Wilson's Children Catalog* slightly forward on the shelves and tag those books. Susan would follow them, notice where the library was missing titles, and mark books that should be kept. The teens would also pull out nonfiction titles and tag them by copyright date so older books could be pulled.

At the end of the summer, when children's books are, for the most part, in disarray, the teens would come to the library and help put everything in order again. So you see, teens can also be recruited, trained, and scheduled by other library departments besides those devoted to teen services, and those departments can also greatly benefit.[30]

Teen Book-Buying Trips

Another way to get teens to contribute to their young adult library collections is to organize a TAB or teen volunteer book-buying trip to a local bookstore. These outings are a lot of fun for both the teens who participate and the adults who join them.

If you and your teens are not extremely familiar with the YA collection, it helps to take a printout of the titles in it, or a laptop on which you may check library holdings. That way, you'll avoid duplication of titles or at least keep it to a minimum. In addition, if you have asked teens who frequent your teen space what new materials they would like to see in it, you will also want to bring along any lists of titles they have recommended.

When Tracey Briseño from the Ames Public Library in Iowa asks her TAG members to meet her at Borders to purchase books, she doesn't require permission slips, because she doesn't transport the teens. The group meets at Borders, with each teen arranging his or her own transportation. Many parents even stay for the event. Tracey says that it works out quite well and that they always get a wonderful selection of new books. She contacts Borders ahead of time to let them know the group is coming and to ensure that carts are available to accommodate all the books the teens choose.[31]

In most cases, library staff members transporting teens to a bookstore will require permission forms to be completed. If you are planning to meet your group at the bookstore itself, as the Ames Public Library group does, you will still want to check with your administrators to find out if permission forms might be needed. If some of your teens have reached the legal age of 18, investigate whether or not they need to sign participation agreements. Be sure to include this important step of handling permissions when planning your excursion, however the outing is arranged.

Barrington Public Library's Teen Book-Buying Trip

At the Barrington Public Library in New Hampshire (www.barrington.nh. gov/Library/tabid/566/Default.aspx), members of the teen advisory group go on a book-buying trip to a local bookstore each year. Librarian Wendy Rowe and the library's director serve as chaperones and drivers. Permission slips are distributed to participating minor teens for parental signatures (see figure 3.6, p. 62). If a volunteer is needed to drive, that person's insurance coverage is verified.

Wendy says that their library director is a "walking catalog," which really comes in handy to prevent duplication—they have had only a couple of duplicates in the past four years! If Wendy did not have her along, she would bring a laptop to check titles already owned by the library.

This is an enjoyable event that the teens look forward to each year. They spend about $200 from their own fund-raising account, and the library matches that amount to purchase teen items. If your teens are interested in a book-buying activity, you might think about replicating this one.[33]

Teen participation benefits other teens in the community in several ways. Having teens planning YA programs and collections means that the Library is more likely to draw in other teenagers. Our TAG members are given a portion of the teen book budget for their semi-annual trips to local bookstores to select materials. During their last outing, they selected approximately $800 worth. They determined which books to purchase, calculated the total cost of the books with the discount for each from the different budgets from which they were selecting, and helped to re-shelve materials that were not selected. The books chosen by the teens have been very popular and representative of a spectrum of interests.[32]

Tracey Briseño
Library Assistant, Teen and Youth Services
Ames Public Library, Iowa

TEENS WORKING WITH CHILDREN

At the Austin Public Library's Southeast Austin Community Branch, TAG members planned craft activities for children at their greatly anticipated fall Fiesta in September. They made beautiful flowers for the event and helped younger children make craft projects during it. Likewise, when their Ruiz Branch celebrated its fortieth anniversary in November 2008, the Ruiz TAG members were involved in planning the commemoration. The teens helped with everything from preparations to overseeing the celebration itself, including monitoring craft activities and even reading stories to the children in attendance.[34]

When there is a special children's event on the horizon, teen volunteers can be a marvelous resource. Always consider asking your teens for assistance in planning and seeing the event through. You will be amazed at how many teens truly savor working with children, in everything from helping them learn, to working with craft activities, to telling and reading stories.

Barrington Public Library Permission Slip for Teen Advisory Board Field Trip

The Teen Advisory Board is planning a field trip to buy books and CDs for the library on Monday, December 1, 2008 at 4pm. We will go to Barnes and Noble Bookstore in Newington where the students will pick out young adult books and CDs for the library's collection. Students will be back at the Barrington Public Library for pickup by 7:00 p.m. Please sign and return this permission slip before the field trip. TAB members *must* have a signed permission slip to attend the field trip.

- ✂ -

I _____, the legal parent/guardian of _____, give permission for him/her to attend a field trip to Barnes and Noble bookstore in Newington. I understand that the library is not responsible for injury, loss, or damages and that TAB members participate in this outing at their own risk. I understand that my child will be properly supervised and driven to and from the bookstore by a chaperone that is properly insured. I understand that my child will be seat-belted at all times while in the vehicle.

I also give permission for library staff and chaperones to obtain emergency medical care for my child should an accident occur. My child's medical insurance information is listed here (Include insurance company name, policy number, phone number of insurer, and any other information needed to use this insurance.)

_____

_____

_____

Phone no. in case of emergency: _____

_____ _____
Parent's Signature   Date

Figure 3.6. Barrington Public Library, Book-buying Trip Permission Form

As teens enjoy working with children, the reverse is true as well. Younger children look up to them and aspire to be like the "big teenagers" someday. They want to follow in their footsteps. What better way to encourage this natural pattern than by connecting children with teens who are good role models?

One day the children with whom your teen volunteers are working will be teenagers themselves. You can bet that they will remember the example of the teens who worked with them when they were small, and as a result might decide to join in on teen participatory activities at your library when they are old enough. By having teens today helping the children of today, who will be the teens of tomorrow, you are preparing fertile ground for future teen support and involvement. When you encourage teens to learn how to effectively assist children in learning about and appreciating the library and to share with them a love of reading, you are also laying the foundation for those teens bringing their own future children to the library and supporting it as adults. It is win-win all around!

Teens Tutor Children at the South Brunswick Public Library, New Jersey

The Teen Tutors at the South Brunswick Library began as a direct result of Saleena Davidson's YAC group asking to do a program that allowed them to feel like they were giving back to the community. (See figure 3.7.) She spent time discussing it carefully with the teens, considering the responsibility level such a program would entail, and confessed that at first she was not very enthusiastic about it. However, she agreed to let the teens start the program, and it has been going well ever since. That was back in 2003.

TAG definitely sparks interest in younger kids who want to participate! At the Ruiz Branch, younger kids are asking all the time: "What is this TAG thing?" When they hear what it's about, they often want to help out, but then we have to tell them they need to wait until they are 13. We feel the anticipation can be a good thing, as it gives them something to look forward to.[35]

Alison O'Reilly
Teen Services Librarian
Austin Public Library—Southeast Austin Community Branch
Austin, Texas

Teen Tutors now runs Monday through Thursday from 4:00 to 8:00 p.m. with teen volunteers each donating an hour a week of their time to the program. To give the teens a sense of ownership of the idea, and to ensure that Saleena didn't have to be present at all times, YAC decided to have teen supervisors in grades 9–12 who would work two-hour shifts and report on the performances and progress during their shift, including how many teens volunteered, how many students showed up, and so forth.

The tutoring program is structured as homework help service for students in kindergarten through eighth grade. Volunteer tutors are in grades 6–12. Middle schoolers are always helped by high school level students, to ensure that tutors have the knowledge and maturity to handle the homework material for middle school assignments. The program works as a drop-in program, which Saleena says "has had its ups and downs, but is basically solid," and the supervisory positions have become a real teen status symbol. Saleena also says that she has four to six teens working on each shift, which means she coordinates and monitors a weekly schedule of about 60 teens, which can be challenging at times. However, she also points out that the program is definitely working, so it is worth it.[36]

Keep in mind that *any* teen participation activities will require library staff time to help plan, coordinate, and monitor, in addition to funding. This staff time must be part of the buy-in by supervisors and administrators in your library, along with financial support for teen participation endeavors. Be prepared with information from this book, information and statistics from your community, and the perspectives of local teens, to substantiate your argument that teen participation activities are very valuable.

Teen Tutoring Guidelines and Expectations

Expectations:

- To be able to tutor general subjects as needed by elementary students.
- To show up on time on the day and time you said you were available.
- To have a good attitude and lots of patience for those you are tutoring.
- To sign in and out in order to receive credit for volunteer hours worked.
- To exhibit proper behavior as an example to those around you.
- To call or e-mail in the event of an emergency or a conflict with your scheduled tutoring hour as soon as possible.

Guidelines:

- Tutoring will be on a set schedule; you need to volunteer for a minimum of one hour per week.
- If you neglect to show up for your shift, and you don't call, you will be dropped from the program. It works on a three strikes and you're out basis. To ensure that your call isn't lost, call only the extension listed above, and if you don't speak to me (Saleena), then make sure you leave a message on that extension only.
- Please note that you may not get your first choice of times for tutoring. If you only have one option, list only that one, but please don't offer days or times that you cannot do. If I cannot fit you into the schedule at the beginning of the season, I will contact you when an opening occurs that matches your schedule. Please contact me as far in advance as possible if your schedule changes.

Please keep this paper for your records.

Saleena Davidson (YA Librarian & Teen Volunteer Coordinator) Contact Information:
Phone: 732-329-4000 ext. 7634
E-mail: southbrunswickteentalk@yahoo.com

Figure 3.7. South Brunswick Public Library, Teen Tutoring Guidelines

Summer Tutoring Program at the Farmers Branch Manske Library, Texas

There is also a teen tutoring program at the Farmers Branch Manske Library in Texas (www.ci.farmers-branch.tx.us/library/). Teens tutor K–4 students in biweekly programs during the summer. The tutoring programs are offered on Mondays and Thursdays for eight weeks, with teens and younger students working in pairs. The first 10–15 minutes of the hour-long programs are spent allowing teens and their young students to read in a "book buddies" atmosphere. The young students read aloud if they are comfortable with that approach; otherwise, the teens read to them. Then the pairs of teens and children move on to file folder games, educational board games, and floor puzzles. All of the materials are organized by grade level, and there is a giant chart to record accomplishments. Teen volunteers write each young student's name on the chart and track his or her progress on the activities throughout the summer.

The population served by Farmers Branch Manske Library is about 26,000, with some patrons coming from surrounding cities. In the summer of 2008, a total of 224 teens volunteered at the library, with each tutoring program session attracting about 40–75 teen volunteers and an equal number of young students. Many of the teen volunteers and young students came to both programs each week. At times, the library had several more teen volunteers than young students, and in those cases other jobs for the teens were usually found.[37]

I think that volunteering at the library is a fantastic experience for our teens. They can help their community and themselves. The majority of our teen volunteers are in the sixth to eighth grades so this is their first job-like experience. They sign up for specific shifts and are required to show up at specific times. There are consequences if they do not do what they say they are going to do. For example, if they have three "no shows," which means they signed up for a shift and did not call to say that they couldn't make it, they cannot sign up for additional shifts.

Working with the younger students in the Tutoring program is especially rewarding for the teens. I think it's great that our teen volunteers are so visible to other teens visiting the library. I think that this lets them see that teens are valued here.[38]

Jennifer Dillon
Youth Services Supervisor
Farmers Branch Manske Library, Farmers Branch, Texas

Corona del Sol Friends of the Library Club Teens Also Help Children

The student members of the Corona del Sol High School's Friends of the Library Club think it is important to work for their library and community in multifaceted ways. One of these is to do projects for the young children at the AZTYKES preschool at their school. The FOTL Club teens have helped inventory the easy reader books for the preschool library collection. They have also created posters reflecting the weekly themes that the AZTYKES students learn about in their classes. When a teacher comes to read to the AZTYKES in the library, the posters are supportive visual aids that reinforce the books chosen for the week.[39]

These projects provide important services to the youngest students in the school community; help the teens reach out to and connect with the children; and, as in other library examples you have already read about, allow the children to see the impressive example of dedicated teenagers they may aspire to be like one day.

Puppet Plays Bring Tweens, Teens, Children, and Stories Together

At the South Brunswick Public Library, Saleena Davidson started a Puppetry Program through which tweens and teens would interact with younger children. She developed it as a fun program that all ages would enjoy, intending that the older teens would mentor the tweens. She decided to incorporate puppetry because it allowed a degree of anonymity for the young adults, and she reworked popular children's tales so that the littlest audience members would be familiar with them.

The tweens and teens prepared for groups of children ages four to seven. They found this age level to be very nonjudgmental, appreciative, and enthusiastic. By doing plays for these children, the older performers had the bonus of allowing themselves to be very silly at times and to regress a bit for the shows, which proved to be a lot of fun for all.

Saleena explained that she has had the typical cyclical success with teen/tween groups, with some shows attracting only three puppeteers, some several more, and once even a large group of thirty, which she divided into two groups of 15. It makes sense that there would be such variations, because this program has been going on in various incarnations for nine years. Throughout them all, Saleena points out that the older young adults watch over the younger ones, which she finds impressive.[40]

The sizes of Saleena's young adult puppetry troupes again bring up an important point. Variations in group sizes often demonstrate that teen programs may reflect *quality* and not necessarily *quantity*. When working with teens, don't be discouraged when on occasion you only attract a few teen participants. What those few are able to accomplish and the pleasure they get from their participation is what counts. You might find administrators questioning the value of working with small numbers and insisting that your teen offerings—both the numbers of teen volunteers and the number of their peers being reached—must attract larger groups to be effective and worth the time and cost. Be prepared with the argument that sometimes it is the smaller teen groups and activities that have the strongest impact.

Reading Buddies Program at the Kirkwood Public Library

A few summers ago, the Kirkwood Public Library in Missouri (http://kpl.lib.mo.us/) started an annual Reading Buddies program. Through the program, young children entering grades 1–4 are paired with a Big Buddy. Reading Buddies meet at the library once a week for about an hour to read together. The main emphasis is on the Big Buddy encouraging and helping the Little Buddy with reading. Big Buddy volunteers must be 13 to 18 years old or newly graduated from high school.

Lynn Bosso, Assistant Director of Programs & Youth Services, pairs a Big Buddy with a Little Buddy at the beginning of the summer program and tries to keep those pairs intact during the whole program. Much of Lynn's program structure is patterned after a program that Chris Miller, at Coquitlam Public Library in British Columbia, graciously shared with her when she was in the planning stages of the Reading Buddies program.

The program starts out in a large group, in which the Big and Little Buddies pair off. Buddy pairs go to the Children's Room of the library, where they read together for about 35 to 40 minutes. Lynn circulates through the Children's Room during this reading time and helps the pairs find more books if they need them. For the last 10 to 15 minutes of the program, everyone gathers into a large group for a game.

Most of Lynn's Big Buddy volunteers return from previous summers. Such repeated participation is evidence of a program that truly satisfies teens. New teens who apply to be Big Buddies are asked to come to the library for an informal interview. Lynn stresses the importance of finding mature, dependable teens for the Big Buddy positions.[41]

Want to start a Book Buddies or Reading Buddies program? Try these resources:

Johnston, Francine R., et al. *Book Buddies, Second Edition: A Tutoring Framework for Struggling Readers.* New York: Guilford, 2009.

Samway, Katharine Davies, Gail Whang, and Mary Pippett. *Buddy Reading: Cross-Age Tutoring in a Multicultural School.* Portsmouth, NH: Heinemann, 1995.

SUMMING UP

As you can see, teen participation through TAGs and teen volunteer programs comes in many forms in both school and public libraries. The examples shared in this chapter present a clear picture of the kinds of opportunities you might consider offering to, for, and with your teens.

Remember, for the staff time and effort you put into developing teen participation activities, you get teens who are able to earn community service credits or who just relish the experiences for the fun and joy of contributing—or both. You get teens who will move on to adulthood appreciating and supporting their library. You also get things accomplished that otherwise might have gone by the wayside in times of financial exigency.

This chapter is just the beginning. There are lots more things to learn about the amazing and varied youth participation activities going on in libraries today.

Making youth participation through our Youth Advisory Council part of my library media center has been incredible. These teens are wonderful—full of energy, insights, and ideas that I would never achieve on my own. It really is one of the most rewarding parts of my career.[42]

Ernie Cox
Library Media Specialist
St. Timothy's School
Raleigh, North Carolina

ENDNOTES

1. Sandi Imperio, e-mail message to author, October 4, 2008.

2. Judy Macaluso, e-mail message to author, December 8, 2008.

3. Sandi Imperio, e-mail message to author, October 4, 2008.

4. Allison O'Reilly, e-mail message to author, September 17, 2008.

5. Saleena Davidson, e-mail message to author, July 29, 2008.

6. Davidson, e-mail, July 29, 2008.

7. Ashwini Dhokte, e-mail message to author, August 6, 2008.

8. Kathee Herbstreit, e-mail message to author, January 11, 2008.

9. Giny McConathy, interview with author, January 6, 2009.

10. Kimberley Spring, Nathan Dietz, and Robert Grimm Jr., "Leveling the Path to Participation: Volunteering and Civic Engagement Among Youth from Disadvantaged Circumstances," *Corporation for National & Community Service* (2007): 2, www.nationalservice.gov/pdf/07_0406_disad_youth.pdf (accessed October 25, 2009).

11. Spring et al., "Leveling the Path to Participation," 2-4.

12. Giny McConathy, interview with and e-mail message to author, January 6, 2009.

13. Kate DiPronio, e-mail message to author, May 8, 2008.

14. Joann Pompa, e-mail message to author, September 9, 2008.

15. Joann Pompa, e-mail messages to author, May 10, 2008.

16. Melanie Limbert-Callahan, e-mail message to author, February 21, 2008.

17. Limbert-Callahan, e-mail, February 21, 2008.

18. Limbert-Callahan, e-mail, February 21, 2008.

19. Kelly Hoppe, e-mail message to author, July 6, 2008.

20. Kelly Hoppe, "Library Aide Antics." *Library Media Connection* 26 (March 2008): 21.

21. Tracy Briseño, e-mail message to author, July 28, 2008.

22. Samantha Nicholson, e-mail message to author, August 28, 2008.

23. Lisa Bowen, "Attracting, Addressing, and Amusing the Teen Reader," *ALAN Review* 34 (Fall 2006): 22–23.

24. Lisa Bowen, e-mail message to author, May 15, 2008.

25. Lindsey Dunn, e-mail message to author, August 19, 2008.

26. Martha Choate, e-mail message to author, October 3, 2008.

27. Valerie Nicholson, e-mail message to author, October 7, 2008.

28. "Next Chapter—A Reading Club for Teens with Developmental Disabilities," *U*N*A*B*A*S*H*E*D Librarian* 149 (2008): 16.

29. Kimberly Paone, e-mail message to author, July 25, 2008.

30. Susan Chappell, e-mail message to author, August 25, 2008.

31. Tracy Briseño, listserv message to TAGAD-L, October 9, 2008.

32. Tracy Briseño, e-mail message to author, July 7, 2008.

33. Wendy Rowe, listserv message to TAGAD-L, October 9, 2008.

34. Allison O'Reilly, e-mail message to author, September 17, 2008.

35. O'Reilly, e-mail, September 17, 2008.

36. Saleena Davidson, e-mail message to author, October 18, 2008.

37. Jennifer Dillon, e-mail message to author, August 13 2008.

38. Dillon, e-mail, August 13, 2008.

39. Joann Pompa, e-mail message to author, September 9, 2008.

40. Saleena Davidson, e-mail message to author, October 18, 2008.

41. Lynn Bosso, e-mail message to author, August 28, 2008.

42. Ernie Cox, e-mail message to author, October 13, 2008.

4

Ways Teens Can Participate: Writing, Art, and Performance Projects and Activities

A tremendous number of teens like to write, draw and paint, perform music and drama, and create artistically in a variety of other ways. Why not incorporate this talent and interest into teen library participation activities? Instead of bringing in a presenter or instructor, or doing it yourself, let the teens plan and run the activities. The teens get a place where they can release their creative energy and express their imagination, and the library gets teen involvement that attracts positive attention. Creative projects, activities, and events that teens design and take charge of are also marvelous ways to positively cultivate the teen traits and encourage resiliency. It is a win-win situation!

If you are not artistically or creatively inclined, you might wonder how you would go about getting teens involved in these kinds of activities. Don't worry—there are plenty of resources to give you information, and chances are there are local citizens who are experts and might be willing to lend you a hand. Ask the teens what they would like to do, and go from there. For example, even if you think you are a ho-hum writer, and your teens want to pen book reviews, you can find examples to share with them as they are learning how to develop this skill. You might even want to try your hand at writing some reviews yourself. Teens really enjoy it when their adult advisors are interested in and willing to learn something new that the teens find appealing.

If you *are* skilled at music, art, writing, or drama, or have some other creative talent, be willing to share those skills with your teens. Let them know that if they have an interest in something at which you are proficient, you will be happy to guide them through developing a project with that focus. Perhaps your teens want to plan a craft program for little children or fellow teens. You might be an expert in creating simple crafts such as magnets, jewelry, or wreaths. Show your teens what you like to do and how you do it, and see if they might like you to give them a few lessons. What you are able to share may be passed on as they manage the creative programs they develop.

Be open to new ideas! If your teens come up with a creative project that seems overwhelming, stop and think about it. How can you help make it happen? If you need advice from colleagues, join a listserv for librarians and send a message explaining the idea and asking for advice on how you might make it work. You will be amazed at what other librarians are able to share based on actual experiences at their libraries and the ideas your question prompts.

TEEN LITERARY MAGAZINES

These days, teens who want to produce a literary or other magazine through their libraries have various options. Teen magazines, also known as "zines," may be printed on paper the old-fashioned way so that they can be distributed in schools, local youth agencies, and the public library. Teens often prefer this method, which allows them and their peers to hold the finished product in their hands and gives them something to keep. Another option is allowing your teens to produce their zine electronically. Online teen zines have become a popular way to offer this creative outlet. Some libraries combine production of a published teen magazine on paper and an online version.

If your teens want to produce a zine, you will need to have some careful discussion with them about format and funding. Before meeting with them, do your homework and be prepared to explain printing budgets and to give cost comparisons between doing printed and online versions. Encourage teens to make a decision with you based on the financial and staff time support you and your library are able to devote to the project. If your library has no money for publishing a zine on paper, perhaps the teens would be willing to do a fund-raiser or gather outside support to be able to do it this way rather than virtually.

Now let's look at some examples of teen-created magazines and how they are planned and function.

Tigard Public Library *Scratched* Teen Zine

At the Tigard Public Library in Tigard, Oregon (www.ci.tigard.or.us/library/), teens create and publish a well-received teen zine called *Scratched*. By providing such an opportunity, the library gives teens a chance to work independently, plan and produce a product that benefits the library and fellow teens, promote the library through their work, learn about publishing, and develop and polish creative writing and artistry skills. That is a lot of benefits from one ongoing program!

Historically, the Teen Library Council (TLC) members at the Tigard Public Library have been the biggest contributors to *Scratched*, but recently they are seeing more submissions from nonmembers, which is a positive step forward. (See figure 4.1.) A project like this offers a great chance to reach out to teens in the community who might not normally connect with the library and to encourage them to contribute to a teen library project.

In the past, issues of the zine were formatted using Microsoft Publisher™. Submissions were scanned, and Publisher was used to compile them electronically. However, after a summer zine workshop with the director of Portland's Independent Publishing Resource Center, the library has changed the zine preparation format. Since that workshop, the Tigard teens now have a more hands-on approach, using collage techniques to put the magazine together without electronic tools, and photocopying it for distribution. This new format requires more work, so more teens are needed for production—which means more teens get involved. Inviting a professional publishing agency, local newspaper, or local magazine publisher to train teens in effective publishing techniques is a great way to support them while working on a literary magazine project and to develop new skills.

Be a Part of the Tigard Public Library Teen Zine

Attention all creative thinkers! Want to express yourself? Want to see yourself in print? Help create Tigard Public Library's Teen Zine, and get published!

What's a zine? Zines (pronounced "zeens") are mini magazine-like publications that can include personal ponderings, poems, stories, photography, artwork, song lyrics, reviews, comic strips, opinions and editorials, and more. It can be whatever you want it to be!

If you would like to submit items or articles for publication in the zine, fill out the bottom half of this form and return it to the Tigard Public Library.

Lisa N Elliott, Young Adult Librarian
503-718-2654
lisae@tigard-or.gov

Please keep this half.

Please return this half to the library.

Tigard Public Library
Teen Zine Submission/Participation Form

Name _____   Grade _____

Phone _____ E-mail _____

_____ I would like to submit an item for publication in the zine (Note: Not every submission is guaranteed publication. All submissions are subject to Tigard Public Library staff's discretion.)

_____I would like to participate in future teen zine meetings to help with designing and organizing publication of the zine.

Figure 4.1. Tigard Teen Zine Submission Guidelines

Tigard Public Library Teen Zine

Zine Submission Guidelines

- You must be in grade 6 to 12
- All creative work must be original (no plagiarizing)
- Include your name, grade, and phone number with all submissions
- For artwork and photography submissions, you may submit your original work, a high quality copy of your work, or a digital picture of your work
- You can submit your work at any time for consideration in the upcoming edition
- Inclusion in the zine is not guaranteed, and is subject to the Young Adult Librarian's approval

What You Can Submit

- Editorials
- Poetry
- Short Stories
- Photography

- Artwork
- Song Lyrics
- Book, Movie, Music Reviews
- Comic strips

Where to Submit Your Work

By mail:

Tigard Public Library
13500 SW Hall Blvd
Tigard, OR 97213
Attention: Lisa Elliott

Or e-mail submissions to
lisae@tigard-or.gov

Questions?

Contact Lisa N Elliott, Young Adult Librarian: lisae@tigard-or.gov or 503-718-2654

Participation/Submission Form is available at www.tigard-or.gov/library/teens

TIGARD PUBLIC LIBRARY
Serving the public since 1963

13500 SW Hall Blvd., Tigard, OR • 503-684-6537 • www.tigard-or.gov

Figure 4.1. Tigard Teen Zine Submission Guidelines (*Cont.*)

With the help of the TLC, the library has formed a Zine Team. This is a group of teens who are interested in influencing the look and layout of the zine, beyond their own submissions. A teen editor has been appointed and helps coordinate the group as they compile each issue of the zine at the Zine Team meetings. The Zine Team decides on themes for each issue and selects materials that fit the theme. For example, last year they used the summer reading program theme, "Metamorphosis," for their summer issue.[1]

Here are two books to inspire, motivate, and guide teen zine creators:

Block, Francesca Lia, and Hillary Carlip. *Zine Scene: The Do It Yourself Guide to Zines*. Los Angeles: Girl Press, 1998.

Watson, Esther Pearl. *Watcha Mean, What's a Zine?* Boston: Graphia, 2006.

Inklings at Monroe County

At the Associated Libraries of Monroe County (www.monroepl.org) in Pennsylvania, which comprises the Barrett Friendly Library, Clymer Library, Eastern Monroe Public Library, Pocono Mountain Public Library, and Western Pocono Community Library, members of the Teen Advisory Board from each of the libraries work together to publish an online teen zine featuring writing by area teens. The zine was conceived by members of the TAB at the Eastern Monroe Public Library, who proposed the idea as a joint effort to the TABs in the other branches. A core group of six TAB teens named the zine *Inklings*, developed the guidelines for submissions, regularly welcomes other interested local teens at meetings, and encourages their contributions to each production.[2]

Started in June 2008, *Inklings* is posted on the Teen Page of the library system's Web site. In addition, a limited number of in-print editions of the zine are available in the library. *Inklings* includes poetry, artwork, reviews, and short stories.

According to the teens who run the project, *Inklings* is "for teens, by teens . . . who want to inspire others and establish a voice in our community; who want to be published; who are aspiring authors; who are artistic, creative, and have nothing better to do . . . and because, let's face it— *Inklings* just rocks!"[3]

Teen Zine Guidelines for Submission

Guidelines for *Inklings* are very straightforward, sensible, and simple to emulate:

- Teens may submit poetry, fiction, or nonfiction (which includes essays, opinion pieces, and book reviews), comics, and artwork.

- All submitted pieces must be original and include the following statement: "This confirms that this work is entirely original," followed by each teen's full name.

- Anyone in grades 7 through 12 may submit his or her work. A special section is even provided for TAB alumni who would like to contribute.

- All work submitted must be appropriate for a teen audience.

- The editors reserve the right to limit the number of items published by one person in each issue.

- Not all work submitted is published. The teen editors reserve the right to choose which pieces will be published in each issue.

- Submissions are not edited for grammar or spelling. Teens are asked to proofread their work before submitting it. At the discretion of the editors, minor changes might be made for publication purposes.

- Written work is submitted by e-mail attachment or on a floppy, CD, or DVD in Microsoft Word™ or plain text format. Floppy, CD, and DVD copies of work are not returned to the creator.[4]

Consider sharing these basic guidelines and the guidelines from the Tigard teen zine with your teen group if they are anticipating the creation of their own teen zine.

How Teen Work Is Submitted

The teens who are directly involved in planning the zine and contributing original work have an outlet to showcase their creativity and feel empowered by planning and providing this project. The planners practice decision making skills in deciding whether pieces submitted are appropriate for the zine, and they also work on constructive criticism as they critique the pieces. The planners make suggestions about layout, colors, graphics, and other details of the online zine. Those who do not directly participate can see the creative work of their peers which might possibly inspire them to try something similar of their own.[5]

Mary Ann Lewis
Young Adult Librarian
Associated Libraries of Monroe County
Stroudsburg, PA

Teens in Monroe County are asked to carefully read and follow the "Guidelines for Submission." They must e-mail their work to Mary Ann Lewis, the young adult services librarian, and add the words "zine submission" in the subject line. As an alternative, teens may submit their work to Mary Ann on an external storage device via one of the branches in the library system.

All submissions must include the teen's first and last names; age; grade; school; town; phone number; and e-mail address, if he or she has one. Published work indicates the first name and last initial of each contributor, plus the teen's school or town if he or she wishes that information to be included.

Teens are encouraged to continually turn in their newly created pieces, as submissions are accepted on an ongoing basis. Once Mary Ann receives the submissions, she gives them to the zine volunteers, who proceed from there. Meetings are held every six months to review and select the featured writing and artwork for the next issue.[6]

Another Way to Get Published: Writing Reviews

Teens who enjoy reading often like to share information about what they have read. A good way to foster this interest is to provide opportunities for them to write book reviews, through venues such as *Inklings* and a variety of other sources of publications. Writing reviews does necessarily stop at books, either. Teens might also enjoy writing reviews of audiobooks, movies, television shows, music, and even plays. If you have teens who are interested in participating in this manner, provide a space for their reviews to appear, whether it be in a newsletter, on your library's Web page, or on a bulletin board.

When you give teens a chance to express themselves and to hone their writing skills through reviewing, everyone benefits. The teen writers have a place that allows their voices to be heard. When you publish or post their written reviews, other teens might discover recommendations through what your teens have evaluated.

Besides any reviewing opportunities your library can offer to interested teens, there are other channels for them to express their views about what they have read. For instance, *Voice of Youth Advocates* (*VOYA*) magazine (www.voya.com) encourages librarian reviewers and teen partners to concurrently read new books and create reviews. When published, the side-by-side "teen partner reviews" provide VOYA readers with both a librarian's and a teen's perspective on the same book.

You will discover additional ways that book reviewing ties in to teen library participation in subsequent chapters of this book. Remember that when you have teens who like to write, encouraging them to review allows them an avenue of self-expression while connecting them to the teen community at large.

Don't forget to include *all* the members of your teen community. Notice that the flyer from the Watsonville Public Library on how to write a book review (figure 4.2, pp. 76–77) has both English and Spanish versions. If your community has a large population of teens who speak a language other than English, provide translated material they can read, understand, and share with their peers. By doing so, you will help to increase their interest in your library participation opportunities.

A SIMPLE LIBRARY TEEN POETRY SLAM PLAN

One of the most popular and often most successful teen participatory programs is a teen poetry slam. Most likely you have heard of poetry slams, but if you have never actually seen or conducted one, you might be wondering what exactly a poetry slam is, and how you can help your teens to arrange one. If you *have* done slams before, you might want to figure out some new approaches.

Starting Out: Planning the Poetry Slam

For those not familiar with the idea, a poetry slam is an event created for performance poetry artists to compete with each other for cash, prizes, or pride. Performance poetry is also known as *spoken word* and is more than mere recitation. It incorporates dramatic elements and allows vocal inflection, movement, and facial expression to express ideas or emotions.[7] An excellent resource for additional information on poetry slams is the frequently asked questions ("General FAQ") section of the Poetry Slam, Inc. Web site at www.poetryslam.com.

For a library-oriented poetry slam run by teens, the best approach is to keep the slam simple. Ten to fifteen registrants is an ideal number for a two-hour library slam program, with a limit of three minutes per poem. You want to allow each teen contestant a chance to perform all of the poems he or she has prepared in three rounds and not cut anyone off before getting a chance to share all of his or her work. This is different from slams in coffeehouses or other forums, which usually have elimination rounds. On the other hand, be flexible if your TAB members prefer a semblance of the elimination round format.

The first step is to set a date and time that works for both you and your TAB. Some libraries do poetry slams as part of Teen Read Week or National Poetry Month, but see what fits in your community. As you would for any program planning, ask the teens and check with the local schools about potential conflicts, such as SAT testing or prom, on the date you would like to set for the slam.

Once the slam is scheduled, you will want your TAB to decide on prizes and to volunteer for the various assigned slam roles. In chapter 1 I mentioned that the teen advisory group from the Maricopa County Library in Arizona selected a bookstore gift card, a box of Twinkies, and a block of Velveeta (and later, a can of Spam) as their prizes. This worked well with the teens in their community.[8] However, when the teen members of our Interesting Reader Society (IRS) at the Poudre River Public Library District planned their slam last spring, they were happy with more traditional first, second, and third place prizes of bookstore gift cards, with journals and pens for the rest of the participants.

How to Write a Book Review

When writing a book review the goal is to write about the book without giving away anything important to the plot itself and to critique the work of the author. If a book is really bad— say so! But don't just say it's bad, explain why it's bad (or good if it's good). As a reader, I want to know why I should pick up that book (or avoid it)! I don't need to read a book review that just says the same thing that is written on the back cover (or front flap) of the book.

Here are some general guidelines you can follow.

1. Be sure to have the title and author of the book written down.

2. What is the book about? Bugs? Pirates? Self-Discovery? You can tell a bit about the plot of the book (or the subject of the book for non-fiction) - but be sure to only write one or two sentences.

3. Was it a good book? Or was it a book that could be passed over for something more interesting? For non-fiction books—was it factual? Or were many of the statements simply opinions?

4. Elaborate on why it was or was not a good book. You can share your feelings—what you thought about the book—but be sure to also include why you think the way you do. If the book is confusing, , say so. If the characters were amazing and seemed totally believable, say so. The goal of the book review is to let other readers share in your experience so that they can better decide if they want to read the book too.

Still stumped? Here are some questions to ask yourself:

For Fiction Books:
Was the book interesting? Memorable? Useful? Entertaining? Instructive? Why?
How did the book affect you?
Is the book clearly written? Did it make sense? Or was it confusing?
What is the Point Of View in the book? Do you agree with it? Why or why not?
Were the characters believable? Why or why not? Were they flat and shallow? Or well rounded?
Could you relate to any characters in the story? Who was your favorite character ? Why?
Was there a problem or obstacle in the story? Was it overcome?
Is the theme new and original? Or old? A new spin? Or boring?
Did you like the book? Or would was another better? Was it badly written or boring?
Would you change anything about the book?
Is it slow to start? Or does it catch you from the start?
Is the plot fully realized? Or does it leave loose ends?
Is the dialogue good? Or stilted?
Is the setting believable? Was a particular atmosphere evoked?
Are all the scenes relevant to the story? Or is there a lot of things that weren't important?

For Nonfiction Books:
Were the sources listed?
Is the information general, or in depth?
Was the writing factual, or persuasive and personal?
Was the book enjoyable? Or was it boring to read?
What is the Point Of View in the book? Do you agree with it? Why or why not?

Figure 4.2. How to Write a Book Review, Watsonville Public Library

Cómo Escribir una Crítica

Al escribir una critica, el objetivo es de escribir acerca del libro sin mencionar detalles importantes del libro y criticar el trabajo del autor. ¡Si un libro realmente no te gusto — dilo! Pero no digas que no esta bueno, explica por qué no esta bueno (o si realmente esta bueno). ¡Como un lector, yo quiero saber por qué yo voy a seleccionar el libro (o evitarlo)! Yo no quiero leer una crítica que diga la misma cosa que esta escrita en la portada del libro.

Puedes seguir las siguientes guías.

1. Asegura de anotar el título y autor del libro.

2. ¿De qué se trata el libro? ¿insectos? ¿piratas? ¿auto-descubrimiento? Puedes decir un poco acerca del complot del libro (o el sujeto del libro) - sólo necesitas escribir algunas oraciones.

3. ¿Fue un libro bueno? ¿O fue un libro que quizás lo haigas cambiado por otro más interesante? ¿Para libros de no-ficción—fue basado en hechos reales? ¿O fueron muchas de las declaraciones simplemente opiniones?

4. Elabore en por qué fue o no fue un libro bueno. Puedes compartir tus sentimientos— que pensaste acerca del libro—asegura incluir porque piensas de esa manera. Si el libro es confuso, dilo. Si los personajes fueron asombrosos y parecieron totalmente creíble, dilo. El objetivo de la crítica es de compartir con otros lectores tus experiencias para que ellos puedan decidir si ellos también quieren leer el libro.

¿Sigues confundido? Aquí están algunas preguntas que te puedes preguntar:

Para libros de Ficción:
¿El libro fue interesante? ¿memorable? ¿útil? ¿entretenido? ¿instructivo? ¿Por qué?
¿Cómo te afectó el libro?
¿Fue escrito el libro claramente? ¿Tuvo sentido? ¿O te confundió?
¿Cuál es el punto de vista en el libro? ¿Concuerda con el tuyo? ¿Por qué o por qué no?
¿Fueron los personajes creíbles? ¿Por qué o por qué no? ¿Fueron ellos superficiales?
¿Podrías relacionarte con un de los personajes en la historia? ¿Quién fue tu personaje preferido? ¿Por qué?
¿Había una problema o el obstáculo en la historia? ¿Fue vencido?
¿El tema es nuevo y original? ¿O viejo? ¿Una nueva innovación? ¿O aburrido?
¿Te gusto el libro? ¿O otro fue mejor? ¿Fue escrito mal o aburrido?
¿Cambiarías algo acerca del libro?
¿Empieza lento? ¿O te empicas a leer mas desde del comienzo?
¿El complot se da a conocer desde el comienzo? ¿O deja detalles?
¿El diálogo es bueno? ¿O forzado?
¿El lugar en donde se lleva acabo es creíble? ¿El autor cree una atmósfera particular?
¿Son todas las escenas pertinentes a la historia? ¿O hay muchas cosas que no fueron importantes?

Para libros de No-Ficción:
¿Fueron listadas las fuentes?
¿La información general, o profundo?
¿La escritura fue basada en hechos reales, o persuasiva y personal?
¿Fue el libro agradable? ¿O aburrido para leer?
¿Cuál fue el punto de vista en el libro? ¿Estas de acuerdo? ¿Por qué o por qué no?

Figure 4.2. How to Write a Book Review, Watsonville Public Library (*Cont.*)

Movie theater or other kinds of gift cards also make good prizes. Allow your teens to help decide what prizes they think will be a draw in your library. They will also need to decide if they want to have a first, second, and third place award scale, honorable mentions, or another system of awarding prizes for winners.

Publicity for the Poetry Slam

A brochure or flyer to advertise your slam can doubly serve as a registration form for your teen slam contestants (see figure 4.3). The brochure should include a definition of a poetry slam; a description of eligibility, rules, expectations, and how the slam will be conducted; a list of prizes and how they will be awarded; the date, time and location; and a detachable sign-up form.

The brochure should also indicate whether there are any content and word choice boundaries for the original poems to be performed. In a school setting, teacher-librarians will have to defer to their school's policies. In a public library, there may be more flexibility. When in doubt about content rules, always check with your supervisor or manager. You want all of the teen participants to feel comfortable expressing themselves, and the audience to understand the perimeters of the contest. Be up front with slam registrants and audience participants about any special requirements by indicating them in the slam brochure.

If your Friends of the Library group is funding the event, a local business is donating prizes, or anyone else is helping in any other special way, acknowledge and thank them in the brochure and during the slam itself. You will particularly want to recognize your TAB.

If your library has developed an online registration system for classes and programs, have your slammers register through that system. For slams at our library, teens bring in their signed registration forms giving contact information and agreeing to abide by the rules, and are also entered into our online registration system. This allows us to take registrations at any of our library branches without surpassing the program's keyed-in sign-up limit. It also provides an instant list of participants for reminders and program check in.

Make sure the poetry slam is promoted in the junior and senior high schools if yours is a public library, or throughout the school if yours is a school library. Public librarians may send copies of the slam brochure or flyer to the school library media staff members and ask them to circulate the information for you. Don't forget the English teachers. Poetry is right up their alley, and they are happy to let their students know about this opportunity. As a matter of fact, you might encourage the English teachers to offer extra credit to any student who performs as a slammer or who attends the program as an audience member to cheer on fellow teens.

Naturally, you will promote the slam on your school or library's Web page, especially on the "teen page," if you have one. Be sure that local media are aware of the program via press releases. Send copies of the brochure to local teen agencies like the Boys & Girls Club, to any poetry-oriented groups, and to local coffeehouses. Finally, encourage your TAB members to distribute flyers and brochures to their friends and classmates who write and enjoy poetry.

What You Need and a Description of Roles

There are a number of items needed and roles to fill for a successful slam:

- *Small whiteboards or pads of paper and markers* for the judges to write and display their scores.

- *A fishbowl or other container* to hold *slips of paper with the names of the slam competitors.* Drawing from the fishbowl determines poet order for each round.

Slammin'
@
Your Library

Saturday, April 18, 2009

1:00 – 3:00 p.m.

For grades 6-12

Harmony Library
Community Meeting Room

Hosted by
The Interesting Reader Society
TIRS
library teen advisory group

Poudre River Public Library District

www.fcgov.com/library

Main Library
201 Peterson
2216380

Información 4162012

Reasonable accommodations
will be made for access to services,
programs, and activities and special
communication arrangements will
be made for persons with disabilities.
Please call 221-6380 for assistance.

Harmony Library
A jointuse facility of Front Range Community College
& the Fort Collins Regional Library District

Harmony & Shields
2048404

Opening March 28, 2009
Council Tree Library
2733 Council Tree Avenue
(Harmony & Ziegler Roads)

FRONT RANGE
COMMUNITY COLLEGE

Teen Poetry Slam Registration for Slammers

Name

Age

School/Grade

Address

Telephone number

Email address

I certify that the three poems I will present
at the Poudre River Public Library District Teen
Poetry Slam on Saturday, April 18, 2009 will be my
own original poems, and that I will adhere to the
rules as given in this brochure.

I understand that a place will be reserved
for me at the Teen Poetry Slam, and if for any
reason I will be unable to attend I will inform the
Library at 970-221-6380 or 970-204-8206 as soon
as possible so that someone else may be assigned
my place.

Signature of Slammer

Date

Figure 4.3. Poudre River Public Library District, Teen Poetry Slam Flyer

Poetry Slam

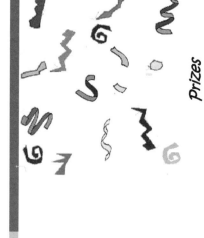

What is a Poetry Slam? Simply put, it is the competitive art of original performance poetry. It is a lot of fun for both the poets ("slammers") and the audience members.

You can participate in two ways:
*As a Slammer
*As an active audience member

Rules

You must register to become a Slammer for the contest, which is limited to 15 contestants in grades 6-12. There will be a waiting list in case of cancellations.

To register, fill out, sign, and detach the form in this brochure. Bring it to the reference desk at either the Main Library or the Harmony Library. Be sure to have the librarian also register you in the online system.

Audience members are expected to be "big + vocal" in response to judging scores.

Audience members do not need to register.

The order in which Slammers will perform will be drawn randomly before each round.

There will be three rounds to the Slam, so each poet should have three pieces of original poetry ready.

Poems presented will be limited to those that do not contain profanity, obscenity, or excessive violence.

There is a three-minute time limit per poem. Timing begins as soon as the poet begins speaking. After three minutes, the poet is allowed a ten-second grace period. Beyond this, points get deducted, a half point for every ten seconds over the grace period.

Each poem is judged on a scale of 1-10, with 10 being the highest. One-place decimal points are allowed. The scorekeeper records every score, tossing out the highest and lowest. The middle three scores (minus any penalties) are added for each round's score. At the end of three rounds, the winning poet is the one with the highest cumulative score.

No props or costumes are allowed. Poets must use only words, voice, and body to communicate their message. (Reading the poem off paper is not considered a prop.)

Prizes

First, Second, and Third place prizes will be awarded for the top three scores. Additional prizes will be awarded to all participants.

First Place is a $50.00 bookstore gift card.

Second Place is a $30.00 bookstore gift card.

Third Place is a $20.00 bookstore gift card.

Figure 4.3. Poudre River Public Library District, Teen Poetry Slam Flyer (Cont.)

- *A "host" or "master of ceremonies" (MC)*. This should be a high-spirited and outgoing TAB member with a good sense of humor who is willing and anxious to fill the role. The host draws names for the order of the rounds, introduces each poet, gives words of encouragement, and announces the winners at the end. The host might tell a few jokes and keep the audience engaged and connected to the performances.

- *Five judges,* who are responsible for numerically evaluating the performance of each poet. Judges must consider both the *performance* and *quality* of each poem to determine the scores. Scores usually range from 1 to 10, with 1 being the worst and 10 being the best.

- *Two scorekeepers,* preferably good at math, to keep tabs on *score sheets* (see figure 4.4, p. 82). For each poem, the middle three scores from the five judges will be recorded, eliminating the two that are highest and lowest. Each scorekeeper must have a *calculator* and *two sharpened pencils* along with the score sheets. Though one scorekeeper is fine, it's better to have two to avoid any confusion. When the final scores are tallied by each scorekeeper, they should match one another, which indicates an accurate accounting of the winners.

- *One timekeeper,* who tracks each poet's allotted time. If a poet exceeds the time limit set for the slam, which could be 30 seconds beyond the allotted 3 minutes for each poem, with a half point deduction, the timekeeper will inform the scorekeepers to take off the designated amount. A *stopwatch* is very helpful for a timekeeper, but a *watch with a second hand* will do.

- *The audience,* which includes everyone who does not have a specific role and is there to witness and enjoy the slam. Since the goal of a poetry slam is to connect the poets more intimately with the audience, the audience should be "loud and reactive," letting the judges know by applauding or booing whether or not they agree with their scores. This strong audience reaction to the scoring is a major difference between a poetry *slam* and a poetry *reading*.

- *The poets,* who read and perform their original poetic works.

Running the Slam

When you are planning a poetry slam, you will start by reviewing the assigned positions with your TAG or other teen volunteers. Someone must be stationed at a welcome table near the meeting room entrance to sign in the slammers and add slips of paper with their names to the fishbowl.

You might allow five minutes' leeway for all slam contestants to arrive, but no longer. A statement in the rules that all slammers must be on time can help to ensure that the program begins promptly. Participants must understand up front that their places will be forfeited if they are late and a "wait list" slammer is there on time.

A Simple Plan for Poetry Slam Rounds

After the host gives an overview of the rules and explains how the rounds will unfold and how final judging will be tallied, the actual competition begins. The host draws a name from the fishbowl and announces poet number 1. This "luck of the draw" permits slammers to perform randomly during each round. The host repeats this process throughout the first round until each poet's name has been called.

Upon completion of each piece, the poet should leave the stage area while the judges quickly mark their individual scores on the score sheets. Once scores are all completed, the judges hold up their score cards. The host reads the scores, the audience responds, and the scorekeepers record the middle three scores on the score sheets, leaving out the highest and lowest scores.

Poetry Slam Scoresheet

Poet Name	Round 1 Score	Round 2 Score	Round 3 Score	Total (round 1 + round 2 + round 3)

Write down all five judges' scores for the poet.
Cross out the highest and lowest.
Add the three remaining scores together.

Write the total in the box.

Figure 4.4. Poetry Slam Scoresheet. Used with permission of Anthology, Inc.

This process is repeated through rounds 2 and 3.

At the conclusion of all three rounds, the host announces the winners and awards their prizes. If other competitors get consolation prizes, those are given out as well.[9]

Additional Points to Consider

Parents and other adults like to come to watch the teens participate in poetry slams. Ask your teens how they feel about allowing this. Some teen groups prefer to keep the program "no adults allowed." Our teen group said they have no problem with parents attending, but the parents should sit in a special "parent area" in the back of the room. Other teens might be amenable to adults being in the audience, without limitations. Talk over the issue with your teens and decide on a course of action that fits at your library.

Provide refreshments for the audience and participants. Something simple like cookies and juice is fine. Be sure to have drinking water available for each teen slammer.

While waiting for the scorekeepers to tally the scores, take a short break. Check to be sure there are no problems figuring out the scores. Let the host know when it is time to get the audience back to their seats. It is guaranteed that everyone will return in a timely fashion, because they will want to know who won!

If you work in a multi-branch library system, consider doing a slam at each branch, with the winners from all the branches competing in a final championship competition. If there are several branches, you might include only the top scorers. If you have a smaller library system, with few branches, you might include all the first-, second-, and third-place finishers from each branch.

Teen Poetry Readings and Open Mike Nights

Hosting poetry readings or open mike nights might be a simpler and more manageable option for the teens at your library. They might enjoy transforming a meeting room into a "coffeehouse" with refreshments and inviting local teens to come and read their original poetry or to listen to the poetry that is being read. No pressure, no prizes—just a casual place to enjoy one another's company, snack, and hear some great original poems. Allow your teens to set up the room as they would like and to arrange the readings in a manner that is most comfortable for them and their peers. They might even come up with an interesting angle to such a program, as the teens described in the next section did!

RaWR: Readings and Wild Recitations

A variation of the poetry reading idea was extremely successful for the teens at the Ketchikan Public Library in Alaska (www.firstcitylibraries.org/KPLhomepage.html). Their TAG advisor, Kelly Johnson, said,

> The RaWR program, which stands for "Reading and Wild Recitations," was the teens' idea. We had planned on doing something for National Poetry Month, but almost no one wanted to read their *own* poetry. But *everyone* had a favorite already-published passage they wanted to read. In fact, when the program was underway, a few complete books were read—Dr. Seuss is still a popular guy! The TAG teens picked the poster graphic too. I found five choices and they voted overwhelmingly for the lioness.
>
> We only had 14 teens at the program since we found out two weeks before that there was a huge Southeast Alaska Choir performance that night, and several of the TAG kids were in it. But they had mistakenly told us the wrong date. However, everyone who came to RaWR had a great time. We had a sign up sheet with scheduled snack breaks, and the TAG kids took turns introducing the

readers and acted as hosts. They declared the evening a total success and it was decided we would do RaWR II next year—*not* the same week as Southeast Choir though![10]

RaWR demonstrates that even a popular program idea may be successfully adapted into a new format when imaginative teens are allowed to be creative. Give your teens the opportunity to share ideas and brainstorm unique approaches like the teens from Ketchikan did.

Remember to work with your teens to develop attention-grabbing publicity like the RaWR flyer. The extra effort it takes to create an especially attractive flyer and matching poster (figure 4.5) is worth it, because they catch the eye of busy teens. Remember also to check the school and community calendar to make sure there are no choir performances or other conflicts the night of your program!

Here's a little secret: Kelly Johnson, the TAG advisor at the Ketchikan Public Library, is one of the former Young Adult Advisory Council members I worked with at the City of Mesa Library in Arizona in the 1980s. Once again, this goes to show that teens who participate in their libraries sometimes go on to work in libraries with teens themselves, following in our footsteps!

Ketchikan Public Library Community Novel

The TAG at the Ketchikan Public Library decided to try something else new and original. They thought that a community novel would be a fun program to get young people *and* adults involved in their library in an entertaining and creative way. People at the library were invited to add to a story idea that the teens dreamed up:

> T.A.G. invites you to write a paragraph (or two) about Thomas Alistair, Jared Mason, and Enid Isabella—three teens hanging out in a laundromat in General-town, Washington. Take them out of the laundromat, give them friends or loved ones, fun times or rough times, and T.A.G. will put it all together to create a novel written by Ketchikan, Alaska!

The final tally was 44 paragraphs contributed by library clientele, with only 2 that were totally unusable. The novel turned out to be nine chapters long, and seven TAG members served as volunteer readers for it. To attract interest in the "novel" reading, the TAG did the program as a cooperative effort with the local college. The college had a program of its own coming up, and the TAG teens tapped into their evening of improvisations, storytelling, and games by adding the presentation of the community novel, complete with refreshments. Those who attended really enjoyed the innovative segment of TAG reading the "novel."[11] (See figure 4.6, p. 86.)

This is an idea any TAG can latch on to, and there may be additional ways to approach it. For instance, it could be a competition to complete a whole story, or a prize could be awarded for the most important or best-written paragraph. It could also be a program that the public library coordinates with the schools. Teachers and other school staff members could be invited to get in on the action, too! Or, it might simply be a program like the one the teens in Ketchikan did, with the public contributing to a community "novel."

The "novel" reading might be an enjoyable addition to another event, such as a poetry slam or a creative writing workshop. If it is done in conjunction with the schools as a contest for the best ending, it might be a fun afterschool program or be added to jazz up a school library's teen volunteer meeting. Perhaps a school or local newspaper would be willing to publish the top three versions of the story. The possibilities are endless!

If your teens are interested in conducting this program, do some brainstorming to see how they think it might best fit in your school or community.

Figure 4.5. RaWR Program Poster

Figure 4.6. Ketchikan Community Novel Poster

ART-ORIENTED PROJECTS AND ACTIVITIES

For some teenagers, art is the main channel of self-expression. For others, creating art might not be their primary focus, but it is still an important one. You will want to encourage not only the teens who like to read and write to become part of your teen participation fold, but also those who are drawn to the more visual aspects of communication.

Consider how important graphic novels have become over the last few decades and how many teens have checked out the various "how to draw" books from your collection. Think about how, for every teen captivated by poetry, there is a teen captivated by drawing. There are many ways that you can attract teens to your library just by acknowledging their appreciation for art and by allowing them to incorporate this kind of self-expression into their library participation experiences.

Display Designers at the Kirkwood Public Library

At the Kirkwood Public Library in Missouri (kpl.lib.mo.us/), teens who enjoy art can apply to participate in the Display Designers Program during the summer months. Volunteers who are age 13 or older work in teams of three to four. Lynn Bosso, Assistant Director of Programs & Youth Services at the library, said that last summer there were four Display Designers teams.

Each team was assigned a specific display area of the library, and team members decided on a book display theme, which Lynn approved. The teen volunteers then selected the books, created signs and visuals for the displays, and put them up. Some of the teams also created brief booklists on a wide variety of topics and genres to go along with their displays.

At the beginning of the summer, the teen Display Designers artists received some basic training with a computer graphics program to create signs and display visuals. The teens greatly enjoyed learning about these support tools and were very creative in putting them and additional supplies to good use.

The teens knew that Lynn was available for help and that she kept tabs on their activities, but she allowed them to work independently, and they did a great job creating the displays.[12] When teens are permitted and trusted to work on their own like this, remarkable results can follow. The Display Designers at the Kirkwood Public Library are an impressive example of empowering teens to use their artistic skills for promoting books and reading at their library.

A Teen Art Show at the Elizabeth Public Library

Each spring, the TAC at the Elizabeth Public Library in New Jersey (www.elizpl.org) sponsors a library art show exclusively for students in grades 6 to 12. Art teachers and students are solicited to encourage submission of one piece of any medium from each student. There are generally 80 to 150 pieces of artwork received and arranged in the library's auditorium, in categories based on the grade of the artist and the medium. Three expert judges—two local artists and a "crafty" library assistant—determine a winner in each category, a "Best in Show" winner for grades 6 to 8, another "Best in Show" for grades 9 to12, and many "Honorable Mention" prizes. On the night of the open-to-the-public show, prizes are awarded to the winners and certificates are given to all of the show's participants.

The TAC is vital to the art show's success. Members are responsible for marketing the event by bringing flyers to school and letting other teens know, via word-of-mouth and through MySpace messages, to submit their work if they are interested and to attend the actual show. They are also responsible for assisting in mounting the pieces for the show and for the creation of printed programs and nametags.

On the night of the show, teens wears badges that say "Elizabeth Public Library, Teen Advisory Council Member." They hand out programs, answer questions about the show, assist with refreshments, help hand out prizes, and clean up at the end.[13]

I am sure the Elizabeth Public Library teens were just as proud of their badges as those long-ago teens at Hutchins Junior High School were of their "Library Service" buttons!

Teen Arts Come Alive at the Boulder Public Library

The Teen Art Gallery at the Boulder Public Library in Colorado (www.boulder.lib.co.us) is a unique school and public library cooperative endeavor. Funded by a grant, the gallery features rotating exhibits exclusively reserved for artwork created by local middle and high school students. Art classes from the local schools take turns presenting their work for the displays. A wide range of formats is featured, including painting, photography, graffiti, sculpture, collage, found objects, writing, and more.

The Teen Art Gallery is not restricted to school groups. It also provides an excellent opportunity for artistic teens to independently prepare and show their individual creations in a public venue, or to do so with a group of friends.

Another interesting facet of this project is podcasted interviews with art teachers and the students whose work is currently being displayed in the Teen Art Gallery. These podcasts are accessed through the library's teen Web page, along with podcasts of original poetry spoken by the teens who participate in the library's Just Write creative writing sessions.

Funded by the Boulder Public Library Foundation, the Just Write sessions are held to expand writing skills and to offer teens a chance to meet with likeminded writers as they work on novels, short stories, poetry, songs, and other creative endeavors.

In whatever way they choose to take part, the teens who are involved gain experience with publicly sharing their work, exposure for their schools or community groups, and an opportunity to enhance their college applications and resumes.[14]

Window Painting at the Poudre River Public Library District

Does the teen space in your library have amazing windows? Ours does! They are tall, bright windows that face away from the sun to keep the light appealing but not overwhelming, whatever the time of year. If your teens express interest in making *your* library's beautiful windows an artistic showpiece that will attract fellow teens to the area, ask for permission to do window painting.

Once we received approval, three members of our Interesting Reader Society came in after school one day and decorated the windows to match the Teen Read Week theme. They had a ball doing it, and it added a wonderful dimension to the other Teen Read Week publicity that was out and about in the teen area. Once Teen Read Week was over, the IRS members knew it was time to get out the paper towels and remove the paint. However, they asked if they could get permission to paint the windows again, this time with an attractive winter theme.

If your teens want to embark on a window-painting activity, smile—don't panic! Here are some tips for a simple and successful project:

- Ask your supervisor and/or administrator for permission to do the window painting, including a request for funding if you don't already have money for such an activity in your budget.

- Have the teens choose a theme, which could even be a hodgepodge of book genres.

- Go to any good craft supply store and purchase water soluble window paints. They come in roll-on tubes that do not drip. You can buy them in a variety of colors. Be forewarned that the metallic colors cost two to three times what the basic colors do! If you stick to basic colors, for $20 to $30 you will be able to purchase a nice assortment of paints.

However, if you keep an eye out for sales, you can get these items at a greatly reduced price.

- Plan ahead for the clean-up part of the project. Spray bottles with water or window cleaner in them and plenty of paper towels make removing the window paints a breeze! However, advise your teens to apply the paints lightly, because heavier applications make the paint harder to remove.

- Be prepared for comments from your library's elderly or conservative set. Some may be appreciative of the young people having fun and promoting reading through their window art. Others might correlate window painting with graffiti. To those who express displeasure, you will need to say a few positive words about the teens using their creativity to promote books and reading to their peers.

- Praise your teens for a job well done! Be sure to take photos of their artwork. Share positive comments you hear about the artwork with the artists.

TEENS AND DRAMA: A GREAT MATCH

Drama is a fabulous outlet for creativity and self-expression, and teens who like to perform may use it to contribute to their libraries in a variety of ways. You read about one of them in chapter 3. The teen puppetry troupe at the South Brunswick Public Library provides enjoyable programs for both the teens who participate in them and the children and parents in the audiences. The puppetry troupe illustrates one way that drama can bring literature to life and allow teens to become involved in promoting it at their libraries.

Following are some additional examples that demonstrate new ideas and approaches for incorporating drama into active teen participation.

Elizabeth Public Library Teen Theater Troupe

At the Elizabeth Public Library, the Teen Theatre Troupe is in its fourth summer. Their very first performance was *Sleeping Handsome*, which was their own adaptation of *Sleeping Beauty*. It featured both male and female fairies, but with a prince and princess who didn't want to kiss at the end, so they exchanged a Hershey's Kiss instead! The subsequent project was an adaptation of the picture book *The Paper Bag Princess*, followed by *The Three Little Elephants (and the Big Bad Mouse)*.

The group meets every Friday afternoon during the summer, when they choose a story to adapt. The librarian writes out the play and then works with the teens on props, costumes, scenery, and everything else needed to perform it. The teens do a run-through each week. Because of time and scheduling constraints, and the fact that they are doing more performances, their latest production is a readers theatre adaptation of *The Ugly Caterpillar* instead of a regular play.

The change to readers theater demonstrates how a teen theater troupe, or any library group, needs to be flexible. In past years, the theater troupe centered an entire program around their performance. They had a storytime at which the librarian read an original book, such as *Sleeping Beauty*, *The Paper Bag Princess*, or *The Three Little Pigs*, and then the teens performed a 15- to 20-minute play based on the story. A related craft, with teen actors assisting little ones with making paper bag puppets or elephant masks, followed. Because the focus has changed to incorporate teen performances as part of the end-of-summer festivities, the children's librarian has planned games and other activities for children after the storytime and play, with the actors still on hand to assist.[15]

Readers Theatre at the San Diego County Library

Readers theatre may also be the focal point of teen dramatic programming. At the San Diego County Library in California (www.sdcl.org), there is an active teen-created, teen-driven readers theatre group. Barbara Sutton, the library's Central Region Youth Librarian II, advises that with such library groups the teens should do as much of the script writing and performance preparation themselves as possible, while also having fun.[16]

Readers theatre is similar to a radio play, with the group reading a script that paraphrases a book or story while using nominal staging or props. Group involvement enhances teen literacy skills and promotes positive youth development in a wide variety of ways, including team building, boosting creativity, and allowing exposure to new literature. An array of teen library participatory options may result, such as performing for young children or seniors or offering playwriting workshops and festivals for peers.

There are a few basic steps to starting an effective teen readers theatre program at your library. Your teens will have to determine their audience; create a simple, original script or select a prescripted play online or from a book; request necessary permissions; and select parts. It is a good idea to start with a familiar story, introduced by a narrator. The play should include several characters, use lots of dialog; add a touch of humor; and incorporate excitement, tension and conflict. Your teens will need copies of the play, folders, highlighters, and any staging items. All participating teens should have the same style and color of shirt, although costume embellishments and props may be added. Rehearsals and performances should be scheduled in advance so the teens know the dates and times to which they are committing.

When teens are performing, they do not read in a vacuum. They must be expressive and use inflection, bring eye contact and simple gestures into play, and turn to face the other actors or the audience as appropriate. Likewise, stage presence is important, whether the teens stand at podiums or music stands, sit on stools, or arrange themselves in a unique fashion that fits the play. Other techniques, such as joining voices for emphasis, playing background music, or having the narrator stand in a peripheral position, should also be incorporated to fit the play.[17]

Offer readers theatre at your library as an option for teens who enjoy acting. It will allow them to use their drama skills without investing time in memorizing lines.

Puppet Pals at the Poudre River Public Library District

In chapter 3 you read about the Library Pals at the Poudre River Public Library District in Fort Collins, Colorado. Library Pals is more than just a volunteer experience for the teens who participate during their first year. It also serves as a "hidden" audition for another library teen volunteer group, Puppet Pals.

After Library Pals teens are inconspicuously observed in their volunteer work during the first year they sign on, those who exhibit the most promising talent for being trained to perform puppet shows are personally invited to sign up the following year for another teen participatory group, Puppet Pals. If they are not interested, they may stick with Library Pals. Another option is for teens to join the Interesting Reader Society library teen advisory group. Remember that, when possible, it really helps to have a variety of options like this for library teen involvement.

Puppet Pals perform all the puppet plays for little children during the summer, in teams of four each. Puppet Pals receive special training prior to beginning their rehearsals. During that training they learn the basic technical skills of hand puppetry, with a minimum of dialog and plenty of action and humorous movements. Learning how to do special effects, such as creating "smoke" or "rain," is also part of the training. Once the teens complete their puppetry instruction, they are ready to move on to rehearsals.

Without extra time available for guiding teens in script writing, the basic puppet play scripts are written by Giny McConathy, the Children's Services Library Assistant who is in charge of Library Pals and Puppet Pals. She then encourages the Puppet Pals to come up with ideas to incorporate into the shows, thereby adding elements of teen ingenuity and creativity to the productions.

After six two-hour rehearsals, the Puppet Pals teens are ready for their actual performances, which run a half hour each and comprise four short puppet plays. Twelve performances are scheduled each summer at all three library branches. The teens are expected to be present 10 minutes before each show as the audience arrives, during which they do impromptu puppet skits. They are also expected to stay 10 minutes after each show to "introduce" the children from the audience to the puppets and to answer any questions they may have. (See figure 4.7.)

Figure 4.7. Puppet Pals Troupe Performs for Children at the Poudre River Public Library District, Fort Collins, Colorado. Photo by Giny McConathy

Puppet shows are offered an additional four times a year after the multiple performances in the summer. Giny indicates that homeschooled teen puppeteers are a wonderful resource for doing these shows and keeping teens involved. Although they are held for young children at a time when most other teenagers are in school, homeschooled teens often have the flexibility and parental support to continue doing shows year-round.[18]

Don't underestimate the capability of homeschooled teens to contribute to your library at odd hours for many other kinds of events, activities, and tasks. Be sure to reach out to them and let them know what teen participatory options your library has to offer and where they are most needed. Likewise, older teen participants who might have finished high school but are still willing to be involved at the library are a valuable resource. Who says teens have to stop their library-oriented activities just because they have graduated?

A good example is a former Poudre River Public Library District teen volunteer named Colin West. Colin was one of the first Puppet Pals and ended up as one of the best puppeteers the library has ever had. His library connections started early, as his mother began bringing him there as a toddler. When he was old enough, Colin spent a summer as a Library Pal, and then he joined Puppet Pals for four more years. He was eventually hired by the library as a storyteller, and he did a superb job in that role (see figure 4.8).

Colin is a talented young man whose debate team won a national championship, and about whom Giny says, "I expect he'll be President of the United States some day." Although his life brims with many interests and abilities, library volunteering was and is as important as any of them. Chances are that his positive experiences as a teen will influence his support for libraries in the future.[19]

Figure 4.8. Colin West Tells Stories for the Children and Parents of Fort Collins.
Photo by Giny McConathy

TEENS AND STORYTELLING

Storytelling is another fun and productive way to empower teens and to give them an opportunity to perform. Sue-Ellen Jones, Teen Services Librarian at the Poudre River Public Library District, teaches storytelling to teenagers and then arranges for them to perform for library audiences. She has shared her viewpoints on why teen storytelling is valuable:

> Storytelling provides a window to the origin tales of other cultures and offers us an understanding of people very different from ourselves. Stories enrich not only the people who listen but the storyteller as well. By getting teenagers involved in storytelling, libraries can provide these insights and this enrichment for both the teens and their audiences.

Teens who perform stories for others learn firsthand about how one can love a story and feel connected to it. A teen who learns a story carries the kernels of truth and identity from that story and its culture inside him or herself until the story is shared with another individual or group. Teens learn that they can repeat the same story and receive unique audience reactions to it each time, drawing out new aspects.

When I teach storytelling techniques to teenagers, I ask them to haunt the folktale sections of their libraries for several weeks and to explore stories from many different cultures. I always ask them to bring two or three stories that they are interested in learning to our first storytelling session. I ask them to identify the elements of the story that call up a response in them and to articulate those to the storytelling group. Some teens like a story's strong character, some appreciate the culture and country in which the story is set, and others are gripped by a story's humor or heroism. Teens encounter all of these things when they learn a story. Like the West African griots of old who held an honored place in their society as keepers of the legends, folklore, and customs for tribal families, leaders, and elders, teens become the "keepers" of their stories and share their own sense of self from each story with their listeners.

As teens learn storytelling, they explore how to imagine scenes and images so that they can remember a story; how to create characters through nuance and subtlety with their voices; and how to use their personalities to "sell" the stories to which they are attracted. When all is said and done, though, teenagers can tell stories to explore other heritages and maybe—just maybe—they will be inspired to develop and share stories from their own time with each other.[20]

SUMMING UP: SELF-EXPRESSION ENHANCES TEEN LIBRARY PARTICIPATION

Consider the ways your teens might constructively exhibit the teen traits through their creative contributions to your library. The examples in this chapter are a start, and you and your teens can probably think of additional innovative ways to approach art, writing, and performance activities. On the other hand, your teens might latch on to a specific idea they discover here and decide to go with it. Give them a chance to figure out what artistic endeavors they would like to pursue and help them to achieve their goals. Your library will not only be encouraging library involvement that enhances positive youth development, it will be outwardly promoting artistic works to other young people in your community and offering an outlet for expression.

At times in history when budgets are tight and cutbacks abound, creative activities are often put on a back burner. Allowing teens to focus on the arts through your library will demonstrate the importance and value of artistic endeavors despite tough times and enhance the permanent positive effects they can have on the lives of youth.

For added information and instruction on puppetry, children's theater, reader's theatre, and storytelling with teens as they create library performances for all ages, here are some helpful resources to read, use, and share:

Bauer, Caroline Feller. *Leading Kids to Books through Puppets*. Chicago: American Library Association, 1997.

Cummings, Richard. *101 Hand Puppets: A Beginner's Guide to Puppeteering*. Mineola, NY: Dover, 2002.

de Vos, Gail. *Storytelling for Young Adults: A Guide to Tales for Teens*. 2nd ed. Westport, CT: Libraries Unlimited, 2003.

Engler, Larry, and Carol Fijan. *Making Puppets Come Alive: How to Learn and Teach Hand Puppetry*. Mineola, NY: Dover, 1997.

Fijan, Carol, and Frank Ballard. *Directing Puppet Theater Step-by-Step*. 2nd ed. San Jose, CA: Resource Publications, 1990.

Friedman, Lisa, and Mary Dowdle. *Break a Leg!: The Kids' Guide to Acting and Stagecraft*. New York: Workman, 2002.

Iakovakia, Laurel L. *Puppet Plays Plus: Using Stock Characters to Entertain and Teach Early Literacy*. Westport, CT: Libraries Unlimited, 2009.

Latrobe, Kathy Howard, and Mildred Knight Laughlin. *Readers Theater for Young Adults: Scripts and Script Development*. Englewood, CO: Teacher Ideas Press, 1989.

Peterson, Lenka, and Dan O'Connor. *Kids Take the Stage: Helping Young People Discover the Creative Outlet of Theater*. New York: Backstage Books, 2006.

Schroeder, Joanne F. *Fun Puppet Skits for Schools and Libraries*. Englewood, CO: Teacher Ideas Press, 1995.

Sima, Judy, and Kevin Cordi. *Raising Voices: Creating Youth Storytelling Groups and Troupes*. Westport, CT: Libraries Unlimited, 2003.

Spencer, Charmaine. *Story to Stage Workbook: A Step-by-Step Guide to Adapting Children's Literature into Stage and Puppet Plays*. n.p.: n.p., 2005. Written by the script consultant from the Puppeteers of America and available for purchase at store.puppeteers.org.

ENDNOTES

1. Lisa Elliott, e-mail message to author, October 1, 2008.

2. Mary Ann Lewis, e-mail message to author, January 18, 2009.

3. Young Adult Services of the Associated Libraries of Monroe County, *Teen Page* (Associated Libraries of Monroe County, n.d.), www.monroepl.org/teenpagemain.htm (accessed September 20, 2009).

4. YAS of the Associated Libraries of Monroe County, "Teen Page."

5. Lewis, e-mail, January 18, 2009.

6. YAS of the Associated Libraries of Monroe County, "Teen Page."

7. Bob Nelson et al., *Introduction to Performance Poetry and Poetry Slam: A Teacher's Guide and 4 Day Course (without Video)* (Mesa, AZ: Anthology, Inc., 2005), section 1.0.

8. Diane P. Tuccillo, "Successful Teen Advisory Groups: Teen Driven . . . with Guidance and Helping Hand," *Voice of Youth Advocates e-VOYA* (December 2005), pdfs.voya.com/VO/YA2/ VOYA200512 SuccessfulTeens.pdf (accessed September 17, 2009).

9. Nelson, *Introduction to Performance Poetry and Poetry Slam*, sections 2.0–4.0.

10. Kelly Johnson, e-mail message to author, May 16, 2008, and May 18, 2008.

11. Kelly Johnson, e-mail messages to author, October 20, 2008, and January 16, 2009.

12. Lynn Bosso, e-mail message to author, August 28, 2008.

13. Kimberly Paone, e-mail message to author, August 2, 2008.

14. Boulder Public Library Teens, *Creative Types: Teen Art Gallery and Just Write Creative Writing for Teens* (Boulder Public Library, n.d.), www.boulderteens.org/creative.htm (accessed September 20, 2009).

15. Kimberly Paone, e-mail message to author, August 13, 2008.

16. Barbara Sutton, e-mail message to author, May 9, 2009.

17. Barbara Sutton, "Readers Theater for Teens" (PowerPoint presentation, San Diego County Library, California, 2009).

18. Giny McConathy, interview with author, January 6, 2009, and e-mail messages to author, January 7, 2009.

19. Giny McConathy, e-mail message to author, January 7, 2009.

20. Sue-Ellen Jones, e-mail message to author, May 4, 2009.

5

Limited Teen Participation: Special Temporary Involvement Without Ongoing Commitment

You might have, or have decided to start, a TAB or a teen volunteer program, or both. You might have a great response from teens who are eager to belong to these groups and to participate in an ongoing fashion. But what about the teens in your community who might be interested in providing service to their library, but who are not able to make a steady commitment? There are ways that you can incorporate involvement by these teens as well. The best part is, they will be empowered and appreciated just like the teens you work with on a regular basis.

How do you make this happen? By being creative, open-minded, flexible, and willing to work with teens who are "just passing through." These teens are probably no less interested in supporting your library than the continually involved teens, but they might have other obligations and interests that prevent them from giving their time as often as your regulars. Having limited opportunities allows more teens from your community to have a voice in their library. A bonus to offering temporary volunteer opportunities is that often several of these teens will most likely decide to make an ongoing commitment at some point, or at least become more regular library users.

The following sections cover some interesting ways that teens can be part of your library without being official library TAB members or volunteers.

DROP-IN YOUTH SERVICE OPPORTUNITIES

Imagine that summer is coming, and you already have your TAB volunteers engaged in designing programs for their fellow teens, plus they are all set to take on responsibility for running your children's and teen summer reading programs. The teens have helped in making plans and preparations, and they are trained and ready to go. When you think about it, though, the number of teens making an ongoing commitment is small compared to the number of other teens in your community. How do you reach out and include teens who might want to help out and be a part of their library, but who do not want to be on the roster of regular volunteers?

If you are at the City of Mesa Library system in Arizona (www.mesalibrary.org), you have additional options that your "one shot deal" teens may embrace. These options surround a special drop-in teen volunteer program, called Summer of Service (SOS). It all began with a single temporary volunteer day opportunity, and grew from there. In days of financial pressure, the library depends even more on the efforts of these teens.

National Youth Services Day and Global Youth Service Day

The basic concept of SOS started on National Youth Service Day, now called Global Youth Service Day, in 2006. At the City of Mesa Library, the one-day service opportunity was named "Get Radical and Read at Your Library," and permitted interested teens to earn volunteer and service learning credit by shelf-reading the nonfiction collection at Main Library in teams of two. With severe budget cuts reducing the library's regular shelving staff and preventing those who remained from keeping up with their shelf-reading tasks, this was a much appreciated project for getting the library collection in order. Snacks and drinks were available for the 14 teens, who spent 42 service hours shelf-reading that day.[1] The teens who participated in this activity had good things to say about their experience. For example, one said, "Volunteering at the library was a fun, helpful thing to do, and it helps with service learning hours."

As a catalyst for nurturing youth participation in widespread settings, Global Youth Service Day (www.ysa.org/NatlGYSD/tabid/59/Default.aspx) offers an excellent opportunity for any library to experiment with a one-day, drop-in teen service learning program. Officially, the "day" is actually a choice of three days in April, which gives flexibility to agencies trying to fit the "day" into their schedules. In 2009 Global Youth Service even encouraged teens to make it a "semester of service" instead of just one day and teens outside the United States were prompted to participate in an international Global Youth Service Day counterpart. The event is sponsored by Youth Service America (YSA) every April (www.ysa.org) in conjunction with cooperating businesses and other agencies, and highly encourages any group or organization that fosters teen participation to get on board.

The YSA Web page succinctly explains the premise for supporting this special day:

> Millions of youth participate in Global Youth Service Day, the largest service event in the world . . . . Global Youth Service Day supports youth on a life-long path of service and civic engagement, and educates the public, the media, and elected officials about the role of youth as community leaders.[2]

The description may be construed to include the wide variety of youth participatory roles libraries might play in our communities. Obviously, libraries fit the mold for promoting teen participation and service on Global Youth Service Day. Does the idea pique your interest? If so, you can find extensive supplemental guidance on working with teens to select and implement Global Youth Service Day volunteer activities at the YSA Web site.

SOS Teen Participation Opportunities

From the roots of its 2006 National Youth Service Day program, the City of Mesa Library created its innovative plan to get teens involved in informal drop-in volunteering, and SOS was born. It gave teens the opportunity to help the library without committing to specific hours or a regular schedule. Teen volunteers ages 12 to 18 or in grades 7 to 12 were welcome one day per week at Main Library to carry out a variety of duties. The teens could sign up for one day or for as many days during the summer that they wanted to volunteer. They were allowed a choice of dates and times and to select the tasks needing to be done.

To publicize SOS, a press release went out to the local newspapers, and posters were sent to the junior and senior high schools. An advertisement was also published in the Mesa Service Learning newsletter (www.mesaservicelearning.org) at the schools. Bookmarks were placed at service desks and checkout areas, and posters for the program were displayed in key locations at all three City of Mesa Library branches (see figure 5.1, p. 100).

Each week a task list was prepared by the volunteer coordinator with duties that the library hoped to see accomplished. Teens would pick from the choices on the list based on what each one was interested in doing. Tasks like cleaning books, bringing in and sorting book drop deposits, organizing donations, shelf-reading, and shelving returned library items were offered every week. Other duties, such as laminating, organizing displays, and pulling books for withdrawal, were added to the task list as needed. Employees from all areas of the library got involved in finding projects that teens could do and in developing a weekly task list with a range of choices.

The task list was a vital element in running SOS. Each time the program was offered, a new list was posted. When teens arrived for the SOS program, they would examine the task list and then pick what they wanted to do for the day. They signed in on the side of the form labeled "What I did" and were taken to the appropriate areas to be trained and to complete the tasks. If they finished and had time to do other things, they could return to the task list and pick another project. Two things that really helped with task lists were having detailed instructions for special jobs, like cleaning books and CDs, or shelf-reading, and having supplies ready and waiting in work areas, such as a paper cutter with bookmarks to be cut, or markers and stamps with books to be withdrawn.

After the success of the initial drop-in volunteer season, the City of Mesa Library again opened its doors to teens for SOS in 2007. This time the program was expanded by offering it at all three library locations in Mesa in order to reach more teens wanting to earn service hours and help their library. One task list was then posted for all teens per location per SOS day. Through this subsequent SOS program, teens once again assisted with daily tasks, were actively involved in their community, and were given the opportunity to learn new life skills.[3]

Figure 5.1. SOS (Summer of Service) Volunteer Recruitment Poster/Flyer

SOS Bargain Basement Bookstore

In 2008 SOS added a book sale component, the SOS Bargain Basement Bookstore, which allowed teens to participate in new ways. They were given an opportunity to plan, organize and run their very own bookstore at Main Library. Kathee Herbstreit, the volunteer coordinator, explained how this came about:

> On the first day of the SOS program, during orientation, an announcement was made letting the teens know that if anyone was interested in running a used bookstore, they would need to meet and plan how to accomplish the goal. They were told that in a vacant room in the basement of the library, shelves were assembled for this purpose. The announcement brought some excitement to the room as practically every teen verbally showed interest in helping. At that moment I knew I had found something that would bring them back week after week during the summer.
>
> Running a bookstore with the teens was a learning experience in design, organization, planning, advertising, and communication. Even though there was not a monetary emphasis, the teens did financially add to the money earned from used items at the library. For the teens, just knowing that people came and bought items that they had chosen to sell gave them the satisfaction of accomplishing the goal.
>
> I believe that giving teens a chance to accomplish something tangible, for which they can actually take ownership, is very alluring. This concept is in line with the basic philosophy of the SOS teen program.[4]

SOS Bargain Basement Bookstore: Teen Decision Making

Before they started their Bargain Basement Bookstore, the Mesa teens were asked to decide how the bookstore would be run. Questions were posed and answered by the teens prior to establishing the bookstore. If your teens want to try a comparable project, you might consider asking them the same or similar questions. Getting teen input from the ground up and following through with their choices is an important element of empowerment. Listed below are the questions, with the teens' decisions:

- **What goals do you want to set for the bookstore?** "Sell books and make money for the library during the summer."

- **Who will be in charge overall?** "The Supervisor of the SOS program."

- **What will be the opening date?** "Next week, the second Tuesday in June."

- **Decide on the hours for the SOS Bargain Basement Bookstore.** "It will be open Tuesdays from 11:00 a.m. to 3:00 p.m."

- **Plan a schedule for who will sit at the desk and take money.** "Two people per one-hour shift."

- **How will money be handled?** "By following sales guidelines and using a money box."

- **How many teens should run the bookstore per hour, including sales attendants, stocking staff, organizers, advertisers, and customer service aides?** "Six teens on each one-hour shift."

- **How and where in the library would you advertise the bookstore?** "Signs will be created and placed by the entrance, at elevators, stairs, and the first floor bookstore. They will be removed at the end of the sale."

- **What type of books do you want to sell?** "Teen books, children's books, classics, fiction, mysteries, health and fitness, biographies, music and movies, and books on tape."

- **How will you arrange and display items on shelves for customers?** "It will be designed as shown in our drawing."

- **How much should the books cost and how will you price them?** "Bargain prices will range from 25 cents to $3.00, based on comparing our prices with the regular library bookstore upstairs. We will make price signs for each end panel and a guide for the sales desk."

- **What supplies will be needed?** "We will need pens, pencils, markers, poster board, a money box, a calculator, tape, and scrap paper."

Kathee acknowledged the teens' decisions and helped them to follow through with the plans they had made for running the bookstore. She was available for assistance and guidance, but the teens owned the project.

At the end of the summer, the teens contributed $433.05 to the library from the bookstore proceeds, reflecting a respectable profit. However, their monetary role was not as important as the fact that they felt a sense of accomplishment and pride that they had given something back to the library. Again, a project like this one, in which teens are empowered, gives them a voice in decision making and allows them to take positive action.[5] A project like this one could even be expanded to teach teens about basic accounting principles and to involve business classes.

A Story of Success

The success of the SOS program demonstrates the importance of flexibility. By allowing teens to have choices, it allowed them to be in control of their volunteer experiences. Even if they could not commit to volunteering on a set schedule for the entire summer, they were still able to offer some help to their community during those months.

This flexibility was inherent in a variety of the program aspects. Besides learning about the program from the regular promotional flyers, teens could attend a teen volunteer job fair, where they learned about SOS opportunities (see figure 5.2). Teens could pick the days and times they wanted to volunteer from the SOS schedule at any or all of the three library locations. They could pick the tasks they preferred from a list prepared each day of the program. They could stay just one hour or all three. They did not need to report absences or that they would be late. The program was constructed to make summers worry free and fun while allowing teens to contribute.

The number of teen volunteers who were involved and the volume of work completed at the library are notable. The first year the SOS program was offered at Main Library, 194 teens provided assistance on "SOS Teen Thursdays," and they completed 826 hours of service. During 2007 SOS was expanded to allow a larger number of teens the opportunity to participate by offering it on a different day each week at one of the three Mesa Library locations. By doing so, it more than doubled the teen participation. That second summer, 439 teens contributed 1,162 hours of service. In 2008, the program ran in similar fashion to the 2007 program, and had 437 teens giving 1,156 hours.

Many teens want to volunteer if the opportunity allows them control of when and how much they will do to help. Through this type of teen program, the City of Mesa Library enriches the lives of teens and builds a connection to service that will last a lifetime.[6]

Figure 5.2. SOS Job Fair Poster/Flyer

Other Options for Drop-in and On-call Teen Library Service

The Glendale Public Library in Arizona (www.glendaleaz.com/Library) offers two variations on the "one day only" and "on-call" aspects of teen volunteering. "Community Service Saturdays" are geared toward teens who only need to do a small number of volunteer hours, or who do not wish to commit to an ongoing volunteer program. Unlike the City of Mesa Library's SOS volunteer program, which is held during the summer months, Glendale Public Library offers its program on Saturday from December through May. Opportunities to contribute are provided on the second Saturday of every month from 10:00 a.m. until 2:00 p.m. Teens earn four hours of community service credit for completing tasks in the library and assisting with a children's craft program. Interested teens must preregister so that the library knows whom to expect. It is not a drop-in program like SOS.

Another choice for teens in Glendale is "On Call Volunteers." This program is for teens who do not want to commit to ongoing volunteering and for whom the Saturday community service hours do not work. These teens are in the wings for particular events held at the library for which extra hands are needed, such as craft programs and special activities. Shifts for on-call volunteers are usually two to four hours, as needed. Teens who are asked to volunteer are notified one week before an event, and they have the option of either accepting the invitation to help out or declining if they have a prior commitment.[7]

Perhaps these kinds of occasional teen volunteer programs would work in your library, and your teens would appreciate having the flexibility they offer. You might want to consider the examples you have read about as well as other alternatives that could work for your library, its staff, and your teen clientele.

Boy and Girl Scout Library Projects

Another wonderful resource for temporary teen involvement is the Boy Scouts and the Girl Scouts. Make sure your local troops know that the library is there and is willing to accept appropriate project contributions. By doing so, you will provide teens with a meaningful setting in which they can give time and effort, help to advance their Scouting accomplishments, and allow the library to be the beneficiary of their good work.

The City of Mesa Library provides opportunities for Scouts to do just that. When the library had its Centennial Celebration in 2007, a Boy Scout helped to run the event to earn his Eagle Scout rank.

Another Boy Scout earned his Eagle rank by helping the library with a "Recycle for Reading" program. The program originated when the City of Mesa offered the library a direct contribution for the purchase of new books, up to $25,000, for materials recycled above the July 2008 total of 35,376 tons. For his project, the Eagle Scout candidate agreed to help recycle the damaged books from the Red Mountain Library branch.

This Eagle Scout's efforts were a crucial part of the "Recycle for Reading" program, which provides extra funds to buy new materials, especially welcome during difficult financial times. His goal was to recycle five tons of books in the recycling blue barrels for the library, and he met that goal. The job was not easy, because the cover of each of book had to be removed before going into a blue barrel, but he persevered, and the project came to fruition.

Another Eagle Scout's project through the City of Mesa Library involved him making book bags for toddler patients at Phoenix Children's Hospital. The Scout sewed cute reversible book bags using donated material, then filled them with the books remaining from the library's discontinued "Born to Read' program and with leftover summer reading program sport ball toys. He made 100 bags to give to the sick children at the hospital.[8]

In similar fashion, the Harris County Public Library (www.hcpl.lib.tx.us/index.htm) in Texas has employed Scouts as volunteers, with great success. Over the years the library has had a number of Eagle Scouts choose their neighborhood library as the focus of their Eagle projects.

They completed a wide variety of projects, ranging from book drives and book sales, to landscaping, to building shelves and other objects.[9]

Don't forget your local Girl Scouts! Girl Scouts seeking their Gold Award may play as instrumental a part as Boy Scouts working toward their Eagle Scout designation. In Frederick County, Virginia, five prospective Gold Award candidates from Troop 525 completed their Gold Award Project, "John Handley High School Library Renovation and Restoration." The girls chose this project because they wanted to help their school and community, and they did.

When the high school library was relocated, it needed to be restocked. The girls took care of this. Because the project made the transition smoother, it allowed the librarians and students to access their library and its books sooner. In collaboration with the school librarian, the girls also improved the library overall by reorganizing it, which made it more useful to everyone.[10]

Like her counterparts in Virginia, a 19-year-old Girl Scout from the San Jacinto Council in Texas earned her Gold Award through library work. She established the first local library in her town of Bremond, Texas (www.bremondtxlibrary.com/index.html), and she even cataloged 6,300 books for the project! Because of her efforts, Bremond now has a three-year provisional membership in the Texas Library System and a full-time librarian.[11]

Scouts are constantly on the lookout for new projects to fulfill their badge and top achievement award requirements. They especially need projects that are unique and community oriented, and libraries are a perfect place for such balanced teen involvement. Remember to contact your local Scouting troops to let them know that your library would be a grateful recipient of their Scouts' efforts if they are interested in a project with a library service focus.

Read One, Pick One

How about a "drop-in" teen collection development program? The Lake City Public Library in Iowa (www.lakecity.lib.ia.us) held a "Read One, Pick One" program to promote the YA collection and to give teen readers a sense of ownership. No prior commitment was required, and teens could participate as much or as little as they wanted. Here's how it worked.

Any teen who read a book from the YA collection during the program got to pick another title, which the library would order and add to that collection. Librarian Kim Olson made a list of potential purchases with small color images of the covers, plus author, title, and a brief synopsis for over 100 titles that she felt would appeal to a wide range of teen readers. She created a colorful form that could be filled out when a book from the collection had been read and was returned. Each teen wrote down the title of a book he or she had read and a new title from the list for purchase. The library then ordered the selected new title.

A special effort was made to get each new title into the collection as soon as possible, with the teen who had picked it being given first reading rights. When the book was ready to circulate, Kim cut the colorful program logo off the request form and taped it on the front of the book. In that way, by the end of the month, the library had new YA books that the teens knew had been picked by their peers, not by the librarians.

The teens enjoyed this program, because it gave them a chance to have a voice in choosing for their collection, and they felt like the library was buying titles they might not have otherwise. In reality, teens could make purchase suggestions at any time, but either they didn't know about that, or they seemed reluctant to do so. Creating a fun program to invite them to take part worked wonders!

Kim feels that the list of potential titles for purchase is important, because it presents possibilities, much like a trip to the bookstore. However, teens were also allowed to propose books that weren't on the list, so their choices were not restricted by it.

The Read One, Pick One program was promoted both in the library and at the local secondary school for grades 7 to 12. Not only did the program bring in new readers, it got the teens talking about which books they wanted. One group of teens even worked together to request all the titles in a particular series.

This program was successful because every teen who used the library could participate as much or as little as he or she wanted, entirely at his or her own pace. It required no meetings or trainings. To heighten interest next time, Kim plans on an ending celebration with pizza and booktalks for all teen participants.

Kim relayed that the library itself really appreciated the Read One, Pick One program because teens had to actually *read* to participate, yet there was no pressure. Another advantage was that the library had the opportunity to buy all the books the teens wanted with their wholesaler's discount, without worrying about travel arrangements—and higher prices—for a bookstore purchasing trip with a select group of teens. *All* teens in the community were encouraged to participate in this project.

Some things to keep in mind if you try this program:

- Be prepared with funding to buy as many books as the teens earn.

- Let the teens know in your publicity that books nominated that are not on the list must fit your collection development policy for the YA collection.

- Be prepared to order frequently, at least every four days, and to process the books quickly.

Allow enough time for each interested teen to read at least one book, make a pick and to get all the requested books processed and into the hands of teen readers. Two to three months might be a good timetable, depending on your budget and the size of the population you serve. Decide whether teens will be limited to selecting just one book, or if they will be permitted to read their own picks, and then continue picking another, and another . . . .[12]

Assisting with a Computer System Transition

When the Ketchikan Public Library transitioned from Dynix Classic to Unicorn with the iBistro Web catalog, a half dozen of its TAG members volunteered to learn iBistro. While the library was closed for three days to do the upgrade and get everything set for the unveiling of the new system, the teens were given special training on how to use it. For the open house day when the library's new system went public, the TAG members came in to the library and stayed by the computer terminals to help people who had problems or questions. This permitted the desk staff to deal with other situations concurrently, instead of being tied up with educating library clientele on the new system.

Although the number of people wanting or needing help was not overwhelming, the TAG members were present and ready to serve in shifts the whole day. They provided quite a bit of guidance on iBistro and even helped a patron set up a MySpace page on one of the dedicated Internet terminals.[13]

When your library has a temporary need for volunteers, as the Ketchikan Public Library did, teens can fit the bill. In this case, teens assisted with customer service by teaching patrons how to use a new computer system. If your library is doing a customer service survey; reorganizing and moving books to new shelving areas; filling packets for an educator's open house that your library is hosting; or any number of other important, time-intensive tasks, ask your TAG members or regular teen volunteers if they would like to add some extra hours, or recruit special teen volunteers to tackle the particular requirement at hand. Be sure to provide snacks!

Simple Yet Important: A Book Cleaning Project

The Harris County Public Library in Houston, Texas (www.hcpl.net/index.htm), has conducted another interesting temporary project that allows teens to participate. Stephanie Robinson Borgman, the Children's Specialist there, explained an easy yet important project that a local church youth group provided for the library:

This project is very simple and very satisfying. It started like this: Some years ago, when I was still working in a branch, I was very concerned about the physical appearance of our picture book collection. The plastic covers were often visibly dirty as well as sticky. Return desk staff members were instructed to put such books on a special shelf for cleaning, but this duty was not even close to their highest priority. At this branch there were primarily adult volunteers, and some were receptive to cleaning books, but it was not one of their most rewarding jobs.

I was contacted by a church youth group leader who wanted to bring a group of teens to the library from 7:00 to 8:00 p.m. one Wednesday night per month to perform community service. They were open to doing whatever we needed done, but time for training was limited. The leader also mentioned that two of the twelve were physically challenged and anything we could come up with that would allow them to participate as fully as possible would be greatly appreciated. I immediately thought of book cleaning. After a couple of days of working through the details, I called the leader back and shared my plan. It was well received and about a week later the group came for the first time.

Our staff had made a special effort to pull as many soiled books as possible. All the books that were normally displayed on the top of our picture book shelves were removed. We set the teens up at tables in the meeting room. The only supplies necessary were multiple spray bottles of "no rinse required" window-type cleaner and lots of paper towels.

The leader divided the teens into two groups and I went over the process with them. I demonstrated by showing them that it was not necessary to saturate the plastic cover with cleaner, but simply to get it reasonably moist and then start rubbing. The dirt on the paper towel was immediate proof of the importance of their efforts.

The physically challenged teens were among the most enthusiastic participants. Their coordination did not permit them to spray the books, but the other teens took care of that part and praised their efforts. The teens stood the books up to allow for final air drying. Periodically, some of the teens would gather up the clean books and take them out to stand on the top of the picture book shelves.

In that hour, several hundred books were cleaned. The teens had a great time and there was no doubt that their efforts made a difference. The waste baskets full of dirty paper towels and the rows of shiny clean books were wonderful proof. They left at 8:00 p.m. to return to their church where pizza was waiting for them.

The leader called me the next day and said that the teens had been very enthusiastic and were teasing one another about their polishing talents and other good natured competition. Over the course of the school year, the group came five or six times. The next year there was a different leader who chose to do something else with the group, but I did continue to see some of the teens who lived in the neighborhood and who became regular library users.

I have used the same book cleaning activity with other groups that were coming only for a single project and I have shared this successful activity in many settings. I know this may seem like a very minor project to some people, but I think having clean and attractive books is an important part of the service we provide and the respect we show to our customers of all ages. No one should be reluctant to check out a library book because it is not reasonably clean.[14]

Community youth groups such as those affiliated with churches, service clubs, or other agencies might be looking for a place to offer volunteer hours but might not think of the library as a recipient. If you would like to get "drop-in" teens involved in a project in your library, be sure to communicate the need to service-oriented places in your community that have eager teens willing and available to complete the tasks at hand.

Drama Club Students Perform Booktalks

In 2005, when I was still working at the City of Mesa Library in Arizona (www. mesalibrary.org), we found that due to budget cuts we would not be able to continue our regular booktalking program in the schools. As an alternative, we decided to record a booktalking video and DVD that could be checked out of the public library and would also be available in the schools through Mesa Public Schools Media Services, now called the Library Resource Center (www2.mpsaz.org/library).

To begin the project, we approached Media Services with our idea, asking if we could partner with them because an audiovisual recording studio was required. They agreed, and we set out to plan the production. Soon we realized that the best approach would be to have teens themselves perform the booktalks. However, because of staffing shortages, we did not have a lot of time available to teach teens how to do this, and we realized that the teen volunteers and the teen advisory group members at the library would definitely need such training.

What to do? The staff from Media Services suggested that we contact the drama teacher at the nearest high school. He recruited three teens from the Drama Club who were willing to learn the booktalking scripts and to be recorded doing three booktalks each. These teens already knew basic performance techniques and were able to provide dynamic booktalks for the production.

The best thing about this project was that none of the teens knew much about the public library before their participation, but the recording project raised their interest. They never became regular volunteers or signed up to join the TAG, yet they were proud and excited that they could be part of the video and DVD recording. All three teens made a connection to the library that we hoped would last, as their contribution to it did.

A Potpourri of Volunteer Opportunities at Cedar Valley Middle School

At the Cedar Valley Middle School in Austin, Texas (http://schools.roundrockisd.org/cedarvalley/), drop-in volunteers are welcome. Students who stay late often stop by the library to help with a variety of tasks. They clean the gerbil cage, put up bulletin board displays, and shelve books. When some art students approached the school librarian about designing a library sign, she readily agreed to let them. The students designed, painted, and put up the sign. Then a group of enthusiastic non-TAB members came by wanting to produce PSA videos to promote the library. Although they were not involved in TAB at the time, they have since joined.

In addition to actual volunteer opportunities, students drop by the library for other purposes. The anime club meets there "unofficially" on occasion (remember that 1924 school library in chapter 2 having the teen Cartoon Club participants meeting in *their* library?). To attract more teens, the Cedar Valley Middle School library has checkers, a chess board, and puzzles available before and after school and during advisory class. When the library is perceived as a fun, exciting place to be like this, more teens are drawn to it and will be inspired to participate.[15]

A Teen Artist at Harris County Public Library, Barbara Bush Branch at Cypress Creek

Terry Domino, the Children's Librarian at the Harris County Library's Barbara Bush Branch at Cypress Creek (www.hcpl.net/location/barbara-bush-cypress-creek), worked out a volunteer arrangement with a talented teen artist who could only volunteer sporadically. Terry shared ideas with her for future bulletin board themes, and the girl worked on them at home or at the library as her schedule allowed. The girl kept track of the hours that she spent monthly on these library art projects so she could receive the volunteer credit hours.

Last fall, the teenaged artist created a manga "back to school" tableau that drew favorable comments and even introduced the manga format to several older adults who had formerly dismissed the genre. Best of all, the library had two beautifully decorated, 35-foot bulletin board displays on which Terry did not need to spend her own time.

Some teens, like this one, might *want* to be a "regular" library volunteer, but without a set schedule. Not every teen is able to attend meetings, training, or other activities that require a timetable, even if it is short term, like being a summer reading volunteer. When you are flexible enough to seek out and allow teens to contribute within their own time frames and at their own pace, you might be surprised at what treasures of talent they can bring to your library.[16]

Teens Can Get Those Required Community Service Hours at the Library!

There is everything right about connecting with schools and organizations that require teen community service hours for one reason or another. Let them know that your library is a welcoming place for the teens to complete those hours. Be sure to send out media publicity expressing your needs and interests and to distribute flyers and other announcements about your willingness to allow teens to serve their hours at your library. By consciously making your library an inviting place for teens to earn this credit, you will be attracting teens who will be excited about their participation with you.

Each year the Kirkwood Public Library in Missouri (http://kpl.lib.mo.us/) offers these opportunities. A significant number of teens needing to complete hours are ninth graders who must each do 12 hours of community service for their civics class. Last year Lynn Bosso, Assistant Director of Programs & Youth Services, had about 25 teens who volunteered over 450 hours during the school year, either for school requirements such as this one, for scouts, or for church. Lynn noted that the community service teens submitted applications like the regular volunteers did, but for them the program was less structured. She works closely with all novice teens in planning their required service hours, which any teen library advisor must do.[17]

TEEN SPACES: PLANNING AND DESIGN

Well-designed spaces for teens in libraries have the potential to supply the resources and environment that promote intellectual, emotional, and social development. An effectively designed young adult space can encourage teens to develop lifelong learning and pleasure reading, provide skills for information literacy on a variety of levels including technological, and allow teens independence in a place where they can be themselves.[18]

A vital component in creating an effective library teen space is gathering teen input. Those who will be the recipients of the dedicated teen space should have a say in the area's content, appearance, purpose, and even associated programming. This may be accomplished by compiling the results of surveys and questionnaires from teens in the community, by engaging a library teen advisory group in the process, or by forming a special teen focus group to address the teen space issue.[19]

It is crucial that your library appropriately size its teen facilities based on the population of those in the middle through high school age bracket, or approximately ages 12 through 18. When you evaluate space allocations for teens in your facility, scale them according to demographics, not personal bias. In public library facilities, the ratio of a teen area to the overall library should be equal to the ratio of the teen population of that community to the overall population of that community.[20] Advocate for a teen space that matches the needs of your locale, so that your teen participants have an adequate area with which to work. Avoid an out-of-the-way or oddly shaped corner that will seem to your teens like the leftovers.

Convening a Teen Space Focus Group

You might be wondering where to start when developing a teen space focus group. The best place to start is with a TAB, if you already have one. Ask TAB members if they would like to serve on the focus group. Explain that you need only a few teens from TAB to represent the group. Once you have a select list of TAB teens to start, begin recruiting others from the rest of the community.

Your goal should be to have a well-rounded representation of teens in the focus group. It should include both library users and nonusers. You might ask teens who frequent your library but who do not belong to the TAB if they are willing to join the group. You might also connect with teachers from the local school or schools to recommend teens who might want to contribute. Remember to include homeschoolers. Likewise, be sure to have teens from both genders and any minority groups from your community in the mix. Ask at the local Boys & Girls Club, the YMCA, or church groups if they have teens who might want to participate. By structuring an all-encompassing group, you will be including your library's entire teen constituency.

As you would at any library teen meeting or training session, plan to have refreshments for your focus group and locate the meetings in a comfortable setting. Be sure to provide all the materials you will need for effective sessions, including a white board or large pad with an easel and markers, relevant handouts, and a suitable facilitator. If you do not feel comfortable in the facilitator role, be sure to enlist the services of someone who is confident, is experienced, and likes teenagers. You will still have to be part of the proceedings even if you are not the person directly conducting the meetings.

The process for the group will vary depending on its purpose. Are members helping to create a brand new teen space from scratch? Is a previously well-used teen space being relocated? Is a poorly designed teen space being renovated? Is an acceptable teen space being expanded? Teen input should reflect the particular circumstances of the teen space at hand.

With those considerations in mind, here are some basic questions you might want to adapt and pose to your focus group:

- What is the purpose of libraries, and why do you use (or not use) them?

- What kinds of things do libraries offer, and what *should* they offer?

- What ideas do you have to improve, change, or design the library teen space, including how you envision furniture, decorations, technology, and the collection?

- How do you think teenagers could be attracted to the library through this space?

- Do you have any additional ideas you would like to share?[21]

Some libraries are large enough or lucky enough to be able to hire a professional planner who will work with teens on designing their teen space. But even smaller libraries that do not have that luxury can work effectively with teens by involving them from the start and throughout the entire process.

I know this from personal experience. In 2008 at my library, our teen space was doubled. I conducted all the planning with our teens to create a new look and feel for the space. I did this by sharing catalogs with them, bringing back photos from conference exhibit halls, and printing out ideas that I found online. The teens did "field trips" through the space and decided what would look and fit best. We now have a very cool teen space that more teens than ever are using due to teen input in its creation.

The Young Adult Center at the Port Jefferson Free Library, New York

In 2007 a unique teen volunteer opportunity arose when the Port Jefferson Free Library in New York (pjfl.suffolk.lib.ny.us/) was planning its Young Adult Center. In order to provide teen input, ideas, and support, an actual teen planning board was created. The teens on the board assisted in the process of deciding what the Young Adult Center would look like, the kinds of materials it would lend from its collection, and what teen programs should take place there.

This may sound like a standard teen space focus group, but it was much more than that. The teen participants went above and beyond their focus group status, attending building and architectural meetings at the village of Port Jefferson and giving their input and reactions. This level of participation demonstrated to the adult planners that teenagers are part of their community and that they will continue to expect an active role in the development of their Young Adult Center.[22]

The efforts of these teens were successful, because the Port Jefferson Free Library now boasts an outstanding building dedicated to teen services. Not every library will be able to offer an entire Young Adult Center like this one, but even the smallest teen space can be at its best, rather than an afterthought, when teens give their input. Remember that teen contributions may be particularly effective when a brand new teen space is being created, especially in a brand new library facility. You will want your teens to be thoroughly involved in the creation or development of any teen space by connecting them directly to architects and planners. Be sure to advocate for them and do your best to keep them included throughout the entire process. Speak up for them at any adult-only meetings and make sure their voices are truly heard.

If you are planning a library teen space and want to have your teens involved, here are some excellent resources to help:

Bolan, Kimberly. *Teen Spaces: The Step-by-Step Library Makeover.* 2nd ed. Chicago: American Library Association, 2009. An updated version of the now-classic resource for developing outstanding library teen spaces, with advice on incorporating the input of the teens who will use it.

PPS: Project for Public Spaces, *Teen Central at Burton Barr Library,* www.pps.org/tcb/teen_central.htm (accessed September 20, 2009). An adaptable project description that tells how a 4,000-foot teen space at the Phoenix Public Library's main library was designed and is run with the help of the community's teens.

"Teen Spaces of Your Dreams," a regular column appearing in *Voice of Youth Advocates* magazine. Gives descriptions of teen-friendly library spaces from around the country which offer exceptional examples for librarians and teens working together to plan and design teen spaces.

Focus Groups May Become TABs

In 2004 the Parker Public Library (www.parkerpubliclibraryaz.org), located on the rural western border of Arizona and also serving a 15-mile stretch of Colorado Indian Reservation across the river in California, decided to transform its once dull and drab young adult corner into a real teen space. How did the library do it? By convening a focus group made up of 12 teens, including 2 homeschoolers. Only 10 teens were invited, but 12 showed up—which proved that teens in the community were interested in what the library had to offer them.

When staff members first met with the teens, they learned right away how important it was to get teen input. They discovered that what the teens wanted was comfortable chairs, low furniture, fast computers, and a current collection of materials. At this point, funding was nonexistent, but staff moved ahead and found grant money to create the new Teen Paradise. It includes a cabana with big, comfy pillows, low wicker chairs, four computers with black leather swivel chairs, two red deck chairs, real-looking palm trees, sand-colored carpet, and wall décor that gives a real feel for being in paradise.[23] Afterward the teens who served as a focus group decided to stay together and became the library's first TAG.

You might discover the same thing happening if you call together a teen focus group to develop a teen space or for some other purpose. If you do not have a TAG in place, the focus group might evolve into an official TAG. This has happened in a number of libraries that have convened focus groups, and a "temporary" group of teen participants has become permanent.

THE TEENS AT PARKER PUBLIC LIBRARY TODAY. The Parker Public Library serves as an inspiration to any small, rural library. Although the town itself is only one square mile with a diverse population of 3,200 people and a county service area of around 20,000 people, it makes teen services a top priority. As a matter of fact, Ariana De Leon, the Bilingual/Children's/Teen Services Librarian, proudly explains that this small library provides more than 100 programs, activities, and events each year, just for teens. Everything from how to open a checking account, to online safety, to cooking, to dealing with health and drug abuse issues, to overnight library lock-ins, to summer reading programs has been offered. Program attendance averages between 30 and 40 teens.

This is a direct result of the 2004 teen space focus group becoming a TAG and continuing its advisory work and support. Because the library staff is small and Ariana wears so many hats, she depends on the 15 teens who belong to the TAG to help extensively, which means they try to meet once every week. She says, "The teens are willing to help because they want to feel like they are needed—which they are. They are able to know what life might bring them and want to try new things that they might not otherwise. They are able to see how different groups of teens who might not 'hang out' together are able to get along, no matter who they are."

Besides the programming they plan for their fellow teens, the TAG members conduct a Homework Helper program at the Parker Library. TAG helps children in first through third grades with homework after school, which especially benefits the teens who are in the National Honor Society, because they earn extra community service hours. The teachers at the schools appreciate the program because it's free, and the children are getting the additional help they need. TAG has also been fund-raising, doing such things as car washes on weekends and selling soft drinks at Parker's "100-Year Celebration," to buy things for the teen room.[24]

"TEENS CAN COOK": AN EXCELLENT BLEND OF FOOD AND ACTIVE TEEN PARTICIPATION. The teens in Parker did not stop there. "Teens Can Cook" was a unique teen participatory program they developed that runs all through the month of July on Friday, while the teens are out of school. Teens from assorted backgrounds make this food-oriented activity a vibrant potpourri of interests, flavors, and cultures. (See figure 5.3.)

Figure 5.3. Parker Public Library TAG, Special Event: Teens Learning Cooking and Meal-Planning Skills and Trying New Foods. Photo by Ariana De Leon

The main premise of this activity is that teens love to eat, which is an expectation in any sort of teen program, orientation, training, or other special event. However, the teens at the Parker Public Library one-upped their peer interest in food by deciding to do a series of programs for which teens would cook things that they felt they could independently make for their families at home. The resulting menus turned out to be diverse and flavorful. For example, they included everything from pasta salad, to semi-homemade chili, to bacon hot dogs, to numerous other culinary creations. The really exciting part of this series of cooking adventures was that at the end, the teens decided to expand the program for a cook-off. Not only that, they planned a challenge of boys against girls.

One of the most interesting aspects of this participatory project was that the teens running the events had requested that selected cookbooks be purchased for the library to support their efforts. The rules for the cook-off included using recipes from one of the books the library had bought for them. This added a "literary" aspect to the competition.

The teens used a small meeting room in the back of the library for the contest. They brought skillets, fryers, and other portable cookers from home to do the cooking. They set up tables for cutting up the ingredients, with a second area reserved for cooking and preparing the food and an additional table for displaying and serving it. The cook-off was even more challenging because the teens were not only competing against each other, they also they were limited by their equipment and the facilities. Among the entries, the girls created a Mexican American shrimp cocktail, and the boys concocted strawberry chocolate cake for dessert.

A few staff members from the Parker Public Library served as judges for the contest, along with the town mayor, the court administrator, and two younger children who came to the library daily. On competition day, the teens worked diligently on their meals for an entire morning, each trying to surpass the efforts of the others. Ariana said that all the teens did a great job cooking, working together, following directions, and serving the food, but in the end the boys emerged as the winners.

The library provided all the supplies the teens needed for their special event, including the food, cooking tools, plates, and, as already mentioned, the cookbooks. Ariana said that the teens went through catalogs and searched online to find just the right cookbooks for the program. She added that a positive outcome is that the teens are still checking out those cookbooks to this day.

What Ariana believes is the most important result of this program is not who won, but that unexpected teens were involved and enjoyed themselves. She says that in addition, the diversity among the teen participants was phenomenal. There were Native American teens and teens from mixed and various ethnicities and cultural groups. The program allowed the teens to sample foods from their own cultures as well as previously unfamiliar foods from other cultures. Even Ariana said that she herself discovered some new delicacies among the teens' fare![25]

NOTE: If your teens want to conduct programming to teach one another about foods and cooking, check into your local public health and safety rules and regulations to ensure that teens are preparing and serving foods accordingly.

Drop-in Participation: A Final Look

Drop-in, or temporary, teen participatory programs are a vital part of teen library involvement. They allow teens who might not otherwise connect with their libraries to do so. They also encourage these teens to consider joining a more permanent volunteer or participatory option later on. However, even if teens do indeed only experience "one-shot deal" contributions to their libraries, they are still being exposed to what libraries are all about, getting a sample of what a library career might hold for them, and coming one step closer to being enduring library users and supporters into adulthood.

Teens who discover an exciting new connection to libraries because of their "temporary" contributions often find that these opportunities provide a bridge to ongoing involvement. Drop-in participation offers flexibility, which can be the key in reaching teens who are managing priorities, looking for a positive focus, and trying to determine a more lasting place to belong.

ENDNOTES

1. Kathee Herbstreit, e-mail message to author, January 11, 2008.

2. Youth Service America, *Global Youth Service Day*, www.ysa.org/NatlGYSD/tabid/59/Default.aspx (accessed September 20, 2009).

3. Kathee Herbstreit, e-mail message to author, August 18, 2008.

4. Kathee Herbstreit, e-mail message to author, August 25, 2008.

5. Herbstreit, e-mail, August 25, 2008.

6. Herbstreit, e-mail, August 25, 2008.

7. Glendale Public Library Teen Turnpike, *Volunteer Opportunities at the Main Library* (Glendale Public Library, 2004), www.glendaleaz.com/Library/teen/happening_html/tt_happening_volunteer.html (accessed September 20, 2009).

8. Kathee Herbstreit, e-mail messge to author, August 12, 2008.

9. Stephanie Robinson Borgman, e-mail message to author, August 25, 2008.

10. Girls Scouts of Shawnee Council, *2008 Gold Award Recipients* (Girls Scouts of America, Girl Scouts of Shawnee Council, Inc., 2008), www.shawneegirlscouts.org/page.aspx?pid=78 (accessed November 25, 2008).

11. Ursula Castrillon, *Girl Scouts Honor Gold Award Young Women of Distinction* (Girl Scouts of America, March 2, 2004), www.girlscouts.org/news/stories/2004/young_women_distinction.asp (accessed November 25, 2008).

12. Kim Olson, listserv posting to TAGAD-L, 23 October 2008, and e-mail message to author, November 12, 2008.

13. Kelly Johnson, e-mail message to author, August 11, 2008.

14. Stephanie Robinson Borgman, e-mail message to author, August 25, 2008.

15. Kate DiPronio, e-mail message to author, May 8, 2008.

16. Terry Domino, e-mail message to author, August 27, 2008.

17. Lynn Bosso, e-mail message to author, August 28, 2008.

18. Sondra Vandermark, "Using Teen Patrons as a Resource in Planning Young Adult Library Space in Public Libraries," in *Planning the Modern Public Library Building*, ed. Gerard B. McCabe and James Robert Kennedy, 161 (Westport, CT: Libraries Unlimited, 2003).

19. Vandermark, "Using Teen Patrons as a Resource," 162–63.

20. Kimberly Bolan, *The Need for Teen Spaces in Public Libraries* (American Library Association, Young Adult Library Services Association White Paper, adopted by the YALSA Board of Directors, January 2008), www.ala.org/ala/mgrps/divs/yalsa/profdev/whitepapers/teenspaces.cfm (accessed September 20, 2009).

21. Vandermark, "Using Teen Patrons as a Resource," 168.

22. Erin Schaarschmidt, e-mail message to author, September 30, 2008.

23. Diane P. Tuccillo, "YA Korner: Teen Paradise at Parker Public Library," *Arizona Library Association Newsletter* (February 2005): 12.

24. Ariana De Leon, e-mail message to author, August 27, 2008.

25. Ariana De Leon, e-mail message to author, January 6, 2009.

6

More Ways Teens Can Participate:
The Technology Connection

Teens and technology go hand in hand. Most teenagers today are not only astute at working with various technological elements in their lives; they are adept at working with multiple ones at the same time. They can do their homework on a computer, listen to their portable hand-held devices, have a show on television, and manage to successfully navigate all three simultaneously.

When the majority of teens come to the library or access the library's online Web page from home or school, they know how to use the computer to do basic searches. If they do not, they are able to learn quickly. To contemporary teens, a card catalog is a virtual one, and they have no concept of index cards filed in a wooden box called a "card catalog." Most are familiar with the latest computer games, how to most effectively use social Web sites, and how to download electronic books.

For the teens in your community who are interested in and knowledgeable about computers and other technologies, there may be a ready made opportunity for them to participate in and contribute to your library. Including teens who have such knowledge and interests can benefit your library and all ages of library users. Remember that is it important to keep track of how current technologies are evolving and what new technologies are emerging as you engage teen volunteers in their electronically oriented library activities.

What are some of the ways teens can provide these kinds of contributions? In this chapter you'll find outstanding ideas and examples that demonstrate the effective pairing of teens and technology in library participation activities.

LIBRARY WEB PAGES FOR TEENS

A library Web site for teens can be a challenge. It must not be too busy, yet at the same time it cannot be too simple. It must provide all the information teens need and want from a library Web site in a very user-friendly format. Think about what happens when *you* access a Web page that is difficult to navigate or is confusing. I know what I do: I try another resource or I give up and look for another way to access the information. Teens who encounter poorly designed Web pages also become discouraged. If the problem is with their local library Web page in general or the library teen Web page in particular, they will simply stop using it. Be sure from the start that you offer a page that is both well designed in appearance and access and has current and useful content.

Once you decide it is time to create a new teen Web page or redesign one, where do you start? First of all, you need permission from your supervisor and library administrators before proceeding. Be prepared for your teens' page with a game plan that includes some well-designed samples from other libraries, a rationale for creating or revising the page, a timeline for completing the project, comments from the teenagers who use your library, and a description of how the teens will actually be involved and contribute.

If you are not already familiar with your particular library or city policies about Web page content and appearance, as well as any restrictions on how your teens might participate, do some research on them. Some libraries allow teens to have direct input on teen Web page design and maintenance; others only permit teens to serve in an advisory role. Develop your game plan keeping any restrictions beyond your control in mind. Make sure that you consult with your teen contributors to the Web page about any restrictions under which they will need to work.

Remember, even if your library or city does require a standardized format for all sections of its Web pages, with careful planning, the use of attractive icons, and well-organized content, you can still provide an eye-catching and helpful teen Web page.

If your library has technical support services staff, it is essential that you consult a member or members of the staff as you proceed with your project. Mostly likely one staff member will be assigned as the technical liaison for your project. His or her guidance, advice, and assistance will be priceless as you work with your teens to develop a new library page for them.

Be sure to get as much teen input as possible during the planning and design stages and to allow your teens to try out a prototype of the Web page before it goes live. Listen to their ideas and recommendations and incorporate them in revisions as the Web page progresses. Remember to actively promote the existence of the teen Web page to the teens in your community!

On that note, if you are developing a teen Web page at a public library, while you are promoting it, check with your local school district about linking your Web site to theirs. In many cases, school districts have strict security measures and policies that block a public library teen Web page from being linked to a school page. You might need to make a special request for your library's teen page to be allowed, assuring the school district that it will be carefully developed and monitored.

A Helpful List of Layout Rules

Although there are a number of teen Web pages currently online that look good and provide a great deal of helpful information, there are many more that are poorly designed and need improvements in content and access. To ensure that your teens' Web page is part of the former group rather than the latter, here are some important rules to follow. Be sure to share these rules with your teen assistants as you are planning.

1. Decide on a **purpose** for your teen page. Enlist the teens who frequent your library in giving it a name that reflects a theme. Ask them to help you develop some goals for it.[1] The Denver Public Library's teen Web page is captioned, "Evolver . . . because evolving minds want to know" (teens.denverlibrary.org/). At my library, the teens dubbed their Web page "Teen Lounge" (read.poudrelibraries.org/teen/). The purpose and theme should be clear and to the point, yet interesting and catchy.

2. Consider the elements of **photocomposition**. Do you have a library logo or a teen advisory group logo that you want to incorporate? What colors will work best together to convey the theme of your page? Where will the navigation menu be located, and will the menu be separated out by colors or by frames? You want to attract the eye of viewers while making the prospect of exploring the Web site inviting.[2]

3. **Navigation** is the most important aspect of your Web page. It should be designed as simply as possible. A good way to start is by making a list with your teens of all the elements that need to be accessed. For most teen Web pages, booklists; online reviews; upcoming programs; teen advisory group and teen volunteer announcements, applications, and activities; homework help links; and self-help and entertainment links are generally included. Other elements might be a blog, podcasts or other audiovisual links, or an online literary magazine.

4. **Decide which links would work best on the teen page**. Pages without links can be pretty boring.[3] Users of the page should always know where they came from and where they are going when they use links. They should be able to go back and forth with ease. Simple and straightforward is best![4]

5. **Create the Web page content**, and consider the time it will take users to load the content from your Web page. Some users will be connecting to the Internet via modem, which is very slow. The simpler your page is, the easier it will be for someone using an older method to access the page. Large graphics and flash animations also slow things up. Use Internet-optimized graphics.[5] Remember to run your spell checker.[6]

6. Make the page **as compatible to the most users as possible**. The best Web sites are the ones that can be viewed in every browser without mistakes or access problems.

7. Create a **banner page** that is inviting and that reflects the theme and name from rule 1. This page will be the introduction to the site, so you want its purpose to be clear. Large pictures or flashy animation might seem "cool" for a teen page, but they can be confusing and inhibit ease of access. Your banner page should be very clear about its purpose and what teens should expect to find within its sections and links.

8. Organize the **content** and make it relevant, interesting, and useful. Be careful how much content you aim for so that you do not overwhelm the page users. Again, flashing colors and animation may seem to attract attention, but in the long run they can make navigation difficult and the Web site's appearance can become annoying. Be sure that you and your teens keep the content current! The quickest turn off to a Web page is irrelevant, outdated information. One really helpful task teens can do on this front is to regularly monitor links for currency and broken links.

9. Increase the quality of the Web page by paying attention to the **presentation of the content**. When certain items or topics need emphasis, use bold letters or italics. Avoid using underlines because users get confused and think this indicates a link. Use the same font consistently. Be sure to leave enough space between information and graphics so that the content looks open and inviting. Use short text segments with appropriate headings, keep links within text to an absolute minimum, and link only with pages with content that is truly relevant to your teen page's purpose.[7]

10. **Publicize your Web site**, but before going live with the new Web page design, give your teen volunteers a chance to experiment with using a prototype. Again, allow them to make recommendations to improve the site. After the site goes live, provide an opportunity for teen users of the Web page to provide **feedback** (and possibly offer some reward), so that keeping the site current, attractive, and effective is an ongoing proposition.[8]

Do you need some additional resources to help you and your teens understand the process for creating and composing an effective library teen Web page? Try these:

Doyle, Miranda. *101+ Great Ideas for Teen Library Web Sites.* Neal-Schuman, 2007.

Selfridge, Benjamin, Peter Selfridge, and Jennifer Osburn. *A Teen's Guide to Creating Web Pages and Blogs.* Prufrock Press, 2008.

Flamingnet

Teens can truly do impressive things with Web pages. One shining example is Seth Cassel's well-designed Flamingnet Web site (flamingnet.com/). Seth is the teen webmaster at McDonogh High School in Owings Mills, Maryland. His story demonstrates a positive combination of teen participation, technology, books, and reading.

Flamingnet was started when Seth was an avid reader in fifth grade and wanted to share his book reviews online. With his father's assistance, he designed the Web site and began posting his reviews. As time went by, national publishers noticed the site and began sending books to Seth for him to review. As the numbers of books increased, Seth decided to open the opportunity to do book reviews to fellow teens across the country. Today, there is a vibrant online community of young readers and book reviewers from fifth grade through college age.

Seth's Flamingnet online book review project is an exciting example of what teens can do online to promote literacy. In case you are wondering, there is a library connection, which expands the site's concept well beyond the perimeters of a Web page. Flamingnet gives its visitors the chance to buy the books that are reviewed. When books are purchased through the site, points are earned toward the purchase of young adult materials for libraries and other facilities in need. Flamingnet has donated hundreds of books to victims of Hurricane Katrina, public schools, and charitable organizations. In addition, it impressively funds teen reading programs with contributions received through the Web site.

The Young Adult Library Services Association (YALSA) selected Seth Cassel's Flamingnet project as the recipient of the 2008 Sagebrush Award for a significant, replicable young adult reading or literature program. The award provided $1,000 for Seth to attend that year's American Library Association Conference, at which he gave a presentation on Flamingnet along with the winners of YALSA's latest "Excellence in Library Services for Young Adults" honorees.[9]

Your teens might take Seth's example to heart and then come up with their own completely unique and innovative ways to use your library's teen Web pages. Ask them to share ideas to see if a spark of something new and exciting materializes as a result. If nothing else, be sure to bring important teen pages like Seth's to their attention.

Getting Teens Involved in Creating Lively School Library Web Pages

You might be surprised to learn that school libraries can be particularly significant places for teens to get involved by connecting them to online technology for more than research. By doing so, students can not only learn more about and have a direct say in what goes on in their school library, but they can greatly enhance their overall educational experiences.

Joyce Kasman Valenza, the well-known teacher/librarian at Springfield Township High School in Erdenheim, Pennsylvania (www.sdst.org/shs/index.php), acknowledged this fact when she realized that the attractive library Web site she had personally created was missing a link—student input and participation. "Here's what I know," she said. "Teens who create or collaborate on online spaces are more likely to feel welcome living in them."[10]

With that revelation in mind, Joyce proceeded to engage students in regular, active involvement in fashioning and maintaining the library Web pages. One group of students teamed up to develop an Art Gallery of original student work. Other students have created a continually growing archive of videos and podcasts in collaboration with the library, classroom teachers, and the video production teacher. Diverse topics are featured, such as grammar, information literacy, and reading list titles brought to life through book videos. In addition. the library site hosts the school's broadcast news production.

Joyce was also inspired by other school library Web sites that she investigated. One is from the library at the Northfield Mount Hermon School in Mount Hermon, Massachusetts (www.nmhschool.org/index.php). There she found the Reading Room blog, a welcoming, student-centered space reflecting the philosophy that "mixing humor and fun with research" is fundamental. All students have a place and a say on the site, from musicians, to writers, to readers, to artists, to "lounge lizards."

"Lounge Lizards" became an actual group of library regulars who take photos of fellow students, get quotes from them, and post them on the Web page. The school's musicians participate in Acoustic Fridays, during which they hold performances that are recorded and posted as podcasts. Students also post reviews of books, CDs, and DVDs, and are creating an online research tutorial. There is even a section for the Library Workjob Crew, where student library assistants share information about their work experiences.

In a changing Web 2.0 Internet environment, where user interaction is a primary focus, it is natural to get teens directly involved in their library's online presence. Keep this in mind when you are developing or improving your library's Web site. Teen involvement can bring such an online space from static to dynamic.[11]

What great ways for teens to learn, grow, have fun, and participate through their school libraries!

Teen Library Web Page Blogs

In chapter 3 you learned about the Wake County Public Libraries' "mock" Newbery and Printz book clubs. Last year the library added a blog feature to its Web site that greatly increased the teen participants' ability to share their thoughts on books as never before. They have used this avenue of expression to best advantage in determining group consensus.

"Mock" book club members from other library locations around the country have found the Wake County Public Libraries' blog and jump in to share their reactions to books as well. Consequently, the "original" Mock Book Club bloggers are not the only ones who comment on the titles under consideration. All the participating teens get a more well-rounded perspective on fellow teens' reactions to each book.[12]

Another kind of blog is used at the Madison Meadows Middle School's library in Phoenix, Arizona (madison.az.schoolwebpages.com/education/school/school.php?sectiondetailid=398). Librarian Sally Roof asks the sixteen library media aides she has every semester to discuss their reflections about each day's library work experiences through a special blog set up for that purpose.[13]

These, and teen library blogs of all kinds, are becoming more popular every day as a discussion venue and a catalyst for teen participation activities. It is easy to set one up online and to offer teens the opportunity to talk about everything from books to library programs to other issues.

How to Start a Blog

You might be wondering, what exactly *is* a blog? "Blog" is short for Web log, a Web site that contains online entries on a specific topic or for a particular organization in reverse chronological order. If you do not have a blog on your teen Web page, here is some general advice on how to get one started:

- Check with your library's computer technology experts to see if adding a blog to the teen Web page is feasible. If so, get their advice on how to proceed.

- Research some blogging providers that might appeal to you and your teens. These include such services as LiveJournal (www.livejournal.com) or Google's Blogger (www. blogger.com). Sites like these are free and pre-made, with templates and push-button publishing functions that don't require much technical know-how. If you choose an outside blogging provider, be sure to get it approved by your technical department before posting.

- Once you sign up, you'll have a gallery of ready-made templates from which to choose. With these, you and your teens may pick a color scheme, layout, and additional enhancements for your blog. Select what works and personalize it by adding your library's name, the name of your teen group, images, etc.

- Decide if want the blog to be private or public. For instance, do you want all teens to be able to read and respond to your blog, or do you just want teens from your library advisory group or school to be able to access it? Most blog sites offer the ability to password-protect your published posts so only approved bloggers may view what has been written. If you want a combination of public and private blogs, you can set up more than one.

- In a library setting, it is important to have a librarian or other staff member to serve as the blog moderator to ensure that the material posted fits the scope and content that you want posted. You might consider appointing a trusted teen to assist with this task.

- After you've set up the blog, write a few test-run posts and make any adjustments to the layout or style that you and your teens desire. Be sure to have your teens try it out as well.

- Post your blog on the library's teen page and send the URL to schools, teens in your community, and local organizations and agencies that serve teens.[14]

Connecting Through Social Networks

You and your teens might also find that connecting with each other through social networks, like Facebook (www.facebook.com) or MySpace (www.myspace.com), is a positive way to relate outside the library. Social networks allow users to join with like-minded individuals in sharing information, interests, and camaraderie through posting messages, comments, photos, and more.

As with blogs, you may set up a social network account for all the teens using your library or for a particular group of teen volunteers. You may set up more than one account with different purposes and also link the social network site or sites you choose on your library's teen Web page.

Opening a social network site a simple process. Just go to the main page of the social network provider you have selected and follow the prompts to get enrolled. Once you are signed up, content may be added that reflects your purpose. Be sure to invite any interested teens to join the social network you have started and regularly monitor what is posted to ensure that participants and content remain on the up and up. Regrettably, unscrupulous and unsavory characters sometimes attempt to infiltrate teen blogs and social network sites, so keeping an eye on content is a vital step for a librarian working with teens to take.

Besides opening the lines of communication between you and your teens, and your teens with their peers, blogs and social network spaces are great publicity for your library and its teen activities. They are also a helpful way for members who have graduated or have moved away to keep in touch.

Setting Up Wikis

Wikis are another way to electronically connect with teens, and Madison Meadows Middle School offers a good example. At the school, there are two Book Clubs, one for fifth and sixth graders, the other for seventh and eighth graders. During the school year, club members read the Grand Canyon Book Award winners, and students decide which books will be read and in what order. Last year they tried something new by setting up a wiki at which they could share personal comments about the books and recommend titles to classmates who were not in a Book Club.[16]

You might find that your teens would like to set up a wiki rather than, or in addition to, a blog or social network space. For specific details and instructions on starting a blog or a wiki, especially in school settings, go to the helpful "Using Blogs and Wikis in Education" Web site at opencontent.org/wiki/index.php?title=Using_Blogs_and_Wikis_in_Education. Public libraries will also find valuable information at this site for setting up and using blogs and wikis with teens.

Videos and Podcasts

Many teens truly relish performing in front of an audience, and when they get a chance to incorporate original material—watch out! You will discover that there are many other anxious teens waiting in the wings to get involved.

At Stapley Junior High in Mesa, Arizona, the Stapley Library Advisory Club (SLAC) members enjoy participating in just this fashion. One member began filming and editing a

---

The Value of Jumping into Facebook

I recently forayed into Facebook at the urging of my sisters so we could share photos of family. I was hesitant, not for the alleged "dangers" of Facebook, but for the overabundant usefulness.

Those concerns were quickly put aside, and I was soon amazed at the number of "friend requests" I received from former Youth Advisory Council (YAC) members and former teen employees as a result of simply being on Facebook. There was so much activity that I was inspired to create a "Jervis YAC Alumni Group." Everyone I invited immediately joined! Now we're going to add pictures and a rumored video of YAC members in an infamous Clifford costume.

I checked out one Facebook site album and there is a picture of one alumnus in the Clifford costume, from over three years ago! There aren't many pictures total, so we really rate! In addition, I received a message from an alumnus who told me that the video he and another YAC member made of themselves in the costume was famous on both of their college campuses as well as in their former high school. He added that those were some great times.

Wow! I truly believe in youth development, and our group is now old enough to show, not tell, the impact we've had. I can't explain to you what a great feeling that gave me.

If you're struggling to get started with teen participation, or to convince your administration that it's a great idea, use this anecdote and point out that it takes time to develop and to see results. However, the results you do get are not merely numbers and percentages. They reflect how we are making an impact on teens' lives. We are not intervention—we are prevention, which is much cheaper! We create active adults and we create community. These teens grow up to be taxpaying, voting citizens. I know how they would and will vote on library issues, and I know how your alumni will, too.

I'm so glad I jumped into Facebook, and am surprised by what I learned.[15]

Lisa Matte, Director
Jervis Public Library
Rome, NY

biweekly booktalking video called *"Bowen's Books,"* in which librarian Lisa Bowen performed. The videos were played during the school's morning announcements. Soon Lisa bowed out when the SLACers' got in on the action and performed the booktalks themselves for the morning shows.[17]

In similar fashion, when a group of teens who were not members of the TAB at Cedar Valley Middle School in Texas asked librarian Kate DiPronio if they could make public service announcement videos for the library, she readily agreed. Like their counterparts at Stapley Junior High, they filmed themselves sharing information about the library for the schoolwide television system. The teens who made the videos have since officially joined the TAB.[18]

Bookends: Teaming Up with a Recording Studio

The Poudre School District in Fort Collins, Colorado (www.psd.k12.co.us), is fortunate to have an elaborate Channel 10 recording studio through which shows can be filmed for the schoolwide television system and local public viewing. An ongoing project involves recording shows called "Bookends," for which booktalking performances are filmed along with other kinds of shows.

One type of show focuses on author interviews. Local or visiting young adult authors are invited to participate in the shows along with teen volunteers from the Poudre River Public Library District's Interesting Reader Society. If you have access to local YA authors in your community, you and your teens are one step ahead of the game in planning an author interviewing project like this one. Even if you do not, be on the lookout if an appropriate author happens to be traveling nearby for a conference, an arranged school visit, or another purpose, and extend an invitation to do a show if your teens are interested in creating one.

For "Bookends," a teacher serves as the host, although a librarian or even a teen could serve in that capacity. During the show the teens pose thoughtful questions to the authors, and the authors carefully respond. These productions are a great way for teens to get involved from a technological perspective; they promote the public library and its teen advisory group; and they serve as a valuable partnership between the school and public library.

Other Approaches to Filming and Sharing Videos Featuring Teens

Besides broadcasting these video shows on school and local television stations, they may also be added to school library or public library teen Web pages, like those at Springfield Township High School and Northfield Mount Hermon School. Doing so gives the videos a more far-reaching teen audience via the Internet.

What if your library does not have any sort of recording studio to create such shows? What if your local school system does not, either? There are still other ways that you can record your teens making library promotionals, performing booktalks, or other creative shows as your teens might devise.

One way might be to use a simple portable recording device to make the shows. Another route might be to investigate options available through a local college or university. If you have one in your community, you may be surprised to learn that it has a recording studio, and that some of its students may be required to complete recording projects for particular courses. Be sure to let the studio administrator know that you have teen volunteers at your library who would be willing subjects for book and library-oriented promotional shows, in case there are college students looking for potential show subjects and ideas.

A third solution might be to contact a local television station about recording your teens doing a show. Be prepared with a proposal for what the show would contain, what its purpose is, and why you believe it would benefit a local community audience.

"Book Trailers"® or Book Videos

Another great way to promote books and reading is to get teens involved in creating "Book Trailers."® These are similar to "movie trailers" or "previews" that are designed to entice viewers to see a particular movie, or booktalks, which are presented to allure readers to noteworthy books by giving a taste of their plots in an audiovisual format. The videos may be shown on television, may be recorded on DVDs for classroom use or to circulate from a library collection, may be accessed online, or a combination of these.

I first encountered this techno-method for reaching teens with "dramatized booktalks" of high interest titles they might enjoy at the Chandler Public Library in Arizona (chandlerlibrary.org) in 2002. In cooperation with the local cable television station, the teen advisory group at the library produced a series of audiovisual booktalks that were broadcast locally and in the schools. The teens wrote the scripts and performed in the videos. This was prior to 2005, the year when user-generated online videos became popular. Now online "Book Trailers"® are becoming a growing faction of teen reader advisory and teen library participation. If you have teens who enjoy both drama and technology, encourage them to hop on the book video bandwagon.

Before you do, you might want discuss labeling the productions differently. The term "Book Trailers" has a U.S. registered trademark, as does "Book Teasers," both of which are held by Circle of Seven Productions/CEO Sheila Clover English (www.cosproductions.com/index.php). This company makes professional book trailers, which they describe as, "A book video synopsis that's fun!"[19] It is highly recommended that, to prevent any potential legal conflicts, you name *your* library's versions with a variation such as "Teen Trailers," "Book Videos," or another descriptive title that does not directly refer to them as "Book Trailers"® or "Book Teasers."®

The Pima County Public Library (PCPL) in Arizona did just that. You will recall that in chapter 1 their creatively named "That's My Take" video trailer project earned the 2007 Sagebrush Award for a program that effectively promotes reading and literature to teenagers. The project has evolved into one in which teens from the community are invited to participate. Every year, the library gives teens an opportunity to win a chance at directing future productions. In February teens are invited to suggest books to target for "two-minute video advertisements." Teens who submit the suggestions for the chosen books work with Pan Left Productions to write and direct the book videos. Teens who watch the videos are encouraged to read the books that are portrayed to see how the stories end and to submit their suggestions for the next round of productions.[20]

In 2008, "The Summer Video Shootout" was added to PCPL's ongoing "That's My Take" project. This program encourages youth voices, creativity, participation in the arts, and literacy, effectively expanding the purpose of "That's My Take." During the summer 20 young adults from Pima County received special training as part of the project. Through participation in workshops and peer mentoring, they learned the ins and outs of filmmaking and helped to write, direct, and produce a short video.[21]

Offering special training to teens so that they can learn the ropes of writing scripts and filming videos successfully may be another important dimension of youth participation. Teens who receive such training may become more knowledgeable and active in the techniques of filmmaking, which in turn creates better films as stronger incentives for reading. It also spotlights the project, which encourages new teens to become involved.

TIPS FOR CREATING BOOK VIDEOS. Unless you have a professional filmmaking company supporting your efforts as PCPL does, you and your teens might be wondering how to embark on a book video project in the first place. Here are some basic steps to follow in creating book videos:

- Have your teens brainstorm about what book to use for a book video. (Tip: See the guidelines for brainstorming techniques with teens in chapter 9.)

- Watch some samples of book videos that other teens have made. A good choice is PCPL's *That's My Take* on their Teen Zone Web site at www.library.pima.gov/teenzone/trailers/#moreinfo.

- Explain that book videos usually run from one to three minutes. Keeping that in mind, guide your teens in developing a storyboard that will convey the mood and very basic content of the book. Because book videos are so brief, teens will have to think carefully about how much time each image, dramatization, or animation will take.

- An important step is selecting music and sound effects as a background to add interest and emotion.

- Discuss what methods teens would like to use in moving from scene to scene. Some options are fading to black, a spiral fade, or creating the illusion of page turning.

- If you or your teens are not adept at the technology required to create or film the videos, ask a local school or television station or someone who has experience making YouTube videos for assistance. You might also investigate whether your library is able to provide funds to hire a professional or to apply for a grant to pay for the project.[22]

Resources for Developing a Storyboard

How do you develop an effective storyboard? If you are wondering, here are some useful resources that effectively depict the principles of the craft, which you can adapt to your teen video trailer needs:

Beiman, Nancy. *Prepare to Board!: Creating Story and Characters for Animated Features and Shorts.* Boston: Elsevier Focal Press, 2007.

Bluth, Don, and Gary Goldman. *Don Bluth's Art of Storyboard.* Milwaukie, OR: Dark Horse, 2004.

Booth, Crystal. *Book Trailers.* www.squidoo.com/booktrailers (accessed September 20, 2009).

Tumminello, Wendy. *Exploring Storyboarding.* Clifton Park, NY: Thomson/Delmar Learning, 2005.

TEENS TEACHING AND PROMOTING COMPUTER TECHNOLOGY

Teen volunteers can play an instrumental role in teaching others to use technology and in promoting the use of technology among their peers. There are some exciting programs going on throughout the country through which teens are incorporating skills they have developed on their own, as well as skills for which they are being trained through library programs fostering technologically oriented teen participation. This section discusses some inspiring examples that demonstrate interesting ways for teens to become involved and to contribute to their libraries via computer technology. Perhaps some of these ideas would work well at *your* library also.

Laguna Hills Technology Library's Teen Volunteer Computer Trainers

In California, the Orange County Library's Laguna Hills Technology Library branch (www.ocpl.org/index.asp) provides wireless Internet access for laptop users, plus high-speed Internet access at 18 workstations. It also offers a full selection of Microsoft Office™ products, including Word, Excel, PowerPoint, Access, and Publisher, in addition to a popular collection of in-print materials.

Because of its intensive technology focus, the community has a fairly high demand from senior citizens for very basic computer assistance such as setting up an e-mail account, sending e-mail attachments, and finding things on the Internet. Teenagers play a special role as volunteer computer trainers, who assist these patrons in learning basic computer applications. This volunteer opportunity came about when instructional tasks started consuming more and more staff time, and the library decided to pair community members needing these skills with teen volunteers who know how to teach them.

Library staff members provide the teen volunteers with basic training and advice on interacting with senior citizens. Each hour-long training session has a specific objective, but beyond that, the teen volunteers may approach the material in any way they see fit as long as patron needs are met. The teens have a fair degree of autonomy during the training sessions, and their input is taken very seriously by library staff.

The volunteer computer trainers program is actively promoted both in the library and throughout the schools because teens who participate in it earn service credits, which are a requirement for high school graduation (see figure 6.1, p. 128). By achieving their credits through this program, they learn very valuable work skills while addressing a vital community need. The hope is that the experience teens take away from contributing to the program will potentially be very useful in their future employment and careers.

To evaluate the effectiveness of the program, staff members consult with both the assisted patrons to make sure their needs are being met and the teen trainers to get their input on how to make the program more effective. As you will discover in chapter 11, evaluation is a key part of this or any other youth participation program.[23]

CyberTeens and iTeens

At the Belmont Public Library in Massachusetts (www.belmont.lib.ma.us), teens offer one-hour computer skills tutoring programs to library users of all ages through prearranged, one-on-one instructional sessions on Tuesday, Wednesday, and Thursday during the summer.[24] After submitting an application, making at least a three-week commitment, and completing the required training and orientation, teen volunteers provide sessions on Mouse Basics, Internet Basics, Yahoo E-mail, Library Catalog, Microsoft Word, Microsoft Powerpoint, and Photo Basics.[25]

The Glendale Public Library in Arizona (www.glendaleaz.com/library) offers a similar program. iTeens volunteers work at the Youth Department Reference Desk, assisting younger children with computers, managing computer sign-ups, and helping to maintain the computers. Like the teens at the Belmont Library, iTeens volunteers receive special training on the library's Apple computers prior to giving computer instruction to the public.[26]

GAMING AND TEEN LIBRARY PARTICIPATION

You might be surprised to learn that libraries have provided games for their clientele since houses of literature in Britain added tables for playing cards, chess, dominos, and billiards in the 1800s. The goal at that time was to lure the public away from houses of ill repute.[27] Of course two centuries later, the purpose for offering gaming in libraries has completely changed. However, it is no less important and has taken on some interesting new technological twists that allow teens to get involved in their libraries in innovative ways.

WANTED:
TEEN VOLUNTEERS !

OC PUBLIC LIBRARIES'
LAGUNA HILLS TECHNOLOGY BRANCH
IS LOOKING FOR:
VOLUNTEER COMPUTER TUTORS

LEARN VALUABLE WORK SKILLS WHILE
ADDRESSING A VITAL COMMUNITY NEED.

Description:
- Volunteers will assist community members who wish to learn basic computer applications (Email, Internet, Microsoft Word, etc.).
- Volunteers will guide these individuals through basic computer applications and will answer basic questions.

Qualifications:
- 13 years old or older, high school and above. Under 18 requires parental permission.
- Familiarity with basic computer applications (Email, Internet, Microsoft Word) and ability to assist others with these applications.
- Interest in working with community members and ability to relate well to, and work patiently with, senior citizens.

Schedule:
- Flexible. Usually 1-hour sessions in the afternoon and evenings and/or Saturday mornings.

To Become a Teen Volunteer Computer Tutor

1.) Contact **Jon Gilliom** (949) 707-2699 or **JDGilliom@ocpl.org**

Or:

2.) Pick up an application at **Laguna Hills Technology Library**: 25555 Alicia Parkway Laguna Hills, CA 92677 (Inside the Community Center)

Training Provided by Library Staff

Figure 6.1. Laguna Hills Technology Library, Teen Computer Trainer Flyer

Julie Scordato, a teen services specialist at the Columbus Metropolitan Library in Ohio (www.columbuslibrary.org), describes the importance of teen video gaming this way: "Gaming is storytelling for teenagers. You get to mingle, play and talk, and you get to really know them. Then when you suggest a book, they listen." Julie's library system has successfully invested $40,000 in teen gaming equipment as part of a program to make teenagers feel more welcome in their library. Investing this much in teen gaming demonstrates the library's belief in and commitment to the value of offering such programming.[28] Although this particular library's investment would be too expensive for most other libraries, remember that basic gaming equipment can cost a fraction of that amount. For an estimated $2,000, you can purchase the required materials to get you started. Ask knowledgeable teens who are interested in volunteering for gaming programs at your library what equipment you will need, what it might cost, and where and how you might set up your gaming programs.

Costs for gaming vary, depending on whether your library or library system purchases equipment for every branch location or school, or equipment is shuttled around. A school and public library might also consider buying equipment together and offering programs as a cooperative effort, if that is feasible in their community. Another option might be to ask teens for parental permission to bring their own equipment from home to share.

If your library does not have the funding or the space to offer video gaming programs for teens, consider still-popular traditional board game activities, like those libraries in Britain did way back in the 1800s. Board games often prove to be a draw in lieu of electronic formats. Keep in mind that gaming of *any* kind is a great way to get teens involved and through the library doors, and to encourage them to use their libraries for other purposes as well.

High School Library Teen Gaming Comes Alive!

Both public and secondary school libraries may be equally perfect settings for hopping on the teen gaming bandwagon. Listen to what Joy Millam, the District Library Coordinator/Teacher Librarian at Valencia High School in Placentia, California (www.vhstigers.org/about_us.jsp), has to say about the successful teen gaming programs she has held at her school library: "I have been hosting gaming events in my school library for almost a year. I had heard about them and thought it would be fun for some of our students who aren't really connected to traditional school activities. The first event we held was absolutely epic! From that great start, the gaming programs have continued."

If you are interested in starting a gaming program, follow Joy's step-by-step instructions for getting teens involved and making a similar exciting program happen at *your* library:

Why Gaming in Libraries?

According to the Merriam-Webster Online Dictionary, "play" refers to any recreational activity. Play contributes to the cognitive, physical, social, and emotional well-being of youth. Games of all types are structured and complex forms that help youth learn skills they will need as adults, including hand-eye coordination, socialization, collaboration, situational awareness, event processing, pattern recognition, and problem solving.

Video games are far from the end all and be all of the gaming experience at the library. "Gaming" in the library context refers to a wide range of other activities, including but not limited to tabletop games (card, board, dice, and miniature) and/or electronic games (on a computer, console or handheld device), as well as puzzles, quizzes, scavenger hunts, geocaching, big games, alternative reality games, and more.

Libraries are about stories and information, not just books. Games at the library should be treated like other new formats, including film, audio, music, graphic novels, and the Internet, which have been integrated into most libraries. Some libraries even circulate toys, puzzles, cake pans, tools, and artwork! Games are just another way to convey stories and information for educational and recreational purposes, and should be treated as valid materials to circulate and build programs around.[29]

Beth Gallaway, author of *Game On*

The Electronic Connection: Getting Your Game on at the Public Library

When you offer video gaming in your library, there's a big bonus: you find gamers. Or rather—they find you. Obviously that's the point, but there's more. Gamer teens in the library are a resource for participatory investment by young customers who might not have thought the library had anything of interest. While many teens come to a game event to get their hands on whatever games you offer, grab a snack, hang with friends, and book out when it's over, some will want more.

The gamer geeks help you set up. They'll help you tear down. They are eager to share their expertise with the technology and their opinions about what games you have or what you should get. Give helpers first shot at playing—they're in the room early, after all, and maybe they get to stay a little late. They'll challenge you to play their favorite games with and against them before the doors open (and after), and they might decide you're cool just for trying, however ineptly. You can connect and then develop the relationship.

And that's just the basics, which isn't bad even if it doesn't go any further. However, even within gaming events, it can go another step.

In my experience, the really invested gamer teens tend to be slightly older than the rest of the game-event attendees. As you get to know them, you may find they self-select to take responsibility, if you encourage them. After all, they want the events to continue running smoothly, often, and with plenty of friendly competition. They teach other kids new games, or how to play better. They might help a younger teen find a fun website, if you have computers running as well as console games. They may be more in tune with what is most fun for what narrow age bracket. They may know about the latest hottest thing you haven't caught onto yet—or what has become passé. For instance, I was still recommending Runescape until someone showed me Toon Town and a couple of driving games. Runescape, I was told, was "what we did back in middle school." By the time you are reading this, there will be another evolution of currently popular games.

These gamers can become formal volunteers, complete with badges of volunteer-authenticity. It gives them credibility among their peers so no one can say, "You're being bossy telling me I have to sign up for the Wii! Who made you king around here?" It also lets them know you value their presence and assistance.

Gamer teens may not be your usual library patrons. They may or may not be avid readers (although many are). Games prove the library does have something relevant to their lives—certainly a theme you've heard before. Coming in our doors regularly, they may find a library is relevant in ways they didn't realize. These are the ones you can recruit to greater involvement in the library's larger world because you'll have time to talk to them about what they love, and share what you love. Ask them questions about their favorite games and systems, experiences they have had while gaming — then take what you hear and see if it applies in the bigger picture. Often gaming is powerfully social, and that's something libraries are doing better and better. Listen to them. (I'm sure you've heard that before!)

Gamers should be represented on your teen advisory councils, or they could help found a new council. Perhaps their tastes overlap to anime, science fiction, fanfic writing, or machinima; those might be the seeds for new activities or clubs. They might have suggestions for ways to make a "boring" teen meeting more fun.

Listen. Ask. Think. Talk. Share. Connect. Because that's how you'll be able to work with them, and have them work with you.[30]

Liz Danforth, with 19 years' experience working in public libraries, presently working for the Pima County Public Library system in Tucson, Arizona, and providing library consulting with Danforth Design & Development

Preparation

When starting the library's video gaming program, Joy's first step was to call area businesses to procure prizes for the gamers. She was able to get several gift cards and certificates to restaurants, which included Subway, a bagel shop, and a fast food hamburger chain, as well as a donation of a five-gallon container of coffee from Starbucks for enjoying during the program.

To advertise, Joy posted fliers around the high school campus about two weeks in advance, made follow-up verbal announcements, posted an announcement on the sign outside the library, and invited the teens to sign up in the library. She also offered community service hours to those who wanted to volunteer as assistants, since the high school has a community service requirement for graduation. By the time the first event was held, there were 12 volunteers and more than 30 gamers signed up to play, with 18 more showing up on the day of the event. What a catchy way for teens to earn service credits!

When teens were signing up, Joy asked whether they might bring a game system to share. In addition, one of the teachers on campus volunteered to bring his PlayStation®2 system as well as one of his classic Nintendo systems. Joy was even able to talk her "gamer" husband into bringing his Xbox360! The program ended up with access to eight systems, including an old Atari reissue, for nostalgia's sake. They had *Rock Band*, which proved to be *very* popular; *Guitar Hero*; Wii games such as *Mario Super Smash Brawl* and *Melee*; and numerous others.

Managing the Equipment/Game Systems

On the day of the gaming event, the teens brought their systems to Joy's office. They labeled each personal system, the controllers, and the games. Then the systems were locked in her office to ensure that no losses would occur. In addition, she asked the students to check their bags upon signing in to the gaming event. This extra step enabled her to reassure students and parents that no one would lose any games or controllers.

Setting Up the Gaming Events

About two hours before the event, Joy and the teens set up the LCD machines and televisions. They used at least three LCDs to project the games on screens. For subsequent programs, they learned that when there is a shortage of the necessary six-foot-square screens, they could improvise using white paper on the wall above the stacks. During the set-up time, the student volunteers and some of the students who own the machines were available to assist. Additional support materials included at least four extension cords and some surge protectors to get it all powered up. Once everything was ready, the lights were turned down, with about a quarter of the lights left on so that Joy and her assistants were able to see and to supervise.

Joy says that the school library is a large room with many little nooks within the stacks, and includes a conference room. The gaming systems were strategically placed around the room after moving tables out of the way to allow space for the gamers. For the initial program, each gaming area was numbered, and there was a directory of games posted on a flipchart. The procedure worked to some degree, but it was later scrapped because teens do not necessarily play the same game at the station for the entire afternoon or evening.

The best teen programs include refreshments, and gaming is no exception. At the Valencia High School library, bottled water and some soda are provided. When the teens check in, they are asked if they want to contribute for pizza. If they do want pizza, $2.00 is charged, and the pizza is ordered an hour into the event. For those who don't want or can't afford pizza, other snacks, such as cookies, are provided.

Running the Actual Gaming Events

Teens were checked in five at a time and then received a claim check for their backpacks and jackets, which were placed in a secure area. The claim check numbers were later used to draw for gift card prizes—an extra element of fun.

Teens were given the option to compete for the Grand Champion prize if they were interested. Competing teens played the individual games, determined an individual champion, and eventually participated in a "game-off," through which the individual champions played a game selected at random. This was done by putting the names of the games in a bowl and drawing them to determine the game to be played. The teens played until there was one person left, and that person became the Grand Champion.

Individual champions received a gift card and a certificate, and the Grand Champion got a second gift card and a special certificate. The Grand Champion also received a "golden" controller. Joy bought an inexpensive PlayStation®2 controller and used gold spray paint to jazz it up. The teens thought it was very cool, and it remains a popular aspect of the current gaming programs. At competitions following the initial one, teens began bringing the controller back to pass to the next winner, like an ongoing trophy.

Post Event Take Down

The volunteers and the owners of the equipment (who were, by default, volunteers in their own right) helped to take everything down at the end of the first and succeeding events. As mentioned previously, all items were labeled to make it easy to return them to their rightful owners at the end of the program. Joy says that it took about 20–30 minutes for the teen volunteers to put everything away.

Some Special Considerations

Joy says that the teens were extremely happy to have gaming at their school library, and they are thrilled that it has continued. She adds that throughout it all, their behavior has been exemplary. The teens mix well with each other, and the gaming aspect seems to be the equalizer. Where teens might never be friends elsewhere on a regular school day, their relationships have changed during the gaming events, and they now enjoy having a good time together. Because gaming activities appeal to every type of teen, from the overworked near genius to the unfocused student who is just getting by in his or her classes, and everyone in-between, teens can participate on many levels.

During the very first gaming event, Joy overheard a freshman telling a senior, "I'm so glad that I'm a freshman, because I get to do this for four years!" This exclamation encapsulates the reason Joy recommends offering teen gaming, and doing it often. She says that teens get so much out of it, and that she has an expanding group of new library users as a result. Many of these students had not previously come to the library, but now she sees them regularly.

Notice that by participating in the success of this program, as in many examples throughout this book, teens have found a place to belong. It makes Joy very happy to know that she is giving these teens, many of whom had been rather disconnected from the school as a whole, a place to fit in and to enjoy being with like-minded peers.

Computer gaming activities are a great opportunity to reach a population that is underserved in regard to youth participation, in any school. They give teens pleasure and give librarians and staff an opportunity to get to know students on another level. Teens are enjoying themselves and consequently seeing the library in a new light. Joy says that there are no negative aspects about doing the gaming activities, except that conducting such programs does "make for a long day." However, as Saleena Davidson said in chapter 3 about the value of time spent coordinating their library's teen tutoring project, Joy adds that devoting the extra time to gaming projects is also absolutely worth it.[31]

Gaming as an Intergenerational Activity

Teen involvement in libraries may become an intergenerational activity not only with younger children but also with older adults. One remarkable way to accomplish this is through gaming activities.

At the Old Bridge Public Library in New Jersey (www.oldbridgelibrary.org) in 2007, the first gaming day for older adults with teens as mentors and instructors began. Teens interested in volunteering for the Senior Spaces gaming events first went through a screening and training process. Afterward they had to demonstrate their ability to introduce older adults to new technologies by showing their librarians how to use a Wii. From the pool of interested teens who completed the training, those who showed the best potential were selected to receive additional instructions on how older adults learn, problem solving, and how to boost confidence in beginners of any age.

Three areas were set up in the library's meeting room, with specific games set up in each one. Each older adult who came to the program was assigned a teen mentor. Within 15 minutes of starting, the program was in full swing. The teens were surprised at the older adults' curiosity. Likewise, the older adults were impressed with the teens' teaching skills. It was an overall positive impression for everyone.

However, the Senior Spaces gaming events at the library did not stop there! For a number of months following the initial activity, teen mentors continued to work with the older adults. Even after their older adult partners became adept at gaming, the teens continued to be involved by introducing their parents and grandparents to gaming. They also continued to play and compete with the older adults they once mentored, and even held an intergenerational Wii Bowling Tournament together.[32]

Again, if your library is feeling an economic pinch and wants to try gaming activities that are less expensive, you might consider starting out with board games. These activities can be surprisingly successful. For example, for a long period of time at the City of Mesa Library we had an active Chess Club. The club was run by the Young Adult Department, and weekly club gatherings were held in the YA meeting room. However, both older adults and younger children also joined in for weekly play, and the teens welcomed everyone. The youth participants enjoyed learning tips from the old timers, and the youth in turn relished the challenging competitions once they learned some new tricks. The best players of all ages ultimately competed against one another in an annual Chess Tournament, with prizes.

If your library is trying to develop intergenerational activities, remember the possibilities of teen volunteers and gaming. Teens can be instrumental in planning and overseeing such programs. As part of the package, you might consider ways that teens can teach older adults, as they did at the Old Bridge Public Library, or ways they might teach younger children about the challenge and fun of library gaming—or both!

Want to know more about organizing successful gaming programs at your library? Here are some handy resources:

Gallaway, Beth. *Game On: Gaming at the Library*. Neal-Schuman, 2009. Teen library gaming expert Beth Gallaway, a proponent of teen gaming from its inkling stages up, shares myriad information and tips for getting the best "game on" at *your* library.

Game On! TTR.08: Texas Teens Read Manual, www.tsl.state.tx.us/ld/projects/ttr/2008/manual (accessed September 20, 2009). As part of its 2008 Texas Teens Read summer reading program, the Texas State Library created this helpful online programming guide to electronic gaming, role-playing games, board games, trivia games, extreme sports, and more.

The Librarian's Guide to Gaming: An Online Toolkit for Building Gaming @ Your Library, librarygamingtoolkit.org (accessed September 20, 2009). This compilation of resources, tips, and best practices guides libraries in providing gaming services for users of all ages.

Neiburger, Eli. *Gamers . . . in the Library?!: The Why, What, and How of Videogame Tournaments for All Ages*. Chicago: American Library Association, 2007. Learn the ropes of conducting successful library gaming programs by using this helpful resource. You'll discover how to plan, run, and publicize exciting gaming events with all ages of library participants.

Digital Filmmaking and Teen Participation

An exciting, high tech approach through which teens may get involved in their libraries is *machinima*. Machinima offers teens a combination of many of the formats and techniques already explored in this chapter. It is filmmaking within a real-time, 3-D virtual environment, which includes video games such as *Halo*, and platforms such as Second Life (secondlife. com/whatis). It brings together the technologies of filmmaking, animation, and 3-D video games.

Machinima uses real-world filmmaking techniques within an interactive virtual environment through which characters and events are controlled by humans, scripts, and artificial intelligence. Video games can supply the settings, props, costumes, and characters to tell an original story. Some platforms also have in-game recording options, though a screen capture software program is required to import game environments where there are no built-in machinima tools. Many machinima enthusiasts enjoy remixing audio and video content for different effects.[33]

Machinima, a concept that combines the terms *machine* and *cinema*, is not new. As a matter of fact, it has been around since 1993, but it has only recently emerged as a widely popular communication method.[34] Because of the increased attention to this medium, the Machinima Institute in Second Life was established on the American Library Association Arts InfoIsland (infoisland.org) and is operated by librarians and educators who provide instructional resources for teaching machinima. Its founder, Bernadette Daly Swanson, who offers a course on the subject at the University of Illinois Graduate School of Library and Information Science, helped create machinima for the Public Library of Charlotte & Mecklenburg County in North Carolina. In 2007 the library held a machinima weekend in Teen Second Life through which teens learned storyboarding techniques and how to capture, edit, and remix with online tools.[35]

If you and your teens are ready to explore the possibilities of a machinima presence through your library's Web page, you might want to investigate ways to approach it that would work in your library's virtual setting. There are a number of platforms available to create machinima, though Teen Second Life has aspects that make it a leading choice. Users can create the scenes that they want for their film, there is a built-in browser for filming, and opening a Teen Second Life account is free. Costs may be minimized by partnering with organizations that have purchased "virtual land," which is necessary to have for building purposes.

Once teens are on board with machinima, there are myriad options for teen involvement. They may use it to create public service announcements or clips promoting library activities, invent stories, or plan a film fest using the format. Let them use their imagination. You will be amazed at what your teens can do by connecting machinima technology with their library.[36]

Would you like more information about machinima? Listed here are some useful resources. Two of the books include CD-ROMs to supplement the printed material.

Academy of Machinima Arts & Sciences: www.machinima.org (accessed September 27, 2009).

Hancock, Hugh, and Johnnie Ingram. *Machinima for Dummies.* Hoboken, NJ: Wiley, 2007. Includes CD-ROM.

Machinima.com. www.machinima.com (accessed September 27, 2009).

Miller, Carolyn Handler. *Digital Storytelling: A Creator's Guide to Interactive Entertainment.* Boston: Elsevier, 2008.

Second Life, *Machinima*. secondlife.com/showcase/machinima.php (accessed September 27, 2009).

Weber, Aimee, et al. *Creating Your World: The Official Guide to Advanced Content Creation for Second Life*. Indianapolis, IN: Wiley, 2008. Includes CD-ROM.

TEEN TECH WEEK: CELEBRATING THE TEEN AND TECHNOLOGY CONNECTION IN LIBRARIES

A fitting final word for this chapter is a discussion of Teen Tech Week. In 2007 the Young Adult Library Services Association (YALSA) launched the inaugural celebration of Teen Tech Week, held in March, as its annual technological counterpart to Teen Read Week, which is held in October. In doing so, YALSA demonstrated how, in addition to its focus on the importance of reading, it has taken the impact of technology on teen library use and teen literacy seriously. As part of the process, through a $1 million grant from the Verizon Foundation, the organization is creating guidelines on how to best use video games in libraries and researching how video gaming affects teen literacy and problem-solving skills.

On its "Teen Tech Week" Web page (www.ala.org/ala/mgrps/divs/yalsa/teentechweek), YALSA carefully explains the value of a week celebrating teens and technology. In an age when a majority of teens report that the Internet is their main source for completing school projects, whether at home, in school, or at the library, multiple studies have shown that they likewise lack the critical thinking skills and technological expertise to use the Internet and other electronic resources effectively. Teen Tech Week was designed to help. Aimed at teens, as well as at the supportive adults in their lives, it recognizes the value of an array of technology. Its weeklong focus engages teens in a positive way to encourage competent and ethical use of all technological formats for both education and recreation. It also focuses on librarians as knowledgeable professionals in the field of information technology.[37]

Keeping the purpose and philosophy of Teen Tech Week in mind, think about all the ways discussed in this chapter that teens can actively participate in their libraries by using and incorporating technology. Consider that when teens are connected with books, reading, and libraries, and they promote these things through their participatory and volunteer endeavors, great things can happen for the teens themselves, their libraries, and their communities. Furthermore, when you add *technology* to the mix, you are helping to encourage another positive aspect of this formula. Teens may find an additional avenue for their library participation while becoming more familiar with and embracing technology—a vital element of everyday contemporary life—as they grow and mature.

In essence, *positive technological teen development* paired with *responsible teen library involvement* becomes an essential part of effective *positive youth development*.

ENDNOTES

1. Bud E. Smith and Arthur Bebak, *Creating Web Pages for Dummies* (Hoboken, NJ: Wiley, 2007), 265.

2. Chomski, Boris, *10 Layout Rules* (10-Layout-Rules.com, n.d.), www.10-layout-rules.com (accessed September 20, 2009)).

3. Smith and Bebak, *Creating Web Pages for Dummies*, 266.

4. Chomski, *10 Layout Rules*.

5. Chomski, *10 Layout Rules*.

6. Smith and Bebak, *Creating Web Pages for Dummies*, 267.

7. Chomski, *10 Layout Rules*.

8. Smith and Bebak, *Creating Web Pages for Dummies*, 269.

9. Young Adult Library Services Association, *Seth Cassel Wins 2008 YALSA/Sagebrush Award for a Young Adult Reading or Literature Program* (American Library Association, 2008), www.ala.org/Template. cfm?Section=pressreleases&template=/contentmanagement/contentdisplay.cfm&ContentID=1720 21 (accessed September 20, 2009).

10. Joyce Kasman Valenza, "Open the Door and Let 'Em In," *Voice of Youth Advocates e-VOYA* (April 2007): Web 1, pdfs.voya.com/VO/YA2/VOYA200704tag_team_tech.pdf (accessed September 20, 2009)).

11. Valenza, "Open the Door and Let 'Em In."

12. Martha Choate, e-mail message to author, October 3, 2008.

13. Sally Roof, e-mail message to author, August 25, 2008.

14. wikiHow, *How to Start a Blog,* www.wikihow.com/Start-a-Blog (accessed September 20, 2009).

15. Lisa Matte, TAGAD-L posting, July 7, 2008, and e-mail message to author, September 9, 2008.

16. Roof, e-mail, August 25, 2008.

17. Lisa Bowen, e-mail message to author, May 15, 2008.

18. Kate DiPronio, e-mail message to author, May 8, 2008.

19. Circle of Seven Productions, *Welcome to Our Circle*, www.cosproductions.com/index.php (accessed February 2, 2008).

20. Pima County Public Library Teen Zone, *That's My Take* (Pima County Public Library, 2009), www.library.pima.gov/teenzone/trailers/2007.cfm (accessed September 20, 2009).

21. PCPLTZ, *That's My Take.*

22. Crystal Booth, *Book Trailers* (Squidoo, 2008), www.squidoo.com/booktrailers (accessed September 20, 2009).

23. Jon Gilliom, e-mail message to author, December 26, 2008.

24. Wicked Local Belmont, *Library Lines* (June 19, 2008), www.wickedlocal.com/belmont/archive/x822803927/Library-Lines (accessed December 10, 2008).

25. Belmont Public Library, "Tech Tips: CyberTeen Guides," blog comment posted on June 2, 2008, belmontlibrarytechtips.blogspot.com/2008/06/cyberteen-guides.html (accessed October 30, 2009.)

26. Glendale Public Library Teen Turnpike, *Volunteer Opportunities at the Main Library* (Glendale Public Library, 2004), www.glendaleaz.com/Library/teen/happening_html/tt_happening_volunteer.html (accessed September 20, 2009).

27. Elizabeth Gibson, "Libraries' Video Games Are Teen Magnet," *Columbus Dispatch*, July 31, 2008, www.dispatch.com/live/content/local_news/stories/2008/07/31/librarygamers.ART_ART_07-31-08_B1_VRAT509.html (accessed September 20, 2009).

28. Gibson, "Libraries' Video Games Are Teen Magnet."

29. Beth Gallaway, e-mail message to author, April 28, 2009.

30. Liz Danforth, e-mail message to author, December 9, 2008.

31. Joy Millam, e-mail message to author, January 28, 2009.

32. Dale Lipschultz, "Gaming @ Your Library," *American Libraries* 40 (January/February 2009): 42–43.

33. Tabitha Tsai and Kelly Czarnecki, "Machinima Goes Mainstream: Digital Filmmaking for the 21st Century," *School Library Journal* 54 (February 2008): 29.

34. Bernadette Daly Swanson, "Second Life Machinima for Libraries: The Intersection of Instruction, Outreach and Marketing in a Real World" (Paper presented at the World Library and Information Congress: 73rd IFLA General Conference and Council, August 19–23, 2007, Durban, South Africa), www.ifla.org/IV/ifla73/papers/133-DalySwanson-en.pdf (accessed February 8, 2009).

35. Tsai and Czarnecki "Machinima Goes Mainstream," 30–31.

36. Tsai and Czarnecki "Machinima Goes Mainstream," 31.

37. Young Adult Library Services Association, *Teen Tech Week 2009* (American Library Association, 2009), www.ala.org/ala/mgrps/divs/yalsa/teentechweek/ttw09/home.cfm (accessed February 8, 2009).

7

❖ ❖ ❖

More Ways Teens Can Participate: Community Outreach and Partnerships

Libraries are a vital part of any well-functioning community, so it makes sense that some activities done by your teen library participants will connect them with the community at large. Although it is important for teens to be involved in the library itself, don't limit your vision only to activities within the library. Instead, encourage teens to reach out beyond the library walls and let other teens know about what the library has to offer them. By doing so, involved library teens will invite other teens to actively engage in the library as they do, through both their words and actions, which ultimately increases your teen participation numbers. Outreach and partnership activities also bring what the teens are doing in your library into focus for the adults in the community and allow adults to see the positive results of teens being part of the library at this level.

Activities that connect teens with the community may be done through partnerships with like-minded agencies and organizations that also work with and serve teens, such as schools, youth clubs, or even youth sporting groups. In addition, teens representing your library might expand their contributions beyond the boundaries of the community to other areas of the country, and even the world!

Now you might be wondering how teen participants in libraries can do all these things. How do teens make connections that allow them to embark on such endeavors? In this chapter you will see some great examples of libraries that encourage teens to become involved in partnerships and outreach activities. The teens are led there by their adult library advisors, who either take an idea presented by teens and help to make it happen, or present an idea to the teens so that the teens may decide if they want to run with it. Either way, consider how you might get teens inspired to try such activities in *your* library.

SCHOOL–PUBLIC LIBRARY COOPERATION

"School–public library cooperation" is a catchphrase that encompasses an old concept almost gone by the wayside, but which is making a comeback. Although examples can be found from earlier decades, in the 1980s the idea of school–public library cooperation was in full swing and became a regular topic for professional education at library conferences and through individualized library training. However, in the past the notion of school–public library cooperation basically meant sharing resources, collaborating on projects and activities, supporting or advocating for one another, and in some cases even sharing facilities. The aspect of collaboration through teen participatory activities was a small part of the picture, although there was some enthusiastic encouragement for it.

In 1979 Peggy A. Sullivan praised young people's willingness and their competency to provide advice about youth services in libraries if they were asked, and she added "that a silver lining in this time of economic adversity could be the availability of young people for volunteer efforts." Further, she said, "Young people need libraries, and libraries need young people; and the more libraries cooperate among themselves, the more and better service they can provide to young people."[1]

Today, that picture is coming full circle as well as into clearer focus as school and public librarians, and even teachers and other youth service workers, mutually encourage teens to become involved in books, reading, libraries, and more through an array of cooperative endeavors. As you read the following examples, think about ways that collaboration might be effective in getting teens involved in *your* library and community.

An Exemplary School–Public Library Cooperative Venture

Each year, the high school and middle school students at Delsea Regional High School (www.delsea.k12.nj.us/cgi-bin/main.pl) participate in cooperative programs with the Franklin Township Public Library (www.franklintwp.org) in Franklinville, New Jersey, to provide a variety of literary events and activities for young children. This partnership has been successful for many years, with teen involvement as its primary basis.

Among the projects that Delsea Regional High School and Franklin Township Public Library have shared are hosting authors for Teen Read Week, rotating the author presentation locations between the school and public library each year, posting notices about the public library's teen advisory group in the school libraries and classrooms, and advertising other public library programs and activities for teens through the school libraries. These cooperative efforts are effective in spreading the word about what each has to offer and even more effective in supporting how the two facilities work together on major teen participatory projects. When you read in the following section how well the school and public libraries collaborate, you might be inspired to investigate similar possibilities in your own community.[2]

High School Story Hours for Children

The Delsea Regional High School media center comes alive with books, reading, and lots of exciting storytime activity each year in December and during spring break. For this cooperative venture, high school students provide coloring pages and activity sheets for preschool children who attend their hour-long programs. During the first half hour, teens read and color with the children. During the second half hour, a teen volunteer dresses as Santa or the Easter bunny, depending on the season. These are exciting interactive projects with many components for promoting teen library and reading participation.

Taking part in the preschool story hours requires some preliminary teen investment and a competitive edge. The story hours are done every year as the culmination of a ninth-grade service learning project. Limited numbers of teens may participate, and teens clamor to take part. The project begins when Mary Moyer, the high school librarian, schedules a children's author each year, who agrees to waive his or her speaking fee in lieu of an earned donation from high school students for a charity of the author's choice. To create some friendly rivalry, the students who collect the most donations in their individual classes get to participate in conducting the storytimes. The idea is to keep everything related to literacy, including the fund-raising project and the ultimate students' reward. The teens enjoy the challenge every year, and it turns out to be a win-win endeavor for all involved.

As an example of how this has worked, in 2008 author DyAnne DiSalvo agreed to be the guest author for the ninth graders, hinging on their pledge to earn funds for DyAnne's selected charity, the Gloucester County Habitat for Humanity. The teens raised money by holding a service-learning oriented "Drop Everything and Read" Pajama Day event in October as their "Make a Difference Day" activity. Students collected monetary pledges based on the time they spent reading. As a reward for their efforts, DyAnne provided a complimentary how-to presentation on writing children's books. The teens incorporated her tips as they created the original books for their upcoming "Read Across America Day" event. In addition, the students who raised the most donations were appointed to prepare and run the upcoming preschool storytimes.[3]

Each year the supplies to run the storytimes are provided by other teen fund-raising endeavors. Cookies, candy canes or Easter candy, coloring pages, crayons, and sometimes children's books are provided by the high school English Club. To raise these funds, the club holds two book fairs a year. They get books from a local bookstore and are able to return what they do not sell. The students man the fair and help with the selection of books. If possible, they plan the fair to coincide with parent conference night, which usually provides enough funds for the storytime activities. In the previous year, the students also sold Read Across America T-shirts to raise money. In addition, Mary sometimes brings back children's books as freebies from conferences, which she donates to the cause.[4]

Once the story hour times are planned and funded, the Franklin Township Public Library publicizes the teen-run events through newspaper announcements and flyers distributed in both the public and school libraries. What's more, the public librarian supplies the children's books for the teens' story hour activities.

During the events, Mary photographs the children and teens in action, then posts the photos on the high school media center Web page, with parental permission. She also sends photos and press releases to the local newspaper. Consequently, a photographer has attended several storytimes, and photos taken during the activities and then published in the newspaper afford additional publicity.

For the storytimes, snacks are provided for the little ones, along with bookmarks and coloring pages to take home. For some sessions there have even been free children's books that the preschoolers could keep.

Participating teens, children, and librarians always find the storytime programs to be a pleasurable experience. As a matter of fact, Mary has noticed that the teens enjoy the storytimes as much as the younger children do![5] (See figure 7.1, p. 140.)

Figure 7.1. Teen and Tot Enjoying Acting Out "I'm a Little Teapot" at Delsea Regional High School and Franklinville Township Public Library Cooperative Storytime. Photo by Mary Moyer

Challenging and Joyful: Teens React to Their Storytime Participation Experiences

Teens involved in the children's story hours found them to be exciting, interesting, and enlightening. Here are some of their reactions:

The holiday story hour was a fantastic experience. The little kids are great to be around. They are very into the stories that were provided. It was a joy to see how happy they were and how much fun they had. It's been worth all the effort that it takes to see them so enthusiastic about the holidays and books.

Samantha Salcedo, grade 11

Story hour has benefited the children greatly for many reasons. One of the reasons is that the children were able to interact with one another as they learned, and were involved all at the same time. The children received an experience that lifted their spirits.

Personally, story hour was one of the experiences that I will never forget throughout my high school career. I believe that it will help me to be more involved and realize how important it is to the children to have something like this for them. Lastly, story hour has made me feel great. I hope that the preschool children had a good time and more importantly, I learned that giving is the most important gift of all.

Kyle McCulley, grade 9

Middle School Storytimes for Children

It is a good thing that reading to young children doesn't stop with the high school students in their library. The public library gets in on the action, too. Delsea Regional Middle School students take part in children's storytimes held at the public library each year, rather than in the school library like their high school counterparts. Denise Saia, who is the director of the Franklin Township Public Library, works closely with the Delsea middle school librarian and trains the seventh-grade students to conduct storytimes for the little ones.

This involvement by early teens includes twice-monthly evening storytime and craft programs for preschool to third-grade youngsters. Denise meets with interested seventh graders at the middle school in late September and demonstrates how to read to the children. After receiving this training, each seventh grader is assigned to a specific storytime/ craft session. These sessions are held at the public library from 6:30 to 7:00 p.m. on scheduled days, and Denise provides the storytime books for the school librarian to share with the middle school students who are involved.

Following the training sessions, the teens are given a month to read the books and practice for the storytimes. The school librarians provide materials and instructions for each craft and, as with the high school storytimes, the public library supplies all the necessary publicity to the newspapers and the schools.

This middle school cooperative project serves as an introduction for the seventh graders who will later be involved in the high school projects. This allows the middle school project to set the stage for continuing participation at the high school level.[7]

Challenging and Joyful: Teens React to Their Storytime Participation Experiences

Reading to the township children was a both a learning experience and fun. Everyone got something out of it. It was nice to see how enthusiastic the children were, which made us like it even more.

The story hour had a few aspects that made it so enjoyable. My friend dressed up as Santa and I was one of his helpers. I liked it especially because of its meaning, being that it was Christmas related. It just brought joy to everyone and I know that the kids had fun.

Shaun Snead, grade 10

My experience showing and helping the little kids was awesome. The kids learned a lot from what I read to them. I read books about counting and finding items in a book. I think it was the best experience I ever did in school and I am proud of participating in it.

Louisa Abiuso, grade 9

Playing Santa at this year's story hour was much more difficult that I originally expected. All I thought I had to do was say "Ho-ho-ho" a few times and ask what the kids wanted for Christmas. The most challenging part was trying to understand what the children were saying! Others asked many questions I found hard to answer, but at the end of it all, I felt proud to be part of the event. I think I can do it again next year as well. Seeing the kids' faces light up made me feel like a saint. It was a wonderful time.

Daniel Wozniak, grade 10[6]

A Read Across America Project: The Cooperation Continues

You might be wondering about all those ninth-grade teens who earned money for the guest author's favorite charity but were not able to take part in the preschool storytimes, and you will be glad to learn that they were not left out. That is because the culmination of the Delsea Regional High School and Franklin Township Public Library cooperation efforts is an outstanding Read Across America Day project.

Each year, Denise goes to the high school and provides guidance for writing, illustrating, and publishing the original children's books that the teens will ultimately create to share with elementary students on Read Across America Day. Denise offers this introduction by spending an entire day with the ninth graders, reading examples of different types of children's books and talking about what children like to hear in stories. After the Read Across America activity ends, the teens' books are collected and placed on display at the public library during the summer so all ages of the local community may read and enjoy them as well.

At the start of the new school year, the books are returned to the student authors. Denise is always delighted to give Mary positive feedback about how much pleasure the community had in reading the students' creations.

Other school and public library teens might find these very successful school–public library reading and storytime projects rewarding and easy to emulate. Think about how such a project might benefit and project goodwill for the teens and children in your community and library.[8]

Volunteer State Readers: Reading Role Models

Another cooperative venture that involves teens reading to youngsters is the Volunteer State Readers Program at Loretto (Tennessee) High School (http://schools.lcss.us/lhs). It was the brainchild of a student, Lucas Hunt, who designed the program around Tennessee's annual Volunteer State Book Award for children. For the project, the 20 titles nominated for the Volunteer State Book Award's primary level are read each year to elementary grade children by Volunteer State Readers Program volunteers from the high school. Approximately 300 elementary students and 10 to 20 high school students participate annually, and the numbers keep growing.

Once a week, the teen volunteers visit kindergarten through second-grade classrooms to read one of the nominated titles. After the children have heard all 20 books, they vote for their favorite. At the end of each school year, copies of the 20 books are given to the high school library, where they become part of a special children's collection.

The Loretto High School students who participate in the program often enlist an organization, like the Lions Club, to fund enough copies of the children's books for the project. At other times the books are purchased through memorial donations. Students also check out books from the local library to secure the copies they need.

The Volunteer State Readers Program began as a means to encourage younger children to read and to be exposed to quality children's literature, as well as to enable high school students to serve as role models for younger children. In Lawrence County, the reading program really makes a difference, because school libraries receive limited funding and sports reign over reading and academics. Special speakers and programs are often not affordable. The Loretto High School students who serve in the Volunteer State Readers Program are positive role models who encourage young readers while personally discovering the rewards of mentoring and community service.

The program kicks off in November and continues until all 20 nominated books have been read at the local elementary schools. The high school librarian oversees the program and works with the student coordinator to schedule the student readers for Friday classroom visits.

Teen volunteers prepare by reading their children's books to the high school librarian or the high school drama teacher, who critique their presentation and reading skills. The volunteer readers also get advice from the elementary teachers on dealing with special needs students. Finally, the student volunteers practice for their actual presentations by reading to their high school teachers and other students.

When teen volunteers read to the children, they sometimes dress as book characters or bring surprises related to their stories. For instance, when one teen read *Jimmy Zangwow's Out-of-This-World Moon Pie Adventure* by Tony DiTerlizzi, he dressed as Jimmy Zangwow and read the book in the first person. He even gave the children Moon Pies, which he said Mr. Moon had sent them! Besides providing entertaining stories, these high school students talk about their love of reading, plus their other hobbies and interests, which strengthens their image as role models.

Each Friday after the reading sessions, the teen volunteers regroup to reflect on the experiences they have had with the elementary students. Through this process, the teens have gradually decided to expand the program and offer additional readings for children in area community clubs. As word has grown about the program, more and more high school students have joined the volunteer ranks.

Lucas Hunt, the teen founder of the project, gave a presentation on the Loretto High School's Volunteer State Readers Program at the 2004 Tennessee Association of School Librarians annual conference. Librarians from throughout the state were enthused about trying similar programs in their high schools. Lucas encouraged them to do so, reinforcing that the program would be very easy to duplicate wherever teens are willing to participate.[9]

Mock Newbery Clubs Extend to the Schools

Here's another cooperative venture that reinforces the concept of promoting literacy. One of the things the Wake County Public Libraries has been able to do is to help other groups begin their own Mock Newbery book clubs, modeled after the Wake Forest one. When the Mock Newbery program was young, some of the teen book club members shared the new books that they loved with their language arts teachers. As a result, a few teachers and media specialists got caught up in the excitement and started Mock Newbery book clubs of their own in area middle schools. This trend has continued. Occasionally the library system has teachers who come to visit the library's book club meetings when they are thinking of starting another group, either as public, private, or homeschool book clubs.[10]

Publicizing One Another

Another important way for school and public libraries to cooperate is to provide publicity for one another's teen programs and events. For instance, the Corona del Sol High School library in Tempe, Arizona, publicizes upcoming teen activities that will be held at both the Chandler Public Library's Sunset branch and the Tempe Public Library, because both are near the school. Mary Moyer posts notices about Teen Advisory Group meetings at the Franklin Township Public Library in the Delsea Regional High School library, and copies are sent to teachers to post in their classrooms. Sally Roof, at Madison Meadows Middle School in Phoenix, does the same thing for the Phoenix Public Library.

Sally received the following message from the Phoenix Library, and she gladly agreed to help spread the word:

> Thank you for your interest in helping us to publicize the Library Teen Council (LTC) at Burton Barr Public Library. LTC participants will be involved in creating and supporting library teen programming, participating in web and blog activities, participating in community service projects, and fundraising in support of library youth services. The LTC will meet twice a month on Saturday afternoons between 3:00 and 5:00 pm.
> We would like to recruit motivated and involved students who are interested in their community. Please share the enclosed flyers with students, teachers, and parents.

Not only did Sally arrange to have this information read to students during the school's morning announcements, she also recommended a few middle schoolers whom she felt would be excellent candidates for the LTC.[11]

Don't forget that this process works both ways, if you work in a public library and the school library helps to promote your activities. If your local school library is holding a book fair or other fund-raiser, an afterschool gaming session, or another special event, be sure to let the library staff know that you are happy to reciprocate and post information in the public library's teen space to help promote the activity.

BOOK SALES AND OTHER FUND-RAISING PROJECTS FOR AND THROUGH THE LIBRARY

You will have noticed that fund-raising was mentioned a few times in the previous section. That's because teens enjoy fund-raising, an important aspect of teen participation. Most teens like the empowerment and the satisfaction of doing something positive for a good cause. Raising money through their own efforts to support their library or community needs is a heady thing. When you give teens the opportunity to do these kinds of activities, you might be surprised at the positive results. No matter what fund-raising activity your teens decide to engage in, their efforts can become a wonderful publicity opportunity for the library and for highlighting the concept of library youth participation. These activities also allow the teens to represent the library while reaching out to and connecting with other parts of the community.

Friends of the Library Book Sales

One of the best ways to get teens involved in fund-raising is to have them take part in large Friends of the Library used book sales. Check with your teen volunteers to see if they are interested, and if so, make the Friends group at your library aware that some of the teens will be available to help with it. The adult Friends group members might never consider teen volunteers as an option for assistance unless you bring it up. Be willing to contact the teens and to provide a list of names and phone numbers of teen book sale volunteers. You might even ask one of the Friends volunteers to come to a teen advisory or teen volunteer meeting to share information about the book sale and discuss what the teens' responsibilities will be.

Friends of the Library book sale participation is a great way for teens to earn extra service hours, contribute positively to the library, and participate in an intergenerational atmosphere. Adult volunteers truly enjoy working with teen volunteers! They are frequently impressed with the dedication and responsibility displayed by their teen coworkers.

If you offer teens the opportunity to assist with book sales, you will probably be astonished at how many teens really want to help. With setup, cleanup, and all the activities in between that comprise a successful book sale, every teen who is interested can get involved. If they have them, ask your teens to wear their TAB or teen volunteer T-shirts at the sale to constructively publicize the library and their ongoing teen library involvement.

As they did when I worked at the City of Mesa Library in Arizona, five to ten members of the Young Adult Advisory Council volunteer for the annual October Friends of the Library book sale event. Teens sign up to help with setup, takedown, restocking of shelves and displays, and ringing up sales. Sandwiches and light snacks during breaks are provided for both the teens and the adults who are helping, which gives them a chance to comfortably get to know one another.

At the Poudre River Public Library District in Fort Collins, Colorado, teens from the Interesting Reader Society serve in similar capacities. Like the Friends group in Mesa, the adult Friends of the Library volunteers in Fort Collins delightedly express their appreciation for the teens' diligent work. Your teens may likewise receive such positive recognition for their contributions. Next time your Friends of the Library group is planning a book sale, remember to make an effort to get your teens involved. You can bet you will be pleasantly surprised at results.

Book Fairs

Another way for teens to earn money and books is by planning and running book fairs in their libraries and communities. At Shepherd Junior High School, the Off the Shelf Book Club members are instrumental in conducting the library's Scholastic book fairs. The students select a theme and also create all the props, backgrounds, displays, and contests to promote the fair throughout the school. They work at the fair as security monitors and make suggestions to perspective buyers. Their efforts have been so outstanding that they earned National Scholastic Book Fair Student Crew Contest honors three times so far, once as first prize winners, the second time for the grand prize, and the third time, in 2008, for second prize.[12]

Planning and holding a book fair like this would be a fun and challenging endeavor for any volunteer teen library group looking for a good way to earn money and materials to support the library. The nice thing about book fairs is that profits may usually be taken in one of two ways. One option is for the library to receive a check to use however it wishes. This is a good choice when the funds received are needed to support a program or to provide certain collection materials. Teens might do a book fair to enable themselves to host a visiting author, to fund a new manga collection, or to buy displayers for the teen area.

A second option is to take book fair profits in books and other collection materials. The drawback to this is that selection is limited to stock available through the book fair provider. The benefit is that the overall profit value is higher when choosing materials rather than cash. Be sure to talk over how profits will be managed if your teens decide to do a book fair.

Book fairs may be conducted through a major book publishing company, like the fairs held at Shepherd Junior High, but there are also other avenues for doing them. Bookstores, independent book distributors, and small publishing houses sometimes offer book fairs. If your teens are interested in supporting this kind of fund-raising effort, investigate the options in your local area in addition to what a national publisher might offer.

Readers to the Rescue

At the Poudre River Public Library District (www.poudrelibraries.org), teens participate through the summer reading program in a unique way. Teens must read a specific number of hours each month to earn prizes and qualify for monthly and grand prize drawings. When they ask if they can get additional prizes or drawing slips if they read extra hours, we explain that we have a better choice for them. For every five extra hours teens read beyond the summer reading program prize requirements, they earn a dollar donation to "Readers to the Rescue."

The Readers to the Rescue project is funded by the Library Trust, which annually gives the reader-earned monies to a preselected organization after all the Readers to the Rescue hours are tallied at the end of the summer. The teen summer reading program piggybacks with the children's program to contribute hours, so the total amount that all young people in the library district are able to donate with their "extra' reading time is impressive. Best of all, if young people choose to forego their regular summer reading prizes altogether, they may donate those reading hours to the Readers to the Rescue pool instead.

In 2008 the recipient of the Readers to the Rescue funds was the African Rainforest Conservancy. Children and teens donated $3,000 to this fund. In 2009 the Fort Collins Cat Rescue was the recipient.[13]

Not only does this extension of the summer reading programs allow a large number of children and teens to participate in a "drop-in" fashion, as we explored in chapter 5, but it allows them to contribute to a bigger picture by using their reading time to support a worthy cause, which teaches valuable lessons about generosity.

If you are finding that the teens who take part in your summer reading program are asking what else is in it for them, you might consider investigating the possibilities of a similar fund-raising tie-in. Check with local organizations and agencies—maybe even your Friends of the Library group—to see if a "Readers to the Rescue" type of project is something they would like to support. You might also have a local individual benefactor who would be interested in providing funds for such an endeavor.

Teen Read-a-Thons

The teen read-a-thon is another interesting approach to teen fund-raising. We are all familiar with telethons and pledge drives on television and the radio to help cure devastating diseases or to fund a public broadcasting station. What if this concept were brought to teen participation in libraries? In some places, it is already happening, with exciting results.

If your teens buy in, you will have an entertaining and exciting project that will benefit others and provide goodwill and publicity for your library. A teen read-a-thon is simple to do and can have very positive results. To conduct a read-a-thon, here are some basic steps to follow:

- Explain the concept of a read-a-thon to your teen volunteers or teen advisory group. Although you might encourage any teen from the community to participate, it is extremely beneficial to have a core group of teens to support the project and enlist other teens to take part.

- Work with your teens to choose an organization, agency, or cause that will be the beneficiary of the read-a-thon donations. You might ask a representative from that intended recipient to come speak to the teens so they will understand where the money earned will be going and how it will be used.

- Decide on a place, date, and time to hold the event. Be sure it is when teens are not in school and they can be involved for an extended period. Be flexible, so that teens have a wide range of time to attend. Some teens will be present for the whole event; others will only be able to stay for a fraction of it. Be sure to accommodate both kinds of participants by allotting a lengthy time span.

- Decide how contributors may pledge and for how much reading time. For instance, you might want to give people the option of donating a flat amount or an amount they designate per hour or half hour of reading. Set a deadline for when donors must turn in their pledges.

- Create a form that teens can use to solicit donations. You might make one side a flyer to advertise the project, the other side a log on which teens may record contributors' pledges.

- Publicize the program in your library as well as in the community. Ask your teen volunteers to spread the word about the event.

- Get funding to purchase snacks and drinks to have on hand for the teen readers during the hours they are participating. Be sure the event location is comfortable for the readers.

- When the event is over, collect any flat rate pledges that have already been given to the teens. At the predetermined deadline, hopefully you will have received the remaining money promised. If not, you might want to call the donors to gently remind them that it is time for them to turn in the contributions they guaranteed.

- If possible, have your library issue a check for the agency that is the beneficiary of the event proceeds. Choose a time to present the check when some of the teens from your library can be present, and use it as an opportunity to promote your teen participation activities.

The following examples demonstrate how library-oriented teen read-a-thons work to promote youth participation and teen outreach for the community.

Poudre River Public Library District

The teen members of the Interesting Reader Society (IRS) of the Poudre River Public Library District have sponsored teen read-a-thons for agencies that also serve youth in the community. In April 2008, as part of National Library Week and on the Young Adult Library Service Association's "Support Teen Literature Day," 21 teenagers participated in a teen read-a-thon that raised $690 for the local Boys & Girls Club. In October 2008, during Teen Read Week, IRS held a second teen read-a-thon, with 18 teenagers participating, which provided $300 for the Turning Point Center for Youth & Family Development (www.turningpnt.org/), a Fort Collins agency that serves high-risk youth and their families. (See figure 7.2, pp. 148–49.)

As you probably noticed, our library did two read-a-thons in one year. The second one earned much less money than the first. We discovered that repeating the event after only six months was too soon. People who financially supported the effort half a year before were not ready to support it again the second time around, even though it was for a good cause. If your teens plan this activity and are quite enthusiastic about the results, and they want to do it again, explain that it is better to wait at least a year between events so that contributors do not get burned out from giving.

Loudoun County Public Library

One larger library system has also conducted teen read-a-thons with impressive results. In 2007 the Loudoun County Public Library in Virginia (library.loudoun.gov/) sponsored their first annual teen read-a-thon to benefit the Loudoun Literacy Council, which supports programs dedicated to helping youth and adults attain and develop literacy skills through individualized tutoring and small group instruction. That year, the 35 teen participants earned over $2,000 for this agency.[14]

Inspired by their initial project's success, teens held a second annual teen read-a-thon in 2008. This time, the library system teamed up with the Loudoun County Animal Shelter in sponsoring the countywide event. Its goal was to promote literacy and build awareness in the community about the shelter's efforts to ensure the safety and welfare of animals.[15] Teen participants were expected to get donations of at least $50 each and to spend a minimum of five hours reading for the event. The read-a-thon was scheduled for three different library branches on three different dates, from 11:00 a.m. to 4:00 p.m. so that teens could choose when to participate. The 36 teen readers who signed up raised $1,700 for the animal shelter.[16]

These impressive results might encourage you to consider doing a read-a-thon event at your library. Ask your teens if they are interested and what agencies they might want to support if they choose to do one. Give them ideas from other libraries like the ones just shared, and see what they can come up with. They may even decide to do this project with your library itself as the beneficiary! If your teens choose this project, you will notice that blending teens, reading, and dedication to a worthy cause is a promising combination.

Other Community Fund-raisers

Helping a School for the Homeless and Books for a Better World

The Friends of the Library Club from Corona del Sol High School (see chapter 3) supports its school library and promotes reading to peers, and under its auspices, members also work on community service projects outside school. For example, they once raised $1,200 for the teachers of the Thomas J. Pappas School for the Homeless in Phoenix after the library was damaged by a storm. However, the teens do not stop with local projects. Their efforts extend internationally.

During the 2007–2008 school year, the Corona del Sol teens raised $500 during the first semester, which they donated to Books for a Better World. The money was earmarked for a project to found a new library in Central or South America. Books for a Better World uses donated funds to start libraries with a basis of 150 books, and every year following its establishment, each new library is supplemented with 100 additional new books.[17]

Fort Collins Regional Library District/Teen Services

TEEN READ-A-THON @ your library

Wednesday, October 15th   3:30 – 8:30 p.m.
Main Library, Ben Delatour Room
201 Peterson St Fort Collins

Open to 6th–12th graders

Celebrate National Teen Read Week!

Participant Name:

Phone & e-mail:

Grade:

Raise money for the Turning Point Center for Youth & Family Development.

Hello! I will be participating in the Fort Collins Regional Library District's **Teen Read-A-Thon @ your library** on Wednesday, October 15th from 3:30 – 8:30 p.m. at the Main Library's Ben Delatour meeting room. We are reading to raise money for a very special cause. **Turning Point Center for Youth & Family Development** is a not for profit 501(c)3 agency that has been working with high risk youth and their families for 40 years. Turning Point's extensive continuum of services includes Community Centered Services, substance abuse treatment and education, residential and transitional services, state approved education programs and aftercare to youth and their families in Northern Colorado, Southern Wyoming and communities along the Front Range. Money raised from the read-a-thon will be donated directly to the Turning Point Center for Youth & Family Development.

You can make a flat donation sponsoring my participation, or pledge an amount per half-hour of reading. For example, you may choose to make a flat donation of $10, as well as pledging $5 (this is just an example) for every half-hour of reading. The Teen Read-A-Thon @ your library will take place at the Main Library at 201 Peterson St. from 3:30 – 8:30 p.m. for National Teen Read Week.

Please make all checks payable to **Turning Point Center for Youth & Family Development.**

For Participants: Please collect any flat donations before the Teen Read-A-Thon and bring them to the event. Please collect any pledges after the event and bring them to Sue-Ellen Jones, Teen Services Librarian, at the Main Library by Friday, October 31st. **Stay for as long or as short a time as you want. We will have a photo release form that you may sign at the event so that we can use your pictures in our publicity.** For more information please contact Sue-Ellen at the Main Library at (970) 221-6380. Visit our Teen page at http://www.fcgov.com/library/teens.php
The Library will provide free pizza and snacks for Teen Read-A-Thon participants.

Figure 7.2. Poudre River Public Library District (Formerly Fort Collins Regional Library District) Teen Read-a-Thon Flyer and Pledge Sheet

Name	Phone	I will make a flat donation of:	I will sponsor this amount per 30 min. of reading:	After the Teen Read-A-Thon		
				Total pledge owed:	Date pledge collected:	Signature:

Figure 7.2. Poudre River Public Library District (Formerly Fort Collins Regional Library District) Teen Read-a-Thon Flyer and Pledge Sheet (Cont.)

A Rock Concert and Three Cups of Tea

Here is another great example of a global teen fund-raiser done through a library. At the Grosse Pointe Public Library in Michigan (www.gp.lib.mi.us/), the TAB Group held a concert to earn money that would support author Greg Mortenson's school-building projects for girls in Pakistan and Afghanistan, which you might have read about in his book *Three Cups of Tea* (Penguin, 2007). For the first time, the TAB members were able to get community service groups in the two local high schools to cooperate with them on a project. The "Playing for Peace" concert (see figure 7.3), was promoted in the high school newspapers and through the local media (see figure 7.4). Through this joint effort, the teens raised $700 and presented a check to Mr. Mortenson following an author presentation he gave at the Grosse Pointe Public Library.[18]

Figure 7.3. Grosse Pointe Public Library Teens Enjoying "Playing for Peace" Concert While Raising Money for Good Cause. Photo by Lynn Maslowski

There are many other ways that teens can become involved in fund-raising, for or through their library. If the library is in need of materials, needs special programming, or has other financial demands, teens might decide on projects to focus their fund-raising toward alleviating those needs. If the teens involved in the library see an outside-the-library community necessity as a target for raising money *through* the library, fund-raising for that purpose is also a worthwhile goal. Tell your teens about your library's needs, and also share with them ideas for helping to solve problems and provide for others in the immediate community and the world at large.

**Figure 7.4. "Playing for Peace" Cooperative Library/High School Concert Flyer,
Grosse Pointe Public Library**

Library Promotional Activities in the Community

Each year the TAG at the Elizabeth Public Library participates in a street fair called July Fest. It is held outside of a community center in the port section of the city, not far from one of the branch libraries. July Fest is sponsored by the Elizabeth Housing Authority, and the city provides refreshments—hot dogs, hamburgers, and soda, plus a disk jockey—for the residents of the community. Various community organizations are invited to set up tables to offer information about their facilities and services. The local hospital has a table, as do the fire department, different outreach organizations, and, of course, the library. At each table, items are given away and some agencies have activities for children.

The library provides a caricature artist who draws any children who are interested, and it hands out materials about summer programs and how to get a library card. TAG members volunteer their time by passing out pamphlets, doing face painting for little ones, and generally representing the library with their advisor, Kimberly Paone, at their assigned table. Teens who volunteer at the July Fest earn community service hours, get raffle tickets for the teen summer reading club, and enjoy the free food. The library and community both benefit.[19]

Participation with a Paycheck?

What about teen library participation that gives a paycheck? This is an entirely different aspect of the teen involvement experience. Let's take a look at an example that offers a monetary reward and has demonstrated its value:

At the Pima County Public Library in Arizona, a special opportunity for teens earns them a stipend of $100 for providing a service for the library. Teens who fulfill their contracts also earn a place at an all-night sleepover celebration just for them at Main Library.

How does this "for hire" activity work? After teens apply for the program and complete the required two-hour Teen Library Advocate training session, they contract to do five presentations in the Tucson schools, during which they talk to other teens about what the library has to offer. In lieu of the school presentations, teens may choose to do sessions for friends, clubs, or religious groups, as long as the total number of presentations given is five. They are expected to arrange their own scheduling for these presentations and to complete them by April 30. Teens fill out all the library paperwork necessary to process payment with their contract agreement, complete with a parent or guardian's signature.[20]

Besides Teen Library Advocates, there are other employment opportunities at the Pima County Public Library that allow teens to learn about working in the library and feel a personal connection to their library experience. Teens ages 14 to 17 may be eligible to become a teen summer intern for a five-week term, and teens who are 16 or 17 may apply for the county's Pledge-a-Job program.

Pledge-a-Job is an employment service created by the Pima County Work Force Development Board to boost the number of paid service opportunities available to youth. The service matches older teens with jobs pledged by local employers who are interested in hiring youth for summer, year-round, or full-time and part-time jobs. Jobs pay an average of $7.50 an hour. To be considered, youth must be functioning successfully at the seventh-grade level or above in reading, math, and language skills. Employment counselors prescreen qualified candidates and match them with appropriate employers. The Pima County Public Library is one of the work sites that provides jobs.[21]

Consider this when thinking about the hired teens at the Pima County Public Library: Are the teens who receive monetary payment for their library-oriented efforts less connected and less responsive to the experience than those who volunteer? That does not seem to be the case. Do you remember reading in chapter 2 about Blanche Janecek's teen library participants at the Laboratory School at the University of Chicago in 1957? She discovered that *all* the students who participated in the library benefited similarly from the experience—those who volunteered, those who worked off library fines, and those who were paid. It appears that premise holds true today. Teens who work as shelvers, circulation clerks, or other paying library jobs often fit the mold of teens who become permanently connected to the library through their work experience.

Whether teens get a paycheck, a special outing for a book-buying trip to build the teen library collection, or a celebratory end-of-summer volunteer pizza party, the positive effects on teens from their library involvement far outweigh the importance of any rewards. That doesn't mean rewards are not beneficial, and that they don't enhance the teens' experiences. It just means that the rewards are not the most important end result. (The topic of rewards and their importance is addressed more thoroughly in chapter 10.)

Court-Appointed Community Service Hours: A Boon or a Bust to Youth Participation?

When teens get on the wrong side of the law, and the judge sentences them to hours of community service, where do they look to complete those hours? Often it is the public library that is contacted to see if they can be placed. This is a cooperative element of teen "participation" that requires flexible consideration.

Some libraries have a strict policy in place against using any court-appointed volunteers. However, if your library is open to discussing the issue, you might want to consider the benefits of allowing teens who have been sent by the courts to serve their time in your library. Remember that there have been both pros and cons in taking on court-appointed youth in libraries. Keep in mind the following observations:

One of the most important things adults can do for youth is to provide positive caring role models. Librarians serve in this role when they mentor or "hire" youth. Youth get the benefit of working with a caring adult to develop strong work and social skills that will benefit them as young adults and adults. Job skills are developed such as how to fill out an application, arriving to work on time, developing customer service skills though working with children, youth, the general public, and library staff. They also learn library skills by working in the library.

Teens then share their experiences with their friends, thereby passing along the benefits of their job and the skills they have learned with their friends. Our Teen Advocate program is based on this premise. If we educate teens about library service, they will then tell their friends about what we have to offer.[22]

Gina Macaluso
Coordinator of Youth Services
Pima County Library, Arizona

- Teens who have been sentenced by the courts for such offenses as illegal driving, underage drinking, truancy, breaking curfew, or offenses that do not indicate the possibility of a direct threat to library staff or the public might greatly benefit from being placed at the library. Your library might want to limit acceptance of court-appointed teens depending on the seriousness of their offenses.

- By providing positive interactions and library staff respect for careful completion of tasks, you could be instrumental in turning around a life that was veering in the wrong direction. Talk to the teens who are assigned to you, and when you feel it is appropriate, give them a chance at some tasks that require extra responsibility.

- Many teens who get into trouble do not know about the library and often are not readers. Placing troubled teens who have been assigned to community service by the courts in libraries might trigger an attitude change that could save a life.

- If you are up front with teens who have been sentenced to community service about the fact that you will not tolerate certain behaviors, and that their placement will be in jeopardy if they pursue those behaviors while on site, you will gain their respect and hopefully inspire them not to engage in actions that will cause you to dismiss them as volunteers.

- If you do take on teen court appointees, be sure to give them exit interviews. You might learn a great deal about their personal perspectives and their impressions of the library by doing so. This information will be valuable when you "hire on" subsequent court-appointed teen volunteers and try to make improvements in relating to them. It will also tell you exactly what you are doing right!

- Remember that these are teenagers who deserve a chance. When you advocate for teens in your library, keep in mind that troubled teens are still teens, and perhaps what you can offer them will not only satisfy their court requirements, but encourage them to become library users and supporters.

- Document everything—work hours, behaviors, and comments, both the positive and the negative. You might need to refer back to this information when a teen asks for a reference later on, or to substantiate a problem you might have encountered with a teen. You also want to document the positive and give praise for a job well done!

THE SILVER LINING

The year 1979, when Peggy Sullivan expressed her thoughts about teen participation in libraries in writing, was a time of economic adversity, and she praised teen volunteers as a valuable asset. Hers is a sensible voice from the past that we can take to heart in the present. Her point that teens can make a real difference assisting in and communicating to others the value of libraries is overwhelmingly valid.

Teens can enhance the library's place as a community partner in an assortment of ways, as you have just seen. The examples featured in this chapter are only a sampling of what can be accomplished. Such activities offer a new angle of recognition for libraries that might not have been there before teens were directly involved.

In times of financial exigency, spreading the word about the place of libraries in all communities is priceless. Teens promoting their libraries through their participatory contributions as they develop into the library leaders and supporters of tomorrow are an important part of that picture. You may help your teens to accomplish similar feats by being on the lookout for partnerships, collaborations, and opportunities to offer community outreach. You may help to make them lifelong library supporters while they influence communities near and far in their discovery of what libraries are all about.

A Positive Outlook on Court-Appointed Teen Volunteers: Some Food for Thought

Nancy Devlin, the Head of Children's Services at the Eisenhower Public Library District in Harwood Heights, Illinois, shares her thoughts about court-appointed volunteers:

Our volunteer opportunities are of two kinds: court appointed and regular volunteers. The regulars comprise high school students, local seniors, church folk, and anyone else not assigned by the courts.

We have a structure for handling *all* volunteers that is based on the court-appointed ones, but the regular volunteers work well within that process too. Basically, our rules make little to no distinction between regular or court volunteers. The only way any staff member knows the difference is that the court appointees have a court identification number on their sign-in sheet, something that is required when I send the document back to the court offices.

All calls about volunteers are directed to me, as the person assigned to this duty. I would recommend only one person be in charge of all volunteers, and for that person to set up interviews with them. When I do, I ask generic questions, such as how many hours they have to complete, what is their time frame, what their skills are, if they have any physical restrictions such as allergies or lifting. Then I let them know what kinds of jobs our library can offer. These include tasks like cleaning, straightening, making felt board stories, doing bulletin boards, and creating book lists.

I also let them know two very important things: I don't chase the volunteers; if they say they are going to be here, I expect them to show up. Also, if I haven't heard from them for four weeks straight, I terminate the volunteer process.

While this may seem harsh, I have found that with court appointees this is crucial. The courts require regular participation, and I am bound by my contract with the courts to maintain my end of the bargain. With regular non-court folks, I am much more flexible.

At the end of the interviews, after hearing my requirements, still-willing volunteers are scheduled for their first volunteer date. However, if during and after the interview I get the sense that the volunteer is not committed, or if I get a bad vibe from them, I let them know that I will have to think about whether or not we can handle them at the current time. After 24 hours of thinking it over, if I still get an uncomfortable feeling, I decline to take on that volunteer. In a couple of instances, through ten years of doing this, I have been compelled to make this decision.

Comments teens make about volunteering can be very positive, such as, "Wow, I never realized how busy it was, or how much work you do behind the scenes." Negative comments might come from teen court-appointed volunteers who resent some of the rules, such as no texting or cell phone use while on the clock. Still, despite occasional negative reactions to the rules, with minimal supervision, we have found that the volunteers can do just about anything in our library. All it takes is the right attitude, from both staff and the volunteers. Because our approach is positive, in 95% of the cases so is the response of the volunteers.

One of our court appointees thanked me recently because I never made him feel "less than" others while he was doing his time. This is an important aspect of working with court-appointed workers.

In short, we love *all* of our volunteers, the court-appointed and the regular ones alike. I couldn't imagine our library being without them.[23]

ENDNOTES

1. Peggy A. Sullivan, "Library Cooperation to Serve Youth," in *Libraries and Young Adults: Media, Services, and Librarianship,* ed. JoAnn V. Rogers, 118 (Englewood, CO: Libraries Unlimited, 1979).

2. Mary Moyer, e-mail message to author, August 18, 2008.

3. Mary Moyer, e-mail message to author, August 21, 2008.

4. Mary Moyer, e-mail message to author, September 7, 2008.

5. Mary Moyer, e-mail message to author, December 23, 2008,

6. Mary Moyer, e-mail message to author, January 3, 2009.

7. Tina Moschella, e-mail message to author, September 30, 2008.

8. Denise Saia, e-mail message to author, September 9, 2008.

9. National Clearinghouse on Families & Youth, *Volunteer State Readers Program, Loretto High School, Loretto, Tennessee* (National Youth Leadership Summit/Youth Leadership Guide, n.d.), www.ncfy.com/publications/guide/vsrp.htm (accessed September 20, 2009).

10. Martha Choate, e-mail message to author, October 3, 2008.

11. Sally Roof, e-mail message to author, September 5, 2008.

12. Melanie Limbert-Callahan, e-mail message to author, February 21, 2008.

13. Lu Benke, e-mail messages to author, February 10, 2009 and April 25, 2009.

14. Loudoun County Public Library Branch Library Advisory Boards, *Teen Read-a-Thon Thank You Flyer* (Loudoun Public Library and Loudoun Literacy Council, 2007), loudoun.vhost.vipnet.org/lcpl/teens/docs/TeenRATThanks85x11.pdf (accessed September 20, 2009).

15. Loudoun County Public Library Branch Library Advisory Boards, *Teen Read-a-Thon Package* (Loudoun County Public Library and Loudoun County Animal Shelter, 2008), loudoun. vhost.vipnet.org/lcpl/teens/docs/janfeb08/2008TEENReadaThonPackage.pdf (accessed September 20, 2009).

16. Loudoun County Animal Shelter, "Students Making a Difference," *Gimme Shelter: News from the Loudoun County Animal Shelter* (March 2008), www.loudoun.gov/controls/speerio/resources/Render Content.aspx?data=6e3ebf8fc0084ae5ae7432625ad84d08&tabid=306&fmpath=%2FNews%2FGimme +Shelter+-+the+LCACC+Newsletter%2F2008+Newsletter+Archive (accessed May 8, 2008).

17. Joann Pompa, e-mail message to author, May 10, 2008.

18. Patricia McClary, e-mail message to author, October 10, 2008.

19. Kimberly Paone, e-mail message to author, August 2, 2008.

20. Pima County Public Library Teen Zone, *Teen Library Advocates* (Pima County Public Library, 2009), www.library.pima.gov/teenzone/getinvolved (accessed September 20, 2009).

21. Community Services Employment Training, *Pledge-a-Job* (Pima County Community and Economic Development, 2008), www.pima.gov/CED/CS/OneStop/PledgeAJob.html (accessed September 20, 2009).

22. Gina Macaluso, e-mail message to author, January 17, 2008.

23. Nancy Devlin, e-mail messages to author, February 12, 2009.

8

Youth Participatory Evaluation and Contributing with Adult Groups

When you think of *youth participatory evaluation*, does the perception of asking teens about their reactions to their involvement experiences at the library come to mind? Although it may *sound* as if that is what the phrase means, it is something totally different. Another term you might find to describe the same concept is *youth participatory action research.*[1]

In chapter 10 you will find out how to evaluate the *effectiveness* of teen library participation, including the teens' reactions. However, when you consider "youth participatory evaluation" in this chapter, you are looking at a very different aspect of evaluation. In the context of this section, and in specific reference to library participation, this term means

- involving teens in knowledge development about and for their library,

- incorporating a process through which adults enlist teens in research and evaluation of the whole library and its offerings,

- allowing teenagers to organize their own research and evaluation projects, and

- encouraging teens and adults to work as partners in intergenerational relationships.[2]

When we consider these elements of "youth participatory evaluation," we mean directly asking teens for their input, recommendations, and evaluations about what is currently happening in the library; finding out what they think could be improved in the library; and giving them a say in the decisions that are made regarding the library. This includes such opportunities as serving with adults on library advisory boards, being encouraged to speak out in focus groups, helping to make choices for the library within and beyond the teen spaces, and adding a young adult perspective to adult library or literacy conferences. It means that teenagers are given an opportunity to participate in *active* decision making, share their perspectives with adults, and expect their recommendations to be respected and acted upon.

TEENS SERVING ON ADULT LIBRARY BOARDS

You might recall from chapter 2 that the 1979 White House Conference on Library and Information Services resolved that youth should be appointed as voting members on library boards to give voice to their ideas and perspectives. As a result, the Young Adult Services Division established its ad hoc Youth Participation in Library Decision-Making Committee in 1981, which later became YALSA's Youth Participation Committee. YALSA ultimately established and supported the premise that all-encompassing teen participation would be a priority and has steered its projects and activities to that end. However, in recent years several libraries have begun to recognize the value of the original White House Conference resolution and have added serving on adult library boards to their youth participation opportunities.

City of Mesa Library and Teen Library Board Representation

At the City of Mesa Library in Arizona, a teen representative from the Young Adult Advisory Council (YAAC) has a voting appointment on the adult Library Advisory Board. This "teen rep" position has been effective for about 30 years, in various formats. At first, teens served on the board as nonvoting members. In the mid-1990s, teen representation became more highly regarded and obstacles related to appointment term limits were overcome.

As a result, the teen voice evolved into a teen voice *and* vote on the City of Mesa Library Advisory Board. As a matter of fact, Dana-Jean LaHaie, the first teen appointed as a voting member, stayed on as she entered college and eventually became its chair!

Her successor, Alyssa Ratledge, served as the YAAC teen representative and full-fledged voting Library Advisory Board member for four years, from 2003 to 2007. In an October 2007 *Voice of Youth Advocates* magazine article, Alyssa described her mayoral appointment to the board, her delight in being selected, and how her perception of the library world changed through her experiences: "When I'm in Library Board mode, everything clicks. I debate, I consider, I manage.... And when I drop by to check out books instead of adjust the budget, I see more than just the shelves and racks that I've always known. I see all the details, all the work that other patrons look right past—because I had a hand in putting so much of it into practice."[3]

When you read Alyssa's story, you can see how important giving teens a voice at this level might be. It is a vital but often overlooked element of youth participation in libraries, and it does take a special teen to apply for and accept such an appointment. The teen selected must be eager and able to engage in discussion about adjusting the budget as well as the exciting new floor plan for the teen space. He or she must be articulate and be able to carefully express personal impressions and perspectives while also conveying the thoughts of his or her peers.

Most teen library advisory groups have at least one competent teen who is attracted to the idea of in serving in this capacity. However, if your library wants a teen appointed to its library advisory board, and there is no apt or interested TAG teen available, there are other options. You can "advertise" in your community for a teen to apply for the appointment, or seek recommendations from teachers or other prominent community members. Although the teen selected might not be a TAG member, the teen voice will still be heard on your board.

A Teen Appointment to an Adult Library Advisory Board: Ketchikan Public Library's Example

In most communities, getting a teen appointed to serve as a voting member on a library advisory board requires an application of intent submitted to the mayor and city council. It also often requires a term commitment of two or three years, so consider a teen's ability to complete a term when you support his or her application. A senior in high school might not be a good candidate, because he or she could not commit to serving beyond one year. On the other hand, a freshman or sophomore could.

A good approach for choosing a candidate is for the library teen advisory group to elect one of its members to serve as its representative to the library advisory board. Another option is for the TAG advisor to nominate a teen from the group after finding out which teens might be interested in serving, or an interested teen from the community at large could be recruited to apply for appointment. In any event, once it is decided who will represent teens in your community's library, the usual next step is for the teen to make formal application to the city or town.

Ask your administrators to let you know when a position on the adult library advisory board is open. You might also check your community Web site and the local newspaper to see when library advisory board position applications are being solicited in your city, town, or county. Find out the proper procedures and protocol for an individual to apply, and assist any interested teens in doing so.

The following example from the Ketchikan Public Library illustrates this process well. The letter accompanied Jasmyne Johnson's official "Application for Appointment, City of Ketchikan Boards and Commissions." The application form states: "I am willing to serve as a member of the (Library Advisory) Board and ask that my name be considered by the Mayor and Council for appointment. I am a resident of the City of Ketchikan." The application also requires a personal resume or letter stating interest in the board to which appointment is being sought.

Jasmyne's Letter

As an example your teens might emulate, here is Jasmyne's letter, composed for her application packet to the adult library advisory board:

September 9, 2008

Dear Mayor and City Council Members:

Hello and thank you for your time. My name is Jasmyne Johnson and I am a member of the Teen Advisory Group at the Ketchikan Public Library, as well as an avid library user. I have been elected by the Teen Advisory Group to represent them as a member of the Library Advisory Board. As their representative on the Library Advisory Board I hope to be able to be a liaison, someone both bringing ideas to the table for the Library Advisory Board, and someone who can take what I learn there back to the Teen Advisory Group. I hope I will hear back from you soon.

Sincerely,

Jasmyne Johnson[4]

Jasmyne was appointed to the adult library advisory board and is now reporting to the board about the TAG activities, library programs and services for teens, and encouraging support for a new teen space. She is also available to answer questions and to give input from a teen's perspective, and she is not shy about doing so!

When you try to get the teens from your library represented on the adult library board, keep Jasmyne's and Alyssa's perspectives in mind.

South Brunswick Public Library's Teen Liaisons to the Friends of the Library Board

Although the South Brunswick Public Library does not have a teen or teens serving on its regular adult library board of directors as the libraries do in Mesa or Ketchikan, it does offer an opportunity for teens to be represented on an adult board. The library's Youth Advisory Council (YAC) has three teen liaisons to the Friends of the Library Board, who alternate attendance at the board meetings, and each reports back to the rest of the teens at their YAC meetings about the topics and ideas that were covered. The format recommending the inclusion of teens was proposed in 2007, and afterward the teens voted to have YAC representatives participating as liaisons. So far this system has been very successful, and YAC and the library are anticipating such representation will continue into the future.[5]

Incorporating teens into the Friends of the Library is just another approach to getting teens involved in the adult library board process. If being on the regular adult library advisory board will not work at your library, then consider the Friends of the Library board option. Another idea might be to have representation on both!

Nonvoting Teen Library Advisory Board Members

You might also propose adding a teen to your adult library advisory board as a nonvoting member. Franklin Eneh is the first teen to serve on the board of the Stratford Library Association of the Stratford Library in Connecticut (www.stratfordlibrary.org), and although he may not have a vote, he does have a voice. He is encouraged to express his opinions about library policies and procedures that affect teenagers. He also testified twice at town council meetings about the value of the library to teens and promotes the library's collection and programs to his peers.[6] Although *voting* positions for teens serving on adult boards is the ideal, securing a nonvoting position is a valuable compromise.

The most important reasons for advocating that teens serve on adult library boards are giving teens a say in how the library operates, which prepares them to support and patronize libraries in the future, and providing representation that encourages the adults on the boards to recognize the value of what teens have to contribute.

Collaborative Community Teen Board or Council Participation

In some cases, teens may become involved in community boards or other groups with which the library collaborates. For instance, at the Pima County Public Library in Tucson, there are a number of ways that teens can have a voice, and in which library teens participate. This is accomplished through the Metropolitan Education Commission's Tucson Teen Congress/ Youth Advisory Council (YAC/TTC). It is made up of over 150 students from middle and high school and includes public, private, and charter school students, plus homeschoolers.[7]

The Metropolitan Education Commission's (MEC) Youth Advisory Council (YAC), which started in 1990, was joined in 1994 by another teen group, Tucson Teen Congress (TTC), under the auspices of the commission. With balanced teen representation from throughout the community, YAC/TTC gives youth a strong positive voice. In October 1993 the Tucson mayor, city council, and Pima County Board of Supervisors amended MEC to include two youth representatives. These young adults are chosen by the YAC/TTC to represent youth in MEC's decision-making process.

The goals of the YAC/TTC are to glean youth input on policies and programs designed to enhance educational quality throughout Pima County and to get youth involved in activities that promote leadership, citizenship, and learning opportunities for all Tucson youth. The group also cosponsors a variety of countywide annual events.

The YAC/TTC has ongoing representation on the Mayor's School District Action Task Force; Metropolitan Education Commission, League of United Latin American Citizens Youth Leadership Conference Steering Committee, Tucson/Pima County Commission on Addiction Treatment and Prevention, Tucson Resiliency Initiative, Tucson Police Department Youth Advisory Committee, and Pima County Public Library Youth Sub-Committee. The YAC/TTC is also an important contributor to the city's National League of Cities (NLC) MetLife Foundation Grant to increase youth civic involvement.[8]

As you can see, the library is a facet of this YAC/TTC partnership. The Pima County Public Library Youth Sub-Committee includes 10 teens who work closely with the library on summer reading, including the development of themes, incentives, and publicity, as well as on the creation of other teen library programs.[9] Investigate how *your* library teens might coordinate representation with any similar action groups that exist in your county, city, or town.

TEEN SUMMITS AND OTHER SPECIAL TRAINING EVENTS: EFFECTIVE METHODS TO EDUCATE LIBRARY STAFF AND ENGAGE TEENAGERS

Bear in mind that when it comes to library work and incorporating teen participation, not every library staff member has a teen focus. In many libraries, there might be little or no focus at all, and staff members might need direction on where to start in their community. If your library staff members are wondering where to begin advocating for, involving, and engaging teens, instigating special training opportunities for them might be key. Even if your library is already promoting teen programming and participation, there is always room for improvement and intensified understanding. One of the best ways to achieve these things is to plan special long-term staff and teen training. That's right—*teen* training. The most effective way to educate library staff members about working with teens is to ensure that teens are an integral part of the training mix.

The library examples you will read about next illustrate learning and training opportunities that any library might offer. Before embarking on such projects,

- consider how and why your library or library system might improve the knowledge and expertise of the library staff working directly and indirectly with teens;

- analyze the current state of advocacy, support, and funding for teen services by library supervisors, managers, and administrators;

- survey library staff and teens in your community to discover their impressions and attitudes about library teen services, what improvements they imagine, and what opportunities there might be for teens to contribute and participate;

- think about what grants and other sources of funding might sustain the long- or short-term training you envision;

- investigate which local and long-distance trainers and presenters might be available and able to satisfy your library's instructional needs; and

- reflect on the best settings in which to hold your special training sessions and how the locations you select might afffect the results of the training.

Nassau Library System: Teen Summit One

The Nassau Library System in New York (www.nassaulibrary.org/) provides an excellent example of how to do this right. In 2006 Youth Services Manager Renée McGrath applied for and received a two-year Library Service and Technology Act (LSTA) "Coolness Factor" grant that enabled the library system to focus specifically on "library services to teens." Linda Braun, well-known teen advocate, technology guru, and 2009 YALSA president, was hired as a consultant for the project, which had many components, including one to hold a teen summit with the ultimate goal of bringing teens and librarians together.

The library staff established several objectives to meet this goal. The first, to foster library youth participation, tied in directly with introducing the "40 Developmental Assets"®, described by the Search Institute® (www.search-institute.org/assets) as "common sense, positive experiences and qualities that help influence choices young people make and help them become caring, responsible adults." Other objectives were to specifically examine teen experiences at the Nassau County public libraries and to discern reactions and ideas for improvement. In conjunction with all of this, a final objective was to provide teens and librarians with the necessary skills to effectively launch the determined changes.

A preliminary workshop held at the Nassau County Library System was facilitated by a Search Institute® trainer and the young adult librarians. The workshop set out to address the 40 Developmental Assets®, making the point that the public library can be instrumental in the healthy development of teens through activities that promote constructive teen outlooks and enhance self-esteem. Group activities to facilitate discussion and networking were the catalysts that reinforced the value of these assets. The ensuing discussions centered on advocating for teens within the family and in the community, empowering teens through purposeful activities, providing teens with boundaries and a set of behavioral expectations, giving teens opportunities for developing positive life values, and helping teens to improve and expand social competencies and positive identities.

Teen Summit was held at the Long Island Children's Museum on a Monday in August when the museum was closed to the public and school was not yet in session. The centrally located museum provided an enjoyable backdrop to the day for the 53 participating teens, 5 staff members from the museum, and the assistant young adult coordinator of the New York Public Library. Staff from 19 libraries in the Nassau County System also attended, mostly youth services librarians, and two library directors. (See figure 8.1.)

Many of the youth services librarians present said that their teens were enthused about the day and talked about it a long while afterward. They also reported that teen–librarian relationships were strengthened as a result of their participation.

A survey conducted at the end of the two-year grant revealed that Teen Summit was very successful for both the librarians and the teen participants. As a result of the helpful training received, eight libraries started a teen advisory group, six libraries created a separate teen space, and three libraries received a budget increase for YA materials and programming. Librarians made a variety of comments:

- "The 40 Developmental Assets® information has helped me advocate with more confidence, and we now have a blog from which I get feedback from several teens."

- "These workshops have provided me with insights into teen psychology; kept me up to date with teen trends and influences; and offered a framework within which to shape the teen program over the next couple of years."

- "My awareness of the importance of teen input and the developmental stages when planning library activities has been reinforced."

- "I am starting a graphic novel club based on the suggestion of a teen who attended the Teen Summit."

- "The grant made my director more aware of the importance of YA services. I have been given more money for books and programs."

Nassau Library System: Teen Summit Two

The following year, in 2007, Teen Summit Two was offered. Because there was strong demand to build upon accomplishments from the year before, Teen Summit Two brought together youth services librarians and 48 teenagers from the member libraries. The goals were to boost teen attendance at programs and to teach YA librarians how to improve and increase interactions with teens. To accomplish these goals, the second summit, like the first, was designed to bring together the librarians and a team of teens from their respective communities.

Teen Summit 2006

What Teens Say They Want and Need in Nassau County Public Libraries

Nassau Library System
900 Jerusalem Ave.
Uniondale, N.Y. 11553
Phone: (516) 292-8920
Fax: (516) 481-4777
www.nassaulibrary.org

We'd like to thank the following sponsors for their generous donations

Funded in part by federal Library Services and Technology Act funds, awarded to The NY State Library by the federal Institute of Museum and Library Services.

40 Developmental Assets

One focus of the Teen Summit was the 40 Developmental Assets; a framework for successful youth development created by the Search-Institute.

By focusing on these assets, teens and librarians were able to consider what is required from their community and from institutions within their community in order to help teens grow up successfully. The assets provided Summit participants with a jumping off point for their discussions.

Areas the assets focus on include:

- Support for teens within the family and the community.
- Empowering teens by giving them opportunities to participate in real-world activities.
- Providing teens with boundaries and a set of behavioral expectations.
- Giving teens opportunities for developing positive life values.
- Helping teens develop social competencies.
- Working with teens to help them gain a positive identity.

The Teen Summit was an opportunity for teens to gain developmental assets. The library programs and services developed as a result of the Summit will continue to help teens in this way.

For more information on the 40 Developmental Assets visit the Search Institute at: http://www.search-institute.org

Figure 8.1. Nassau County Library Teen Summit Brochure

Summit Ideas

Services

Libraries should:

- Sponsor teen advisory groups so that teens can provide input on programs and services
- Have later hours
- Provide more volunteer opportunities
- Offer large selections of books for boys
- Offer more new books
- Keep better track when new books come out in a particular series
- Offer reading incentives
- Have better ways for teens to request materials
- Make technology available for checkout including laptops and MP3 devices
- Offer virtual service components including chat, blogs, etc.
- Keep their web site up-to-date
- Have tutors available to work with teens
- Give free replacement library cards
- Make easy renewal procedures
- Have teen staff visit schools so teens get to know them
- Foster cooperation between school and public librarians
- Have clear signage so teens can easily find materials
- Hire fun teen staff

Summit Ideas

Programs

Teens help plan and implement:

- Field Trips
- Political discussion groups
- Current events based discussions
- Fashion events
- Arts discussions and craft-making
- Author visits
- Teen cafe and open mike nights
- Movies
- Intergenerational programs— teens reading to younger children
- Murder mystery programs
- Presentations on topics of interest to contemporary teens
- Book discussion groups and clubs
- Concerts

Space

Library teen space should:

- Have comfortable furniture – including couches
- Include food courts, coffee corner, etc.
- Have many computers
- Be sound-proofed
- Include listening stations
- Include a big-screen TV and viewing areas
- Provide gaming equipment and game play
- Have study-areas and social areas
- Be a place to socialize and hang out

Figure 8.1. Nassau County Library Teen Summit Brochure (Cont.)

Teen Summit Overview

In August 2006 the Nassau Library System hosted a Teen Summit. The Summit gave teens and librarians an opportunity to meet together and talk about what teens are looking for in and from libraries in Nassau County.

Over 50 teens, from all over the county, participated in the event. The teens had many ideas about how libraries could support and serve them. You can learn about them in this brochure.

Their ideas are organized by content areas. You can read about what they want in relation to library programs, space, and services.

To learn more about the Summit contact the Nassau Library System's Youth Services Manager, Renee McGrath at rmcrath@nassaulibrary.org

This summit gave teens and their local librarians a forum through which to enhance their relationships, discuss how library usage by teens could be increased, learn how to create a more welcoming library environment for teens, and reinforce the library as a place to foster positive youth development. The creation of action plans was the targeted method for implementing these changes and improvements.

For the second summit, the library system again hired a facilitator from the Search Institute®, and part of the day was devoted to reinforcing the 40 Developmental Assets® through enjoyable activities. This time the event was held at the Lynbrook Public Library, a member library with a meeting room that could accommodate a large audience of teens and librarians and provide space for workshop activities.

There were advantages and disadvantages to using the public library setting. Planning was easier, but the library was a bit more confined and restrictive. The teens still appreciated a serious day filled with relevant activities and a chance to share their views in a library setting. On the other hand, the museum setting of the first summit had offered the teens an opportunity to walk around, relax, and recharge their energy while exploring the exhibits. Having the event at the museum had also enhanced its relationship with the library. Despite these caveats about the meeting location, Teen Summit Two was very successful.

A big reason for this success was the variety and focus of sessions offered. One session was directly targeted at library directors to help them understand the needs of teens. Another, called "Everyone Serves Youth," was aimed at all library staff, those who work directly with teens and those who don't. Other sessions focused on particular issues, such as social networking, serving gay/lesbian/bisexual/transgender/questioning youth, and youth participation in libraries.

The second summit's outcomes were impressive. Some libraries started new programs, such as a Winter Reading Program. Seven young adult librarians started blogs for teens in their communities, and seven also started teen advisory boards. Five libraries created teen spaces. One library received a budget increase for YA materials and programming, and two others saw an increase for YA materials. Three libraries more than doubled the amount of YA programming offered. As the impact of the Teen Summits took hold, many more teen spaces were completed, increased circulation and programming were noted, and additional teen services staff members were added.[10]

"Year of the Teen" at Central Massachusetts Regional Library System

When Maureen Ambrosino started her job as Youth Services Consultant at the Central Massachusetts Regional Library System (CMRLS) in 2005, she decided to apply for a grant to promote understanding of and participation by teens in the system's libraries. One of the first things she did was go "on the road" to visit libraries and meet the librarians with whom she would be collaborating.

Maureen came to Massachusetts after working at the Houston Public Library in Texas, where the 40 Developmental Assets® and youth participation were the foundation of programming. As a matter of fact, because of its outstanding focus on youth involvement, Houston Public Library's "After School Programs Provide Reading Enrichment" (ASPIRE) program was selected as one of the "top 50" teen programs nationwide in the 2000 edition of ALA's *Excellence in Library Services to Young Adults*, with Maureen serving as an ASPIRE facilitator. Later, at Fort Bend County Libraries, where Maureen worked from 2000 to 2005, a DeWitt Wallace/Reader's Digest Foundation grant to build youth participation was awarded. Obviously, Maureen came to the CMRLS as an expert on planning and promoting teen involvement in libraries.

When Maureen began visiting librarians in the CMRLS (www.cmrls.org/), she inquired about what teen programming was being done. She discovered that many libraries were not doing *any* teen programming and did not have teen advisory boards; some had few teens using their libraries. The librarians told Maureen that they didn't know what to do with teens, how to manage problematic behavior, or how to get teens to use their libraries. Maureen was concerned when she realized that teen services and participation sorely needed a boost in her new library system. But how would she begin to remedy the situation?

She found the answer when the Massachusetts Board of Library Commissioners (MBLC) announced its upcoming Library Services and Technology Act (LSTA) grant awards. Maureen applied for a grant she called "Year of the Teen" so that she could offer training to and increase knowledge of librarians working with this age group. Through the grant funding, she was able to bring in experts in the field like Patrick Jones, Linda Braun, and others, who covered a wide range of important topics, including adolescent development, library teen advisory groups, teen library collections, gaming, technology, teen spaces, and long-range planning.

Coincidentally, during the 2006 grant round, the MBLC also began offering a "mini grant" program called "Serving Tweens and Teens" (mblc.state.ma.us/grants/lsta/opportunities/targeted_grants/09_tweens_teens.pdf). Grant recipients under this program receive up to $20,000 to build and/or enhance a teen advisory board, do a limited redesign of their teen space, and develop teen programs and collections. A few libraries in Maureen's region qualified for the program, although many more did not. The Year of the Teen sessions provided the skills and knowledge those libraries needed to apply for and receive the grants, which are helping to raise the profile of teen services in the region and continue today.

The Year of the Teen project made a tremendous difference for libraries in central Massachusetts and beyond. Attendance was good at the workshops, and participants were very happy with their training. As a matter of fact, there is even a Year of the Teen blog where like-minded librarians can correspond.

I happened to be the trainer who provided the workshop session on teen advisory boards for Year of the Teen, and Maureen was pleased to inform me that those libraries without a TAB who responded to the post-program survey had ultimately added TABs during the 2008–2009 school year. The addition of TABs demonstrated a clear dedication to the inclusion of youth participation in their services.

As Year of the Teen was coming to a close, Maureen realized that she had quite a bit of money left due to out-of-town speaker costs being much less than projected. After a budget revision, she was able to supplement shared gaming equipment to circulate among the libraries. The extra grant funds allowed her to buy more consoles, accessories, and games, which in turn allowed more of the CMRLS libraries to offer programming. She also purchased six handheld video game units with accompanying games, to help with crowd control while teens wait their turn for the console-based games. The system's librarians are absolutely delighted with the new equipment, as gaming has quickly become a popular and rewarding teen program offering.

Maureen says that one noteworthy outcome of the Year of the Teen project has been a huge increase in the number of libraries offering teen summer reading programs. In 2006 only 8 libraries offered them, but after the Year of the Teen, 23 libraries did. Maureen attributes this improvement directly to increased awareness of effective teen services brought to light by Year of the Teen training.

Year of the Teen's last scheduled workshop was an important one on long-range planning. Susan Babb gave careful instruction on developing a teen-specific plan that could be incorporated into individual library plans. Although teens were not directly involved in these training sessions, their related "youth participatory evaluation" contributions kicked in when library staff members returned to their home libraries. Because teen input is paramount for incorporating long-range plans in teen services, along with staff, director, and trustee input, Year of the Teen participants repeated the training exercises with all of these stakeholders at their libraries.

Although the entire Year of the Teen project was set to end in December 2007, funds still remained, and Maureen was able to add two additional workshops in the spring of 2008. The first was a full-day workshop in April called "Make Way for Teens," presented by Kimberly Bolan, a nationally recognized consultant on library space planning for youth. The workshop encompassed teen participation, collection development, use of a teen space, furnishings and materials, and vendors. To build enthusiasm, a $500 gift certificate to Demco Library Interiors was supplied as a teen space raffle prize, along with smaller gift cards and giveaway items. Kim's goal was to encourage library directors, trustees, or others who control funding to attend with their teen or youth services librarians. Since many teen librarians attend workshops, get excited about making changes, then return to their libraries to be told that there is no money to implement changes, buy-in from administrators is essential. By having librarians and administrators attend together, they return to their libraries energized and ready to start new projects. You will want to keep this important concept in mind if you are attending similar special training for your library.

The final Year of the Teen event was held in May, during which authors Jack Martin and James Murdock presented a half-day workshop, "Serving Gay, Lesbian, Bisexual, Trans-gendered, and Questioning Teens." Massachusetts is one of the few states permitting gay couples to marry, so this topic affects teens across the state. However, before Year of the Teen, many libraries did not purchase materials for or understand the needs of gay teens. Jack and James made an incredible impact with their supportive presentation and provided an extensive list of books for collection development.

Looking back, and ahead, Maureen says:

> Year of the Teen has been such a rewarding experience—for the Region, the librarians, and the teens themselves. On the Regional level, it has helped us greatly enhance our services to teen librarians and show them that we think teens are important to the future of libraries. It has also helped us provide them with equipment that many of them could not afford to buy on their own. Teen librarians benefitted by learning how to attract teens to their libraries, how to make their libraries inviting and welcoming, and how to make their collections and services reflect the input of their teens.
>
> A full 80% of the respondents to the post-program survey report that more teens are using their libraries and that teenage behavior has improved. Teens themselves have benefitted by having library staff members who understand them, want to have them in their buildings, and who are open to new ideas. Teenagers now have a voice in many Central Massachusetts libraries, and have books and other materials that meet their needs. However, the most dramatic Year of the Teen outcomes are the increased number of libraries with teen advisory boards, and the number of librarians who feel more comfortable and effective working with teens.[11]

Ocean County Library's TAB Forums

Libraries with already-established teen advisory boards and dedicated administrative support may still greatly benefit from holding training and discussion sessions to improve the way things are working and to add new ideas. One such library is the Ocean County Library System (theoceancountylibrary.org), which has its headquarters branch in Toms River, New Jersey, and has 21 branches with 12 teen advisory boards (TABs). The library TAB members earn volunteer hours for their participation and a TAB T-shirt. They are involved in a great variety of activities, from planning and running programs for teens, seniors, and children, to providing collection advice, to fund-raising, and much more.

To keep the teens engaged, teach them how to be better volunteers, and help adults learn what the teens perceive about teen services at the library system, an annual TAB Forum brings together TAB members from all the TABs in the county. The teens experience a day filled with teambuilding, sharing ideas, brainstorming, and spirit. In past years the TAB Forum attendees voted on what teen authors to host for the annual Bookfest; created a banner of support for teens at the libraries of Hancock County, Mississippi, after Hurricane Katrina; brainstormed ideas for improved teen library services in their library; and voted on a new TAB T-shirt logo (see figure 8.2).

**Figure 8.2. Cool-looking Logo, a Surefire Way to Draw Teen Attention.
Design by Jeff Bittner, Ocean County Library Printing and Graphics Department**

When planning for the fall 2008 TAB Forum started in the spring, the library administrators were immediately confronted with a dilemma: The Friends of the Library Fall Forum was inadvertently scheduled on the same day! As discussions ensued about how to share the time and meeting room space at the headquarters branch, it occurred to the administrative planners that if you can't beat them, join them! Rather than struggling to find additional meeting space, they decided to bring these two groups of library advocates together. After all, the TABs and Friends groups in the branch libraries did interact on occasion, and the Friends had supported TABs by providing funds for special programs, gaming equipment, and more. The opportunity for these groups to develop a stronger connection was imminent, and the timing was right.

It was determined that, at the forum, each group would meet and conduct business separately, but they would also join together for several activities. The goal was to have both groups learn more about each other, deepen understanding between adults and teens, and brainstorm how the groups could better serve their library branches separately and together.

The planners came up with three activities. The first took place before the forum, when TAB members made posters thanking the branch Friends for their support of the library system, its teen activities, and the TABs. The creative and fun posters were brought to the TAB Forum for display, and afterward the Friends groups requested that the posters be displayed in their branches and showcased at Friends meetings. (See figure 8.3.)

Don't miss out on

TAB Forum 2008

Celebrate Teen Read Week and join TAB members from all over OCL for team building, gaming, and brainstorming.

Saturday, October 18
10:30 am to 3:00 pm

Toms River Branch of OCL
(Meet in the Teen Zone)

Special guest Patricia Kingman
will take you for a journey into the world of the unknown and unexplained.

Call your local YA Librarian to RSVP!
Carpooling options available.
Missing Tab Forum 2008 would BITE!

FREE pizza
and drinks!

Figure 8.3. TAB Forum Flyer. Design by Pham Condello, Ocean County Teen Services Department

The second activity was "Games Old and New," which was an hour-long session allowing adults and teens the opportunity to play timeless games of the past, such as checkers, dominoes, and jacks, and then vice versa, with teens showing adults their modern video games like Wii and Guitar Hero. What another great example of gaming as intergenerational interaction!

The last activity was a brainstorming session on how the groups could better work together. Led by a proficient facilitator with a flip chart, the group, numbering 70-plus young and older people, brainstormed ideas such as starting a column in the Friends newsletter featuring TAB activities; working cooperatively on large library system events; holding periodic joint meetings; having TAB members assist with the Friends annual Book Sale and earning a percentage of profits; creating lasting and visible legacy projects in each branch, such as a mural, photo exhibit, or physical improvement; collaborating on the library Homebound Services program; and many more. At the conclusion of the brainstorming session, the TAB teens and Friends from each individual library branch put their heads together to discuss even more concrete plans for partnerships.

This TAB Forum was a complete success. Each group emerged with a better understanding of how it supports the library and also felt energized and poised to begin working with the other group. Even greater was the follow-up a week later, when the TAB teens at the Berkeley Branch Library met with the Berkeley Friends of the Library group to demonstrate their activities. In a meaningful expression of camaraderie, one of the senior TAB members, who was 18 and was ageing out of TAB, joined the Berkeley Friends group and was voted in as the group secretary. Everyone then realized that building a bridge between the library TABs and the Friends groups is one path to maintaining lifelong library advocates. This is proving to be a very good thing for members of both groups, and for the whole library system.[12]

PROJECTING TEEN VOICES THROUGH THE PROFESSIONAL LIBRARY ASSOCIATIONS THAT ULTIMATELY SERVE AND SUPPORT THEM

The reason many of our professional associations exist is because *teens exist*. We join and become involved because we want to improve library services for teens and share the expertise we have developed to encourage and inspire others to successfully work with teens in their libraries. We want to be sure that teens have a voice and an active role in what their libraries do and for what they stand.

National Education Association (NEA)

The National Education Association (www.nea.org), which was founded in 1857 to "elevate the character and advance the interests of the profession of teaching, and to promote the cause of education in the United States," also encourages teen participation. It has readily supported and encouraged the educational role of both school and public libraries. As mentioned in chapter 2, the root of this connection was the NEA's acceptance in 1896 of Melvil Dewey's recommendation that the organization start a Library Department in support and promotion of libraries as vital facets of the educational process. Public libraries were added to school libraries in various locations around the nation, and in 1916 school libraries were standardized.[13]

In 1998 the NEA declared its sponsorship for the first annual "Read Across America Day," held on March 2, Dr. Seuss's birthday, during which five million youth and one million adults shared the joy of books and reading in events that stretched across the nation. One of the many partners for this event was and still is the American Library Association.[14]

As I look back at the first "Read Across America Day" events held at the City of Mesa Library in Arizona, I recall an exciting time. Adults and teenagers from our community donned tall "Cat in the Hat" red-striped hats and volunteered to spend time reading to children during the day. It was exhilarating to see the response of the teens in particular as they read and provided an example for other youths to follow.

If you are looking for a catalyst to get teens active and involved at your library, encourage them to take part in "Read Across America Day." Besides reading to younger children, as teens did in the example from the Delsea Regional High School and the Franklinville Public Library's cooperative effort (see chapter 7), the NEA suggests various other ways teens may participate, including running poetry slams, readers theatre' events, and book fairs (www.nea.org/home/ns/13023.htm).[15]

National Council of Teachers of English (NCTE)

Another significant professional association that encourages youth participation is the National Council of Teachers of English (www.ncte.org), which was founded in 1911 to improve the teaching and learning of English and the language arts at all levels of education. The organization still provides learning and growth opportunities for those in the profession, channels for partnerships, and the discussion of issues pertaining to the teaching of English. Members comprise teachers and supervisors in all levels of English education, college and university faculty members and students, and professionals in related fields.

One of those related fields is librarianship; NCTE even had a Library Section from 1913 to 1919. Through the years the group has acknowledged the importance of libraries in encouraging teens in their exploration and appreciation of English literature and has partnered with other prominent groups to do so. For example, on the NCTE Web site there are links to the International Reading Association's "Read-Write-Think" summer literacy-enhancing activities (www.readwritethink.org/beyondtheclassroom/summer/grades6_8/). These activities, such as writing and publishing reviews, making podcasts and videos about books, and creating original comics and graphic novels, require much teen thought and involvement and could be a spark for igniting teen participatory ideas in libraries.

Assembly on Literature for Adolescents (ALAN)

In 1973 the Assembly on Literature for Adolescents of NCTE (ALAN) was formed (www.alan-ya.org). Membership in ALAN is an associated but separate organization from NCTE and comprises teachers, authors, librarians, publishers, teacher-educators, their students, and others who have particular interest in young adult literature. The aim of ALAN is to promote knowledge, use, and appreciation of young adult literature as a unique and important body of work. Any librarian looking for resources to learn more about and to promote books with teens would do well to investigate ALAN.

In addition to the various awards and opportunities ALAN offers in its support of adolescent literature, the association has its own special ALAN Award, which honors an outstanding contribution to YA literature each year. ALAN also publishes a journal called *The ALAN Review*, which contains articles about all aspects of adolescent literature, including book reviews, author interviews, how to teach YA literature effectively, dealing with challenges and controversy, and partnering with libraries. "The Library Connection" column, for which I am the editor, offers ideas and inspiration for promoting books and reading through libraries and getting teens involved in them.

Every year in November, ALAN sponsors the two-day ALAN Workshop in conjunction with the NCTE annual conference. This workshop features author talks, panel presentations, breakout sessions, and special events that focus on building knowledge and understanding of YA literature and its positive uses for an audience of around 500 people.

Teenagers have played participatory roles in ALAN Workshop presentations. For example, in 2005 teens from the Carnegie Library of Pittsburgh (www.clpgh.org) performed an excerpt of Paul Fleischman's play *Zap* when the workshop was held in their city. The teen participants, who had a special interest in the performing arts, were recruited from the Carnegie Library and were led by a teen director. Their excellent performance earned a standing ovation from the all-adult ALAN audience.

At the ALAN Workshop in 2007, New York City's popular teen "spoken word" group, Urban Word (www.urbanwordnyc.org/uwnyc), gave a breathtaking demonstration of their remarkable techniques for sharing original poetry. They too received a standing ovation. In this case, the teen poetry group was not directly library related. However, the presentation did foster teen involvement and exemplified and encouraged teen spoken word activities in libraries and schools as an exciting prospect where there might be teen interest.

International Reading Association (IRA)

The International Reading Association (IRA) was founded in 1956 as a nonprofit professional organization for those involved in teaching reading to all ages of learners (www.reading.org). Although the group mainly consists of reading teachers, it is highly supportive of libraries and their role in getting teens connected with books.

IRA encourages this in a variety of ways. Overall, the organization advances adolescent literacy, reading, and writing. It has a support statement advocating for school libraries, which insists on increased funding and providing an adequate number of books for each student. It also encourages student participation in classroom library development, management, and organization. Furthermore, IRA encourages students to use their school libraries to evaluate literature and to lead and engage in book discussions.

Since 1987 IRA has sponsored a Young Adult Choices annual booklist (www.reading.org/ Resources/Booklists/YoungAdultsChoices.aspx), which reflects titles selected as the best of the year by 4,500 participating middle and senior high school book reviewers, organized in teams, from all parts of the United States. The goals of the list are to provide an opportunity for young adults to voice their opinions about the books published for their age group; to develop a list of titles other teens will enjoy reading; and to assist teachers, librarians, parents, and others in finding books that will encourage teens to read more.

In addition, IRA offers its Read-Write-Think ideas for summer activities, some for ages 11–14 and others for ages 14–18. These require action and involvement and might serve as a basis for creating library teen participation activities. As mentioned in the section on the NCTE, Read-Write-Think is promoted as a partnership with that organization.

Colorado Teen Literature Conference

Every April a special event takes place in Denver—the Colorado Teen Literature Conference. It is a collaborative venture among Metropolitan State College of Denver, School of Letters, Arts, and Sciences (www.mscd.edu); University of Colorado Denver, School of Education and Human Development (www.cudenver.edu/Pages/home.aspx); Colorado Language Arts Society (www.clas.us); and Colorado Young Adult Advocates in Libraries or C'YAAL (www.cyaal.org).

In 2008 the conference celebrated its twentieth anniversary, with 425 teachers, librarians, parents, and teens in attendance.[16] At the conference, publishers set up small booths with samples of their products. Each year there are also plenty of authors on hand, who give keynote and lunchtime speeches, conduct workshops, and answer questions during a teen-conducted author panel. Other presenters share information about exciting teen programming and activities, such as holding successful poetry slams, developing effective booktalks, creating online book videos, and more.

The best part of the conference is the great number of teens who are part of the mix. The teens learn about exciting programs that might work at their libraries and hear popular authors share details about their books and writing. Some of the teens get to serve on the afternoon author panels. Those teens prepare questions to which the authors respond.

Holding such a state or local conference brings local young adult literature fans together, allowing teens to participate with adults as they explore not only books but also methods for library programming that will attract fellow teens. You might want to explore the possibility of starting such a conference in your area, perhaps through the teen services division of your state library association. You might also investigate the possibility of doing such a program as a joint effort with another organization that cares about teens, books, reading, and youth participation, such as the English Education Department at a local university.

The Colorado Teen Literature Conference (www.aclin.org/~cyaal/yalc) demonstrates that adults respect and appreciate YA literature and that they know the importance of getting teens to read because they *want to*, not just because they have to; encourages teens to support and promote libraries in their schools and communities; and empowers teens to participate side by side in a professional activity with adults. (See figure 8.4, pp. 174–75.)

YALSA Promotes Teen Participation

The Young Adult Library Services Association (YALSA) of the American Library Association (ALA) has long been a proponent of teen participation in libraries. If you recall from chapter 2, the organization, first as the Young Adult Service Division (YASD) and now as YALSA, has been and still is instrumental in promoting the cause of youth services in libraries extending from the early years of young adult services to the present. The concept of youth participation has been an important part of that picture. YALSA created pivotal publications in the 1980s and 1990s that helped to increase teen participation in both school and public libraries, and it has since created policies and guidelines that support the variety of dimensions of teen involvement in libraries today.

An Interesting Reader Society (IRS) Teen Viewpoint from the 2008 Colorado Teen Literature Conference

The Colorado Teen Literature Conference was a great place to meet and talk with like minded book fans. It also provided a good opportunity to get to know the fellow members of your library group better.

The conference started off very well with an excellent welcoming speech by author Alane Ferguson and tasty breakfast snacks. We then were given the option to choose any session we wished to attend. The selection of sessions was very broad and included everything from technology, to library programs, to writing.

For my first session, I went to a presentation on creating fun teen programs because it is part of my job on the IRS teen library board to come up with new programs to host. For my second session, I chose one about different ways to read more books by using technology.

After the sessions, we attended lunch. The food was decent, but the best part was getting to walk around and see the publishers and their books. At the end of lunch we were given a very humorous speech by author Gail Giles.

Everybody then went to listen to the authors' panel, my favorite part of the day. Authors Alane Ferguson, Gail Giles, Linda Collison, Hilari Bell, Donita Paul, and Laura Resau answered teens' questions. The extemporaneous responses were funny and honest.

This ended a very full and exciting Colorado Teen Literature Conference. It allowed the kids of Colorado who have their hands on a book more often than their cell phones to converge in one spot to celebrate our love of books. I am already looking forward to next year.[17]

Tyler Rudolph
IRS Member
Poudre River Public Library District
Fort Collins, Colorado

One of those documents is YALSA's National Youth Participation Guidelines (www.ala.org/ala/mgrps/divs/yalsa/aboutyalsab/nationalyouth.cfm), which define effective youth participation as, "Involvement of young adults, ages 12 through 18, in responsible action and significant services for their peers and the community." In this regard, YALSA further states that as an organization, it "recognizes the need for a framework to facilitate the process of having young adults . . . participate in any American Library Association activities at the national level."[18]

Poudre River Public Library District
IRS (Interesting Reader Society)
Colorado Teen Literature Conference
Denver, CO
Saturday, April 4, 2009
6:45 a.m.—6:00 p.m.

Permission Form

In order to participate in this off-site library activity, IRS teens and parents/guardians must read this form, complete the permission slip, and return it to one of the Teen Librarians at either Main Library or Harmony Library by March 1, 2009.

Parent and Teen Information

The Colorado Teen Literature Conference will be held from 8:00 a.m. to 4:30 p.m. on the Auraria Campus at the joint-use Tivoli Student Union of the Community College of Denver, Metropolitan State College of Denver, and University of Colorado at Denver.

The number of IRS teens who are able to attend this event is limited to 10. Priority will be given to active members before and/or since April 2008. If there are more than 10, names will be selected via a drawing. Teens who still wish to go but whose names are not on the final list may request to be on a waiting list in case last-minute emergency openings occur. To be on the "on-call" list, you must turn in a permission form.

Teens *MUST* meet *PROMPTLY* in front of the Main Library at 201 Peterson Street no later than 6:45 a.m. for a 6:50 a.m. departure.

Return time to the Main Library is approximately 6:00 p.m. (Teens may call ahead of time via cell phone to let parents know exact pickup time.)

Parents must arrange transportation to and from the Main Library for their own sons and daughters.

Registration ($30) will be provided by the Friends of the Library.

Transportation will be provided by the Poudre River Public Library District and the Friends of the Library.

Lunch will be provided with registration.

No teen will be allowed to leave the group or the conference site during the activity hours.

Teens must agree to follow the directions of library staff chaperones.

Teens are expected to be on their best behavior during travel and during the event.

Teens will *only* be allowed to participate if a *completed permission slip* and *a completed conference registration form* are turned in by March 1.

Sue-Ellen Jones and Diane Tuccillo will be driving a designated van to and from the event and will be the chaperones in charge.

Sue-Ellen's cell phone number in case of emergencies is (970) 222-1234). Diane's is (970) 412-3421.

Poudre River Public Library District will make reasonable accommodations for access to its services, programs, and activities and will make special communications arrangements for persons with disabilities. Please call (970) 221-6380 for assistance.

**Figure 8.4. Poudre River Public Library District CO
Teen Literature Conference Permission Form**

Poudre River Public Library District
Parent/Guardian and Teen Release Statement

As parent/legal guardian of (**teen name**) _____, I have reviewed the information about the **Poudre River Public Library District's off-site trip with the IRS (Interesting Reader Society) to the Colorado Teen Literature Conference** at the Tivoli Student Union of the Auraria Campus in Denver, and give permission for my son/daughter to travel to and be involved in this daylong event.

I/We understand that teens attending this event must be dropped off at the Main Library's front entrance, 201 Peterson Street, at 6:45 a.m. on Saturday, April 4, 2009 and will be picked up at the Main Library's front entrance at approximately 6:00 p.m. I/We have reviewed the attached information about this activity and have discussed it with my/our teen. I/We are also submitting a completed and signed conference registration form (minus the $30 fee, which will be funded by the Friends of the Library).

I/We authorize any emergency medical treatment as deemed necessary.

I/We agree to make no claims against the **Poudre River Public Library District**. I/We understand that all reasonable safety precautions will be taken at all times by the **Poudre River Public Library District** chaperones of the IRS trip to and during participation in the **Colorado Teen Literature Conference**. I/We agree not to hold the **Poudre River Public Library District**, its trustees, chaperones, employees, or volunteer staff liable for damages, losses, or injuries incurred by the subject of this form, including any claims for negligence.

Parent Guardian/Signature(s)_____ Date _____

IRS Member's Signature _____ Date _____

Person to call in case of emergency_____ Telephone Number _____

Alternate emergency contact _____ Telephone Number _____

Medical Insurance PolicyNumber_____

Medical Insurance Policy Company_____

****

You **do not have to sign** the following Photo Release in order to attend the Activity.

Photo Release: I hereby consent that photographs of my teen taken at the **Colorado Teen Literature Conference** may be used by the **Poudre River Public Library District** in library publicity, newspaper articles, and audiovisual presentations; furthermore, I hereby consent that such photographs and the plates from which they are made shall be their property, and they shall have the right to duplicate, reproduce, and make other uses of such photographs and plates as they may desire free and clear of any claims whatsoever on my part.

Parent/Guardian Signature _____ Date _____

**Figure 8.4. Poudre River Public Library District CO
Teen Literature Conference Permission Form (*Cont.*)**

Various efforts to achieve these goals have been put into gear on a number of levels. YALSA has developed the nationwide Teens' Top Ten/YA Galley Project, for which teen participants from across the United States read extensively to determine the "top ten" teen book choices each year. The association invites teenagers to attend the ALA Midwinter and Annual Conferences to speak out about their impressions of each year's Best Books for Young Adults nominees. Whenever applicable, teens are also asked to serve as speakers at ALA conferences for special programs or panel presentations. Teen Read Week and Teen Tech Week offer additional opportunities for teens to be involved. If you are interested in finding out more, check out the YALSA Web page (www.ala.org/yalsa) to further explore these and other teen participation ideas.

YALSA Teens' Top Ten/YA Galley Project

In 1999 Teens' Top Ten/YA Galley Project was born as a pilot project of YALSA, designed to allow teens to both nominate and vote for their top 10 favorite books each year. The seed for the idea was planted in 1988, when members of Cathi Dunn MacRae's Young Adult Advisory Board (YAAB) at Enoch Pratt Free Library in Baltimore created an original "Youth-to-Youth" booklist during an all-day conference with teens from several Pratt branches, then offered it to YALSA's Youth Participation Committee as a model for a nationwide teen-produced list.[19] Over the last decade, Teens' Top Ten/YA Galley has become an official YALSA teen participatory project that has grown and evolved. In 2003, the project's first official year, 1,700 teens nationwide took part in online voting for their "top ten" favorite books during Teen Read Week. In 2008 the number of votes increased to over 8,000.[20] In 2009, to encourage an even higher turnout, the timeline was revised to allow teens to vote online for a lengthier period during the fall, with the final "top ten" titles *revealed* (rather than voted for) during Teen Read Week. This time more than 11,000 teens voted!

How does Teens' Top Ten work? Every two years, librarians or others who work with teens in school and public libraries across the country nominate their teen reading groups for potential appointment for YA Galley. From those nominated, 15 groups are appointed based on criteria that prove the teen members are capable of reading, discussing, evaluating, and nominating books for their peers from the books published the previous year through March of the year in which the books will be considered for Teens' Top Ten. For instance, books published in 2009 (eliminating those already nominated for the 2009 list) through March 2010 are eligible for the 2010 national Teens' Top Ten vote.

Publishers play a vital role in this process. They generously mail advanced reading copies of books to the participating teens, sending at least two copies of every book being published to each appointed reading group. Teens are expected to read and consider each book they receive and complete evaluation forms on them, which are sent to the publishers by the groups' advisors. The publishers value the teens' opinions and use their feedback as they decide what YA books to publish in the future. Sometimes they quote the teens in book publicity. Teens may nominate galley books or *any* books released for *any* age group during the publication date perimeters of each year.

Group leaders or advisors must be members of YALSA, and teens must demonstrate that they are willing to read regularly and to complete evaluation forms on the books they receive. Appointed teens are also expected to nominate books that they feel are outstanding enough to appear on the Teens' Top Ten national voting list. Nominations from all the teen groups are compiled into one large list, from which the teens in the YA Galley groups select their top 25 favorites in April. The resulting list of 25 titles becomes the national Teens' Top Ten list for that year's nationwide vote.

Consider applying to get your teen reading or advisory group involved in Teens' Top Ten/YA Galley. Information on how to apply to be considered for appointment is posted on the YALSA Web site (www.ala.org/ala/mgrps/divs/yalsa/teenreading/teenstopten/

teenstopten.cfm). This project is a great way to foster teen participation, encourage reading, and give your teens and your library some notoriety.

If you or your teens do not apply to become or are not selected as a YA Galley appointed group, you may still be part of the project and use Teens' Top Ten to encourage reading and participation. Here are some ways you and your teens might promote Teens' Top Ten:

- Share information with your teen readers about the books the nominating groups have selected as soon as they are posted on the TTT Web page.

- Once the final list is posted on the TTT Web page in April, plan to order and promote titles for summer reading.

- See if your teens want to start a TTT promotional team within your TAG or reading group to encourage other teens to read the nominated titles.

- Provide incentives for teens to cast their ballots during the TTT voting period.

- Encourage teachers to use the reading/voting as a fun extra credit or other reading assignment.

- Ask teens to design bulletin boards to promote the project.

- Add a link to the TTT Web site on your library teen Web page.

- Have teens prepare special public address system, podcast, or written announcements.

- Describe TTT during booktalk presentations.

- Create bookmarks or flyers that list the nominated titles.

- Include TTT titles as part of library summer reading program events and on summer reading lists.

- Have teens run book discussion groups using the nominated titles.

- Ask your teens for other brilliant ideas!

Teens' Top Ten: Want to Know More?

Try the following articles to discover more about Teens' Top Ten and how your teens can get involved:

Cummings, Edith, Tracey Firestone, and Diane Monnier. "FAQs Answered by the YA Galley Committee." *Young Adult Library Services* (Fall 2006): 39–40.

Meyer, Nadeen, and Heather Acres. "We Love YA Galley/Teens' Top Ten Books." *Voice of Youth Advocates* (June 2004): 108–9.

Monnier, Diane P., and Diane P. Tuccillo. "Get Out the Vote for Teens' Top Ten." *Young Adult Library Services* (Summer 2007): 31–32.

Paone, Kimberly, and Members of the Elizabeth (NJ) Public Library's Teen Book Discussion Group. "Teens' Top Ten Redux." *Young Adult Library Services* (Winter 2008): 15–17.

Tuccillo, Diane. "Teens Meeting the Challenge: Young Adults Gain a Voice Deciding What's Hot to Read." *The ALAN Review* (Winter 2004): 23–26.

Teen Participation Opportunities at ALA Conferences

The Wake County Public Libraries' Eva Perry Mock Newbery Book Club, first mentioned in chapter 3, has been to two ALA Conferences that were within driving distance, in 2002 and 2007. Teen members of the book club spent their conference weekends listening to and talking with authors, publishers, librarians, and others from across the country about books. They collected autographs and bags full of advanced reading copies of new titles. While in Atlanta for the 2002 convention, they were part of a teen panel discussion about books and answered questions from the attendees.

Best of all, the teens attended both Newbery Award banquets and chatted openly with the adults at the banquet tables, who loved meeting and listening to the teens. It was evident to all that the teens had not only read the books, but had also thought carefully about what they had read. A big part of their ability to do that came from their ongoing participation in the mock book club discussions at their library and the guidance of their librarians.[21]

When the Mock Printz Book Club members attended the 2007 ALA Conference in Washington, D.C., they went to the Printz program and reception, where author John Green remembered the group from the webcast when they had chosen his book, *Looking for Alaska*, as that year's Mock Printz Winner—the same book the actual Michael L. Printz Award Committee had selected! In addition, Printz Honor winner Marcus Zusak had joined the teens for lunch after the teens sang "Happy Birthday" to him earlier in the day during a book signing. What great opportunities for teens to connect with actual, award-winning authors!

The Mock Printz Book Club teens wore specially designed T-shirts for this ALA conference, which said, "We're in Your Library, Reading Your Books.—Teens." Many people stopped the group during the convention to comment on the shirts. Likewise, when our teens from the Poudre River Public Library District participated in the Best Books for Young Adults teen forum in Denver in January 2009, they sported their "IRS" T-shirts, and they were able to share that the letters stand for "Interesting Reader Society." Keep in mind that T-shirts are one of the very best publicity techniques you can use to promote your teen involvement!

Besides participation at the ALA conferences, the teens involved in these groups have received national attention in other ways. Members of the Mock Newbery Book Club had the opportunity to be part of the YALSA Teens' Top Ten/YA Galley project nominating committees for the 2005–2006 appointment years. The Mock Printz Book Club and the IRS were both selected to serve as 2 of the 15 nationwide YA Galley groups for the 2009–2010 term.[22]

American Library Association Conference Participation: A Teen's Viewpoint

Jenny Knatz, a former member of the Young Adult Advisory Council (YAAC) at the City of Mesa Library in Arizona, shared her reaction to participating in YALSA activities at an ALA Conference:

> I attended the 2006 American Library Association Conference in New Orleans with two other teen members from YAAC, a trip our parents funded after we were invited. There was also a fourth teen from Grand Junction, Colorado, who joined our group in Louisiana.
>
> The entire experience was beyond amazing. As I toured the massive convention center and wandered down aisle after aisle of publishers, editors, authors, and vendors, my awe continued to escalate. It startled me to realize just how big this world—which, for all my volunteerism I was only just getting a taste of—really was.
>
> The people at the convention were friendly and courteous. I received more free stuff than I could take with me on the flight home. At the convention center, I met author after author that I had never dreamed of seeing face-to-face. I was able

to get books autographed by some of my favorites, and I admit that I was more than a little star-dazzled from that experience.

When not wandering through the city or the convention center, my time was well occupied. I participated in a YALSA panel on the importance of teenage reviewers, which was incredibly cool. I'd been to other, non-library conferences before, and seen panels like this, but to be the one *behind* the long table? To have people want to hear *my* opinions, reactions, and experiences? It was a whole other, exhilarating world.

This feeling was duplicated when I went to the Best Books for Young Adults forum. There were a bunch of us teens sitting up there, speaking to people about the books we'd read. Some of the people we spoke to were from the committee that decided this prestigious book list. They wanted *our* input to help them make their decisions about which books should rise and which should fall. I remember afterwards how one gentleman approached me, impressed with how my opinions had so coincided with his own: "Yes, that's exactly the way I felt about that book!" he said. I can't begin to describe how powerful the feeling was that not only had he been paying attention to what I was saying, but that it mattered enough to him to tell me so.

All of what I have described so far was still at the convention center. The very best parts of this trip were the other things we were invited to do. My group and I were fortunate enough to attend several publishing dinners, including those given by Little, Brown; Scholastic; and Simon & Schuster. Even if the food hadn't been as wonderful as it was, the company would have been. I was able to speak to authors privately, ask them about what drove them, what inspired them. I was even able to inquire into the publishing business with one of the editors, because at the time I was considering that field as a career choice. I made connections at those dinners that would have been impossible had I not attended the conference.

There was one last event we attended that really put the icing on the cake. At the *Voice of Youth Advocates* reception, my group and I signed people in, helped people find their seats, and even did a raffle. However, the part that is most clear in my mind is my discussion with author Scott Westerfeld. Although I had so far only read one of his books, Scott was enthused when I described some of my life to him. We talked about the realities of being an author, the seclusion he often went into to write, and the relief he felt at human contact. He asked me about my hobbies, and I was able to tell him about Academic Decathlon and how I had recently earned my black belt. It was the most in-depth, personal, friendly conversation I had the entire time. I'll never forget it.

Overall, my trip to the ALA conference was a true life-changing experience. It helped put me on the path I'm on now, to being a librarian myself. Realizing how much the library world has to offer inspired me and helped me realize what an impressive career this could be. It was an incredible, unforgettable opportunity that I feel very privileged to have had.[23]

Jenny's exuberant reaction to attending and participating in the ALA conference says a great deal about the honor and respect adults afforded her during her travels. Read on for another teen's perspective.

STAB, BBYA, and Books: A Teen Explains Her Enthusiasm

As a member of the Shoreline Teen Advisory Board (STAB), advised by librarian Rick Orsillo, Chelsea Cooper was eager to share her views on being an active teen library participant at the King County Library System in Washington State (www.kcls.org/) and her involvement in the ALA Midwinter Conference in Seattle in 2007:

> Our STAB group ended up on the Best Books for Young Adults program. I was getting free, unreleased books to read and review. This was really fun for me because you could either worship the book or blow it to pieces, both of which are entertaining.
>
> And ALA in Seattle was truly heaven!!! I came home with about seven bags full of books from the publishers. I think I still have some of them.
>
> If we get teens more involved and take them to stuff like this, it will really change their perspectives on books. The typical teen viewpoint is that books are boring and teachers make you read them. But going to a convention when you are most definitely top class and the publishers are glad to have you read their books—that is a life changing experience and a huge promoter for book people! Teens totally need to be involved with libraries too.
>
> I remember a girl who came to one of our STAB meetings and told us how she had said to people she knew that she had to leave to get to our meeting. They just looked at her and asked, amazed: "You read books for fun?" And she said, "Yeah, reading can be fun—especially when you get to come to the library to eat pizza, make fun of Rick, and then talk about books!"[24]

Teen Participation in Strategic Planning and on Library Focus Groups

Teens like Jenny and Chelsea have unique voices that ring loud and clear about their participatory experiences. There are plenty of other teens out there just like them, waiting to be heard. Maybe you are not able to take your teens to ALA or other conferences, or you have not yet been able to get a teen on your adult library board, but there other ways that teens can be heard while being directly involved in their libraries. One was demonstrated in Massachusetts, when teens from around the state participated in a massive campaign to get voters to reject a proposal to eliminate the state income tax, which would have had dire consequences for libraries.[25]

Here is another means to consider. If your library is embarking on a strategic plan to improve and enhance library services in your community, are teen members of the community directly taking part? If your library is, and if teens are not, then it is time for you to take action.

Many libraries have begun to see that surveying their clientele and making beneficial improvements to overall library services is an important and realistic way to do business. One way that libraries effectively make these improvements across the board is by incorporating teen voices while ideas are investigated, preparations are made, and concrete decisions are put into effect.

To successfully integrate teen perspectives, teenagers must be part of any groups that influence assessments. Sometimes adults talk about what *they* think teenagers want or need, without teens being present, but the only way to get accurate input is to have *teens* giving it. Be sure that if your library is setting out to create a strategic plan, teens are proportionately represented.

A major problem many libraries have in including teens in the mix is school. Often strategic planning meetings are scheduled when most teenagers are in class. In some cases this "conflict" serves as a reason to exclude teens, by adults who cannot appreciate the real contributions teens might make. At other times, adults simply do not understand that there are options to ensure teen representation in strategic planning and in associated focus groups, despite potentially conflicting school hours.

One solution to this dilemma is inviting teens and having them get permission to miss school during times when strategic planning events are being held. Parents and school principals are often willing to approve these kinds of activities that provide a boost to a student's extracurricular record and increased attention for the school. Furthermore, there is another avenue that library strategic planners often overlook when recruiting teens to give input and feedback: including the homeschooled teen population.

Because homeschoolers do not have to report to school every day, they are usually much more flexible with the hours that they can come to the library. Teen homeschoolers are usually very receptive to the idea of expanding their horizons by participating in an activity in the community. Homeschoolers can often meet to discuss library goals at a time when other teens are unavailable, and when it might be convenient for adults in the group to meet with them. Make it a point to advocate for teens to be an instrumental facet of any strategic planning on which your library embarks, and if the question comes up about scheduling, suggest homeschooled teens if you know they are available.

Homeschooled teens might also serve the library in a number of other welcome capacities. Because of their flexible hours, they could help with children's storytimes, assist with Friends of the Library and other fund-raising events, serve on teen advisory boards, and provide endless potential for other teen participatory activities.[26] For instance, at the Poudre River Public Library District, after most teen summer Puppet Pals have long since returned to their classrooms, homeschooled Puppet Pals are called upon four times during the school year to play parts in preschool puppet plays on regular school days.[27]

Whether incorporating homeschooled teens or teens who attend regular school, it is important to encourage the young adult voice in the library decision-making process. Speak up for your teens and work to get them represented in as many ways as possible.

ADVOCATING FOR YOUTH PARTICIPATORY EVALUATION: A SUMMARY

By far the most difficult aspect of teen library participation advocacy is proposing active teen associations with adults where they do not exist and actually getting them underway. However difficult this might be, it is not impossible. Think about all the positive examples in this chapter, be sure to do your homework in providing justification for teen involvement, and prepare carefully as you present a case for having your library incorporate an active teen voice. Then follow through to make it happen.

An imperative first step is establishing a teen library advisory board or building up one that already exists. A viable teen advisory board or other active teen library group is usually the springboard to gaining teen acceptance on adult boards, focus groups, and in serving as teen representatives at adult-oriented events.

Next, talk to your teens and figure out what approach they would like to take. Do they think that having representation on adult boards of directors is a good place to start? Is there an opportunity for teen participation at an adult special event or conference? Is your library developing a strategic plan that could benefit from teen involvement?

Examine the situation in your library and community and determine in what ways your teens might play an active part and have their voices heard.

ENDNOTES

1. The Freechild Project, *Children and Youth Voice, Youth Involvement, Youth Engagement, Youth Organizing and Youth Participation in Participatory Action Research* (The Freechild Section Investigating Youth Involvement, 2007), www.freechild.org/PAR.htm (accessed February 17, 2009).

2. Kim Sabo Flores, *Youth Participatory Evaluation: Strategies for Engaging Young People* (San Francisco: Wiley, 2008), 7.

3. Alyssa Ratledge, "One Teen among Adults on the Library Board," *Voice of Youth Advocates* 30 (October 2007): 313.

4. Kelly Johnson, e-mail message to author, January 16, 2009.

5. Saleena Davidson, e-mail message to author, July 29, 2008.

6. Campaign for America's Libraries. "Speaking Up for Library Services to Teens: A Guide to Advocacy," *Young Adult Library Services Association* (2007), www.ala.org/ala/mgrps/divs/yalsa/advocacy_final.pdf, 39 (accessed February 1, 2009).

7. Gina Macaluso, e-mail message to author, August 11, 2008.

8. Metropolitan Education Commission, *Youth Advisory Council/Tucson Teen Congress Seeking Representatives* (City of Tucson, 2006), www.tucsonaz.gov/mec/yac.html (accessed September 20, 2009).

9. Macaluso, e-mail, August 11, 2008.

10. Renee McGrath, e-mail messages to author, July 30, 2008, August 15, 2008, and November 4, 2008.

11. Maureen Ambrosino, e-mail messages to author, August 7, 2008, and August 13, 2008.

12. Judy Macaluso, e-mail messages to author, November 17, 2008, and December 8, 2008.

13. Alleen Pace Nilsen and Kenneth L. Donelson, *Literature for Today's Young Adults*, 7th ed. (Boston: Allyn & Bacon, 2005), 63–64.

14. National Education Association, *Background on Read Across America*, 2002–2009, www.nea.org/grants/13003.htm (accessed September 20, 2009).

15. National Education Association, *13 Seuss-gestions*, 2002–2009, www.nea.org/grants/20122.htm (accessed September 20, 2009).

16. Dodie Ownes, "Writing, Killing, Slamming, Reading," *School Library Journal* 54 (April 22, 2008), www.schoollibraryjournal.com/article/CA6551739.html (accessed June 20, 2008).

17. Tyler Rudolph, e-mail message to author, 23 June 2008.

18. Young Adult Library Services Association, *About YALSA: National Youth Participation Guidelines* (American Library Association, 2001), www.ala.org/ala/mgrps/divs/yalsa/aboutyalsab/nationalyouth.cfm (accessed September 1, 2008).

19. Diana Tixier Herald and Diane P. Monnier, "The Beasts Have Arrived: The Blooming of Youth Participation in the Young Adult Library Services Association (YALSA)," *Voice of Youth Advocates* 30 (June 2007): 117.

20. Young Adult Library Services Association, *YALSA's Teens' Top Ten* (American Library Association, 2009), www.ala.org/teenstopten (accessed September 20, 2009).

21. Martha Choate, e-mail message to author, October 3, 2008.

22. Valerie Nicholson, e-mail message to author, October 11, 2008.

23. Jenny Knatz, e-mail message to author, May 18, 2008.

24. Chelsea Cooper, e-mail message to author, June 21, 2008.

25. "Teens Helped Save MA Libraries Campaigning Against Tax Cut," *Library Hotline* 46 (November 17, 2008): 2.

26. Maureen T. Lerch and Janet Welch, *Serving Homeschooled Teens and Their Parents* (Westport, CT: Libraries Unlimited, 2004), 122–24.

27. Giny McConathy, interview with author, January 6, 2009.

9

Getting (and Keeping) Teens Involved

In order for solid teen participation endeavors to happen in any library, you must have a plan for designing participatory opportunities and for recruiting, training, supporting, evaluating, and acknowledging teens who take part. It takes preparation and publicity to fulfill such a plan. In this chapter you will learn important ways to develop positive, workable youth participation activities that fit the setting of your school or public library.

LADDER OF YOUTH PARTICIPATION

Effective teen library involvement depends on where that involvement falls on the "ladder of participation." Dr. Roger Hart, a professor in the Ph.D. psychology program of the Graduate Center of the City University of New York and codirector of the Children's Environments Research Group, came to some profound conclusions about children and teenagers and their role in society. (See figure 9.1, p. 184.) Through his research, Hart carefully defined how young people must play a role that is positive, respected, and acted upon in society in order for them to grow into upstanding and self-reliant adults. His determinations concur with the premises of resiliency and fostering the teen traits discussed in chapter 1.[1]

When you are developing, planning, and promoting teen participation in your library, it is important to consider the level of respect and responsibility that you and your library are willing and able to give your teens. The higher up on the "ladder" you can place your teen involvement opportunities, the better the results, and the stronger the teen voice and actions, will be.

Roger Hart's Ladder of Youth Participation

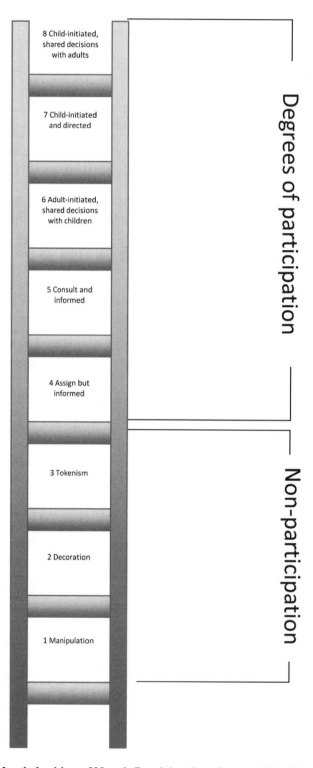

Figure 9.1. Roger Hart's Ladder of Youth Participation. *Source:* R.A. Hart, "Children's Participation: From Tokenism to Citizenship," *Innocenti Essays* no. 4 (Florence: UNICEF International Child Development Centre, 1992). Used with permission. Adapted by Mick Tuccillo.

The Five Top Rungs: Participatory Involvement

Advocating for involvement opportunities on the five highest rungs of Hart's ladder is important to achieving retention of teen participants. Teens want to feel that their efforts are significant and valued, and that they have a say in what is accomplished and how.

Let's take a look at the rungs of this ladder, described from top to bottom, to see the reasons that this is so. Some examples described elsewhere in this book are provided for the first five rungs, to show how they might fall on the ladder.

According to Hart in the definitions that follow, the top five rungs are considered to be "participatory," with the highest rung being the one with the most substantial teen input, and descending from there. The bottom three rungs are considered by Hart to be "nonparticipatory" and should be avoided.

Youth-Initiated Actions; Shared Decisions with Adults

Projects or programs on the highest rung are initiated by young people, and decision making is shared between young people and adults. These projects empower young people while at the same time enabling them to access and learn from the life experience and expertise of adults.

A project that illustrates this rung is that completed by the Girl Scout who decided to earn her Gold Award by starting a library in her community. She established its first local library and even catalogued 6,300 books for the project. Because of her efforts, her town now has a three-year provisional membership in the Texas Library System and a full-time librarian. To complete this project, the Girl Scout was completely empowered and was supported by the adults who enabled her to see it through.[2]

Projects as striking as this one, at the very top of the ladder, are usually few and far between. However, our goal as librarians who support teen participation should be to encourage and empower teens to accomplish similar projects for and in their libraries when an opportunity arises.

Youth-Initiated and Directed Actions

The second rung from the top step occurs when young people initiate and direct a project or program. Adults are involved only in a supportive role.

Here is an example. Teen library advisory group members come to their adult advisor and say they want to do a read-a-thon for the local Boys and Girls Club. Their adult leader approaches the club, finds out that the contribution would be appreciated, and then helps the teens to set up the event. The teens get donors, recruit their friends to take part, tell their teachers and school librarians about the project for increased publicity, and hold the event. The adult advisor provides snacks and drinks and a place in the library for the teens to do their reading. After the event the teens turn in their pledges for the agency, and the director of the agency attends a teen advisory group meeting so that a check prepared by the adult advisor may be presented to the director by the teens from their proceeds. The teens are recognized as the ones who instigated, planned, and conducted the project, but elements of the project would not have happened without adult support.

Adult-Initiated Actions; Shared Decisions with Youth

A project or program on the third rung down is initiated by adults, but the decision making is shared with the young people.

A program that illustrates this rung is Puppet Pals. For this program, young teens are invited, recruited, and trained to provide puppet plays for young children. The teens who participate are encouraged to improvise during the rehearsals of the adult-written plays to make them funnier and more interesting for the children. The teens are also expected to independently interact with their audiences before and after the shows by creatively encouraging children to learn more about the puppets and the stories on which the plays were based.[3]

Youth Are Consulted and Informed

The purpose of activities on the fourth rung down is to gain advice from young people on projects or programs designed and run by adults. The young people are informed about how their input will be used and about the outcomes of the adult-made decisions.

A teen space remodeling project, in which teens are consulted about what furniture to buy and what items to add to the collection, aptly exemplifies this rung. When teen recommendations are taken to heart by the adults who are coordinating the project, it ultimately reflects the teens' influence. The teen space ends up being a very "cool" and appealing area for *all* teens in the community through the guidance of the participating teens.

Youth Are Assigned But Informed

Teen participation on the fifth rung down means that the young people are assigned a specific role and informed about how and why they are being involved.

One event that exemplifies this rung is a Friends of the Library book sale for which teens are enlisted to help. The adult Friends group might plan and run the sale, but they need additional hands to help set up, take down, and sell the books. The library's teen volunteer group is approached to assist with the sale. Several teens sign up to help with particular shifts, and they readily pitch in. Afterward the teens are praised by the Friends of the Library for their role in the fund-raising efforts. Although the sale was an adult-oriented project, teen involvement was instrumental in its success.

Adultism

The bottom three rungs on the youth participatory ladder fall into the category of *adultism*. This type of discrimination against young people occurs any time children or youth are ignored, silenced, neglected, or punished because they are not adults; situations falling in this domain are *not* youth participation.[4]

NOTE: The following situations are completely fictional and are included to clarify how adultism *might* take place in libraries.

Tokenism

On the rung "tokenism," young people *appear* to be given a voice, but in fact have little or no choice about what they do or how they participate.

A situation like this might be when a librarian puts a "suggestion box" in the library's entryway, inviting teen clientele to share program ideas for the coming year. The librarian is praised by his supervisor for soliciting teen input. Likewise, the teens are glad to be asked, and they put their recommendations in the box. However, when the librarian looks through the submissions, he decides that those the teens offered are too much time and trouble. He thinks about programs he would rather do and arranges the teen event schedule based on his own assumptions and preferences, ignoring the suggestion box ideas. On the surface, it looks like the teens were consulted, but in reality their ideas were dismissed.

Decoration

"Decoration" is when young people are used to help or "bolster" a cause in a relatively indirect way, and adults use them for effect. Adults who use youth for this purpose do not pretend that the cause is inspired by young people.

Here is a scenario to illustrate this rung. A library is seeking money for a building expansion. During a presentation to convince the city fathers of the need for a new wing where adult materials will be housed, photographs of children and teenagers at the library are added to a supporting slide show. Young people are not asked for their opinions, and there was never any intention to add either a new children's room or a new teen space in the expansion. Yet pictures of youth using the library are displayed for effect in an attempt to maneuver funding approval.

Manipulation or Deception

When adults use young people to support causes and pretend that the causes are inspired by young people, it qualifies as manipulation, or even deception. It is very similar to the previous rung, except the deception is blatant.

Such a situation might occur if adults get a grant to completely plan and design a new library computer center. Although teens are expected to be regular users of the center, which was reflected in the grant application, teens are not asked for input at all. The adult planners feel they are too immature to express their opinions. Still, at the grand opening of the center, a librarian targets and interviews some teens about their reactions to it. She takes photos of the teens, who give her lukewarm feedback because the center is not particularly teen-friendly. Afterward the teens' photos and exaggerated quotes appear in a library newsletter touting the new service.

As you are advocating for teens and their involvement in your library, be on the lookout for situations in which adultism might rear its head, and speak out about your observations in a tactful fashion. Adults often resort to adultism due to a lack of knowledge or awareness (think back to chapter 1!), and bringing it to their attention might turn a negative attempt to use young people into positive action to incorporate youth participation.

WHAT TEEN PARTICIPATION OPPORTUNITIES SHOULD YOU OFFER?

If you are going to develop a formal teen participation program based on elements from the first five rungs of the youth participation ladder, you will first want to be sure that your volunteer opportunities have a focus. As you have seen from the many examples in the previous chapters, there are a variety of ways to approach the kinds of involvement for teens and how frequently they are able to take part. Even an occasional or drop-in format requires some foresight and planning.

The County of Los Angeles Public Library (www.colapublib.org/) has created a document called "Teens: The Community Service Solution," which is funded under provisions of the Library Services and Technology Act as administered by the California State Library. It is designed to outline the kinds of teen participatory opportunities the library system might offer in various locations and to give practical guidance for helping them to take place. In the document, some excellent models for effective youth participation and community service opportunities are described and outlined. Think about the qualities and criteria for each model, and which would best apply to your library setting based on the examples you have read about in this book.

Remember, although these models were created for a public library system, school libraries may apply them as well.

Teen Technology Task Force Model

In the teen technology task force model, teen volunteers work as a group on and with technology in the public service areas of the library and behind the scenes. Initially the teens are trained together by a member of the library staff. Once a group has been successfully recruited and trained and has gained experience, these students may then proceed to train future teen task force members.

Some suggested tasks and duties for these volunteers:

- Assisting library customers with the use of the library's online public access catalog and other computer resources

- Offering suggestions to library customers searching for information via the Internet

- Providing troubleshooting with equipment

- Assisting library staff with training sessions and scheduling for library customers who need to use the online public access catalog, word processing, and the Internet

- Using technology to produce flyers, posters, or other materials for the library

This model would suit your library if

- you have a number of terminals offering the Internet, word processing, and the library catalog;

- your staff has the technological expertise to train the task force members; and

- you have the time to organize and train a group of volunteers during the early stages of the program.

Teen Advisory Board Model

In the teen advisory board model, a member of the library staff is assigned as supervisor, and teen volunteers serve as an advisory board for the library. Where appropriate, each person may have an allotted role, such as chair, secretary, treasurer, or coordinator of a specific activity. Teens who intend to volunteer for longer periods of time may form the core of the group and assist with continuity of the program; those who want to volunteer for shorter periods may become involved in just one or two shorter-term activities.

Some suggested tasks and duties for these volunteers:

- Advising library staff on ways to make the library more teen-friendly

- Producing a library publication that includes original poetry and prose, book reviews, drawings, and articles

- Developing or maintaining a teen area in the library

- Creating and running programs for younger library customers

- Organizing a used book drive

- Creating artwork and decorations for the library

- Advising library staff on collection development, services, and programs for teens; conducting customer satisfaction or needs surveys

This model would be suitable for your library if

- you have space where a group of teens can meet on a regular basis;

- you have the time to organize and monitor the teen advisory group;

- you do not have many teen programs currently taking place in your library; and

- you have a staff member willing and able to serve as advisor or mentor.

Peer-Tutoring and Working with Younger Children Model

In the peer-tutoring and working with younger children model, teen volunteers may work as a group, in pairs, or individually. The volunteers may work in the children's and teen areas of the library. Before beginning the program, all the teens should receive specialized training for the tasks at hand.

Some suggested tasks and duties for these volunteers:

Peer-tutoring:

- Helping teens to understand and complete homework assignments

- Helping teens use the online public access catalog and the Internet to locate information

- Playing educational games

- Advising library staff on collection development, services, and programs for teens

Working with younger children:

- Reading to children

- Listening to children read

- Helping library staff with storytimes

- Developing afterschool activities for children

- Working on crafts projects

This model would be suitable for your library if

- you have a number of teens and younger children using the library for information and recreation;

- you have a youth services librarian to train and guide teen volunteers; and

- you have a large afterschool latchkey population.

Task Menu Model

In the task menu model, library staff draw up a list of activities for the teen volunteers to carry out. Volunteers meet with library staff to discuss which tasks are most appropriate to their skill sets, abilities, and preferences. Each volunteer is assigned an activity most suitable to him or her. Teens then carry out their assigned tasks, much as they would if they were being paid to work in the library.

Some suggested tasks and duties for these volunteers:

Homework center helper:

- Working with children as they do their homework and helping them to understand their assignments
- Helping children use the computers
- Playing or demonstrating educational games with or to children
- Guiding art projects
- Reviewing books for youth, including writing brief annotations and indicating target age and grade levels
- Advising library staff on collection development in the teen area

Technology assistant:

- Following the teen technology task force model listed above
- Instead of working in a group, accomplishing the tasks on an individual basis

Shelver:

- Shelving a portion of the hundreds of books returned to the library every day
- Helping staff trace missing books and videos
- Checking the library shelves for books in need of repair and helping to repair them
- Keeping the shelves looking tidy
- Reviewing books for youth
- Advising library staff on collection development observations in the teen area

Artist:

- Creating artwork for a bulletin board
- Creating decorations for the library
- Creating flyers and posters advertising events at the library
- Creating bookmarks and booklists that appeal to youth
- Creating attractive notices for everyday use in the library

This model would be suitable for your library if

- you cannot accommodate teen volunteers working together as a group;
- you have staff who can train and supervise teen workers; and
- you have enough miscellaneous tasks to keep volunteers busy.

Teen Worker-Apprentice/Job Shadowing Model

In the teen worker-apprentice/job shadowing model, volunteers work individually as part of the library team. They are assigned to a specific professional or paraprofessional library staff member, whom they job-shadow. The teen assists this person, carries out tasks that are relevant to his or her job, and experiences the way in which this person's role contributes to the functioning of the library as a whole. To provide additional variety and experience for the teens involved, you might devise a rotation system whereby the teens take turns shadowing different library staff members at different times.

Some suggested tasks and duties for volunteers:

Library page shadow:

- Evaluating the condition of library materials
- Organizing returned books on the book carts
- Placing library materials on the appropriate shelf, in the proper order
- Reorganizing library materials to provide ease of access and aesthetic balance
- Collecting stray library materials from tables and other public areas
- Reviewing the placement of materials on the shelves to ensure they are in the correct location
- Assisting customers in completing application forms for new library cards
- Advising library staff on collection development observations in the teen area

Library aide shadow:

- Evaluating the condition of library materials when returned
- Documenting the nature of damaged materials
- Participating in the processing of library materials
- Preparing property labels for library materials
- Preparing new and gift books for circulation
- Answering directional questions for library customers
- Taking customers on tours of the library and explaining library policies

Children's librarian shadow:

- Preparing felt-board stories and storytime areas
- Reviewing books for children
- Reading to children and listening to children read
- Creating artwork for the children's area
- Developing afterschool activities for children
- Constructing craft activities and designing coloring activity sheets

Reference librarian shadow:

- Organizing pamphlets into broad subject areas
- Typing and applying subject labels for pamphlets
- Filing pamphlets under the appropriate subject
- Answering directional questions for library customers
- Assisting library customers with their use of the library's online public access catalog, the Internet, and word processing facilities
- Assisting with the development, organization, and promotion of programs in the library

This model would be suitable for your library if

- you cannot accommodate teen volunteers working as a group; and
- you have staff who are willing to serve as mentors to young people.[5]

Moving Forward

After considering the outlines of the teen participation models above, which sum up many of the examples given in this book, reflect on and plan for those that would be a good fit for your library or library system. A really helpful approach is to poll local teens to find out what they would enjoy doing for the library and what teen interests they perceive the library might address. This could be done in-house as well as through the schools if you are in a public library, and in your school if you are in a school library. Conducting such a survey will reveal whether library anticipation and teen thinking mesh. You might even follow up with a teen focus group.

Once you have evaluated and decided on which teen participation model or models suit your library or library system, you will have a basis on which to proceed. Deciding who will be in charge, when meetings and training will be held, why they will be held, and what your teen participants will hope to accomplish will all stem from the initial decisions and perceptions about what your library and community need; what they are able to support with staff, funding, space, and time; and what teens envision they can and want to contribute.

If you have a volunteer coordinator at your library, solicit that person to help in recruiting teens, managing the application and membership process, assisting with evaluations, and managing other supporting tasks he or she might be willing and able to do. With the volunteer coordinator's input, you can develop job descriptions that will help the teens and staff alike to be clear about teen volunteer positions and job duties. (See figure 9.20.)

Some Basic Considerations for Starting a Teen Participatory Program

Once you decide on which teen participatory activities to pursue, there are a few fundamental planning points to consider. As mentioned previously, be sure to have an adult at the helm who is skilled at working with teens and leading volunteer activities, or who is capable of learning such techniques. That person and other staff members may promote potential participation to those teens who frequent your library. One way to do this is to create a volunteer recruitment toolkit and to offer on-target training and orientation for teens who sign up, including introducing them to all library staff with whom they will be working. Assign these teens challenging tasks and assignments, but remember that not every task fits every teen volunteer, and try to match the right teen to the right situation or setting.[6]

Youth participation opportunities represent some of the best practices in young adult librarianship. The most successful teen programs are those that engage teens in all aspects of activities and collections. We need teens to communicate their interests, concerns, and ideas, and we need them to promote the library among their peers, as no amount of press releases will equal the incredible advertising power of teen word-of-mouth.

We have tried to take advantage of many of the technologies and media that are relevant to teens. Our gaming programs and graphic novel collections are wildly successful, and our blog and zine are very popular as well. These are all formats and forums that have been pioneered by other libraries, but I believe what makes us unique is the incredible support we've had from our library administration and community. While some libraries struggle to make teens feel welcome, our library is conscious and respectful of their need for space and autonomy. While some libraries struggle to find financial support for teen programs, our Friends have never hesitated to provide funds for give-away books or gaming equipment.

We have been able to build strong YA collections, including music and graphic novels, with the input of our teens and the support of adult library patrons who also use items selected for a young adult audience.[7]

Lisa Elliott
Young Adult Librarian
Tigard Public Library, Tigard, Oregon

APPOINTING THE RIGHT ADVISOR

The deal maker or breaker for any library in its youth participation efforts is *finding and appointing the right advisor for the job*. This person may be a school or public librarian, a support staff member, or even an adult library volunteer, depending on the size of the library and its staff and who might be available for appointment as advisor. No matter what the circumstances, it is *crucial* to choose a person who honestly likes and appreciates teenagers and is completely willing to work with, advocate for, and reward them for their library involvement. An advisor who does not have these qualities *will not be successful* in connecting with teens.

City of Mesa Public Library

JOB TITLE:	Young Adult Assistant
REPORTS TO:	The Young Adult Room in the Main Library
PURPOSE:	To assist the Youth Services Librarians. To gain references and work experience. To develop knowledge of the library and its services.
TIME COMMITMENT:	One 1½- to 3-hour shift weekly.
QUALIFICATIONS:	The volunteer should enjoy books and people. This volunteer should be committed to being on time and consistent in attendance. This candidate should be polite, well mannered, and easy going.

DUTIES:

- Call the volunteer coming on the next shift after yours
- Answer phones
- Check out games and magazines
- Provide directional assistance to patrons
- Cover paperbacks
- Shelve, clean, and mend books as needed
- Other special projects include cutting out soup labels, color coding books, helping with mailings on occasion, and stocking displays

TRAINING:	On the job. This position should teach youths about responsibility.

Figure 9.2. City of Mesa Library, Young Adult Assistant Job Description

When a library is selecting a person to serve in this role, those hiring or appointing might focus on someone who is younger, with the expectation that a younger person may relate more readily to the teens. This could be very true. However, libraries should not dismiss an older librarian, other staff member, or adult volunteer who has a strong background in working with teenagers, who enjoys them, and who is "young at heart." Teenagers relate just as well to both kinds of adults, *as long as the adults have the basic traits described above.* Anyone of any age can be educated in the ins and outs of teen psychology, sociology, and culture, but *a personality fitting for work with adolescents is inherent and cannot be learned.* Libraries should remember this when choosing an adult who will be the catalyst for teen participation.

Furthermore, there is no reason that only one person in a given library must be in charge of teen participation activities, or that such an assignment should be limited to teen or youth services specialists. As shown in examples in previous chapters, a children's librarian, volunteer coordinator, library director, or other member of a library staff may also take youth participation duties under his or her wing, in addition to or instead of an "official" teen services staff member.

Another factor to keep in mind is that those working with teen involvement may work successfully in pairs or teams. The position may be a joint venture *or* a solo responsibility. At my library, Sue-Ellen Jones, the other teen services librarian from our Main Library, and I work as partners. We empower, connect with, and engage our teens together. Sometimes the best results come from such partnerships.

These considerations apply to school libraries as well. Middle, junior, and senior high school librarians are usually people who enjoy working with adolescents, and they should select support staff and volunteers who have a similar perspective.

Joann Pompa, who started the Friends of the Library (FOTL) Club at Corona del Sol High School, is a perfect example. You have already read about the wonderful things the club has accomplished through the school library under Joann's guidance. I use the past tense, because Joann moved to a different high school in the fall of 2008. Her natural enthusiasm and strong leadership with teens have followed her. She says, "I have started a FOTL Club here at Mountain Pointe High School, ten members strong and such a great inaugural group! We've been decorating the library with themes and will decide on our community service project soon, perhaps collecting gently used books for our Special Needs students."[8]

Such natural ability with teens is at the center of fostering teen involvement in libraries. No matter how your library does it, make sure that you have the *right* adult or adults assigned to the very special and important task of getting teens to be active. Once this first step has been addressed, your library is ready to move on to recruiting teens and getting them involved in the best ways possible for them and your library.

Leadership = Inspiration + Cooperation:
A Teen's Reflection

I am a teen volunteer at the South Brunswick Public Library. Working with Saleena is fun and enjoyable. Her leadership is based on inspiration and cooperation, not domination and intimidation, a role which Saleena has fulfilled copiously.

My library experience has made me a better person and fun to be around. I could not imagine a teen volunteer program without Saleena; simply put, there really is no better person for this job.[9]

Chirag Bansal

Funding Youth Participation Events, Activities, and Projects

It is important for the astute advisor of any teen involvement ventures in a library to be aware of ways that teen participation activities might be funded. Some activities, such as helping with a weeding project or serving as a computer trainer, will probably not require extra funding besides staff time for training and supervision. However, if you and your teens decide to embark on a project that goes beyond the regular library budget, there are funding options available.

Suppose your teen volunteers want to develop a new career center with associated programs for the teens of your community, or they want to start a homework assistance service for children and young adults. These are the kinds of projects that will most likely need additional funding.

Seek funding from the standard channels first. Prepare a proposal and ask if the project might come from the next year's library budget. Present the idea to the Friends of the Library to see if they might offer monetary support.

Another way is to approach local businesses and service organizations to see if they might assist your teen group with its projects. Don't forget unconventional sources for funding library activities, either. For example, at the Laramie County Library System in Cheyenne, Wyoming, one branch applied for and received a Youth Engagement Grant from the state's Department of Health. The grant funded the new, teen-named Chimera program, which focuses on gaming and other technology-based activities.[10]

If local funding does not pan out or your project is intensive and requires a large amount of monetary support, there are additional avenues to pursue. One of the best for libraries is a Library Services and Technology Act (LSTA) grant.

LSTA Grants

LSTA grants are issued through an application process at the state level. Check with your state library to find out how to apply. Each state library has a Web page at which you may find application forms, information about grants already approved, LSTA budget projections, and more.

If you are new to the grant process, or if you want to follow the process effectively and correctly, you might want to take a free online course offered by Indiana University's Institute of Museum and Library Services. It is called "Shaping Outcomes: Making a Difference in Libraries and Museums." It takes you through all the grant stages of planning, building, evaluating, and reporting. You can find the course at www.shapingoutcomes.org/course/index.htm.

Additional Sources for Youth Participation Grants and Awards

If you are interested in other sources of money to fund your youth participation ideas and activities, there are several choices available. Following are just a few of the sources you can ask for such financial support:

YOUTH SERVICES AMERICA, SERVENET.ORG. Youth Service America lists "grants and awards to support and motivate youth, teachers, service-learning coordinators, and youth-serving organizations to plan and implement projects for National and Global Youth Service Day and on-going service throughout the year. Grants range from $250-$2000." Numerous options for funding are listed. The grant list, complete with descriptions about each source and how to apply, is available at servenet.org/tabid/122/articleType/ArticleView/articleId/85/Funding-Sources-for-Youth-Projects.aspx.[11]

In addition, Youth Service America offers a "Project Plan-It" toolkit (www.ysa.org/planit). "Project Plan-It" is an easy, interactive series of questions and templates that can help teen library participants (or any youth service volunteers) plan service projects or programs. It includes step-by-step guidelines for producing a project plan, a funding proposal, and an effective press release, as well as additional helpful resources. It also allows teens to post their projects on SERVEnet and convert their project or program into a Web site.[12]

FUNDING FOR SOCIAL CHANGE BY AND WITH YOUNG PEOPLE. The Freechild Project sponsors a Web page called "Funding for Social Change by and with Young People." The philosophical basis for this list of resources for funding is that "young people are seeking to make change in their communities around the world *right now*, and are often left lurching about for money to fund their action. A growing number of funders are realizing that young people are not simply 'the future.' They realize that young activists are making significant and meaningful change in their communities today."[13] The lengthy list of those organizations was created by the Freechild Project to make financial support for positive youth-led action easier for young people to obtain (www.freechild.org/funds4progress.htm).

LEARN AND SERVE AMERICA GRANT OPPORTUNITIES. Learn and Serve America, as part of the Corporation for National and Community Service, which is included in the USA Freedom Corps, contributes to and supports the volunteer service efforts of individuals, organizations, and communities. Both school-based and community-based programs needing support are included in the mix.[14] School and public libraries that wish to be considered for youth participation project funding can find valuable information and instructions on how to apply for and receive it by visiting and exploring the "How to Apply/About the eGrants System" Learn and Serve Web page (www.learnandserve.gov/for_organizations/funding/apply.asp).

RECRUITMENT

Once you and another advisor or advisors have been appointed to work with the teens in your library, the next step is recruiting those teens to serve as library participants. It might seem like a daunting task to start a teen group or participatory activity from scratch, so remember to take it one step at a time.

Once you have a core group of teens to work with, you will be amazed at how they perpetuate the recruitment process. However, while your newly involved teens are enlisting their peers, you yourself will continue recruiting on an ongoing basis. You must view recruiting teens as a regular job duty, as you would collection development, being on the service desk, or providing programming. There is never a comfort zone to take a break from recruiting teens—you must always be on the lookout to invite new teens if you want your youth participation activities to thrive.

The reason for this is that currently actively involved teens will eventually fly the coop and head to college or on to other adult endeavors. That is part of the beauty of working with youth—watching them grow up. The great reward comes when, after you have truly offered them a memorable library experience, they keep in touch with you even after leaving young adulthood, and you can enjoy connecting with them as adults who use their library and perhaps bring their own children to it.

Because of the nature of the maturing young adult, you will have gaps to fill when teen participation places are suddenly left vacant due to graduation. Other reasons for gaps are that teens join the swim or debate team, decide to become more involved in their churches, have too much schoolwork, or are involved in myriad other situations that force them to draw some lines. You can probably relate to this, if you think about how overbooked your own life sometimes gets and what enjoyable things you might have to decline or eliminate. Teens must make similar choices, and sometimes what they decide to give up is their library volunteer work. Also understand that some of them simply reach their involvement limits and are ready to move on to other adventures. It is not necessarily a negative reflection on you or your library—it is just a choice. At the same time, there are other teens in your community anticipating an exciting opportunity to meet new people and to have a say in the library. They might not even know it yet, until you tell them! These teens will be your new recruits.

It is important to have an open door policy that lets teens who have left your TAB group or who have resigned from other library activities know that they may return if they wish, or that they may partake in different volunteer opportunities. If you keep bridges intact, you might find teens returning later on, perhaps in another capacity.

Likewise, if your library has a policy that teen involvement will cease after teens graduate from high school, consider asking if that policy may be flexible. If you are open-minded about older teen volunteers returning as "guests" for advisory group events or to fill other teen involvement niches, you will be doing the teens and your library a favor. Sometimes 17-, 18-, and 19-year-old adolescents *are not ready to break away from their teenage support systems*. They might be too attached and unprepared for full-fledged adulthood. For those particular teens who stay local and still need the association, encourage a *gradual evolution* away from teen volunteering. One way might be to help them transition to any adult library volunteering opportunities that are available. You will even find that some teens who go away to college want to stay connected and join in when they are home on breaks. Welcome them!

In most cases, you will encounter only a few teens like these, maybe one or two per year who might still need the social and emotional benefits of teen-oriented library participation. Be sure to let your supervisors and administrators know about flexing the rule for these young people, and ask for clearance to do so.

With all this in mind, we will move on to enhancing or building teen participation through the process of recruiting new teens. Where to start? The following steps will help you to begin and to do it successfully.

Publicity: Producing an Eye-Catching Flyer

An eye-catching flyer will entice teens to find out more about a teen advisory board or volunteer activity and to consider joining the group. It is worth the extra effort and any additional expense to design and print a flyer that teens will take seriously. The flyer created by Patrick Hughey, graphic designer for the Austin Public Library (see figure 9.3, p. 198), demonstrates a high-interest graphic to which teens will be drawn and provides concise information about the group, meeting locations and times, and where they can get more details. An enlargement of the flyer could also be used as a poster in high teen traffic areas.

Signing Up: The TAB or Volunteer Application Form

The best first step in getting teens enrolled as TAB members or library volunteers is the development of a membership application form. An application form might be printed on the reverse side of a promotional flyer, as mentioned above, and made available in-print at the library or online. Copies may be ready for prospective teens at meetings, or on hand for interested teens to take at booktalks, at other teen library events, or from the library's information rack. The application should include a straightforward description of what membership entails and should allow space for listing all the contacts, background information, and signatures your library requires.

Like other styles of teen application forms reproduced in previous chapters, the Eva Perry Regional Library (www.wakegov.com/libraries/default.htm), of the Wake County (North Carolina) Public Libraries, form provides an adaptable example (see figure 9.4, pp. 199–200). Notice that this flyer and application could be printed two-sided, or as two one-sided pages stapled together. With the one-sided and stapled version, teens would be able to keep the front page for reference and detach and turn in the back page as their application.

Figure 9.3. Austin Public Library, TAG Flyer. Design by Patrick Hughey,
Graphic Designer, Austin Public Library

Teen Advisory Board Application Packet

The Eva Perry Library is pleased that you are interested in becoming a member of the Teen Advisory Board. We want to better serve our teen public through this program. We encourage you to complete this application thoughtfully and thoroughly. Members will be asked to attend one meeting a month (for a couple hours on a Saturday) and help with as many programs as possible. Community service hours will be granted but only to those that fulfill the responsibilities listed.

Questions? Call Lindsey at 555-2120
E-mail: Lindsey.dunn@co.wake.nc.us

What is the Teen Advisory Board?
It's a forum for teens
- to meet other teens who enjoy the library and reading
- to have a voice planning the activities for teens at the library
- to help promote our services to your peers

Qualifications for a Teen Advisory Board Member:
Must be:
- between the ages 13 to 16 at time of application.
- willing to commit to 1-2 hours a month for TAB meeting

Responsibilities of a Teen Advisory Board Member:
- Attend all meetings
- Set an example of appropriate library behavior for peers
- Promote the library, its services and activities in school and community
- Plan teen programs, by brainstorming, marketing and publicity, setting up/taking down (meet with planning team as needed)
- Suggest books for teens
- Help with the upkeep and decoration of the teen corner

Meetings
We will meet as a group at least once a month. During the meeting we discuss and plan upcoming activities, talk about good books and websites, and ways the library can help teens. Meeting times are the second Saturday of each month from 2-4 pm. You will be given community service hours for any of the time you spend on TAB.

What programs will TAB help plan in the upcoming year?

Whatever the group decides; it's up to you! The possibilities are endless.

Figure 9.4. Eva Perry Regional Library TAB Information/Application Form

Teen Advisory Board Application

Please fill out the following information and return it to the Eva Perry Library Children's Desk.

Name: _____

Phone No. & E-mail if applicable: _____

Address, including city and zip: _____
_____

School name & grade: _____ Age: _____

Please help us get to know you by answering the following questions. Use the back of this page if necessary.

What are some of your hobbies and interests?

Tell us why you are interested in being a part of the Teen Advisory Board.

What skills, traits or special talents do you have that would make you a good TAB member?

Can you suggest any changes or additions to improve the library's services to teens?

Would you be able to attend most meetings on the Saturday afternoons once a month?

Reference and Parent Signature: _____
Reference Name (not a parent): _____ Phone of Ref: _____

Relationship to you: _____

I am aware my teen is applying for a position with the Eva Perry Library Teen Advisory Board, and I have read the information sheet on TAB. I understand my teen is applying for a year of service. Their service as a member of the Teen Advisory Board can be used on a college or job resume.

Parent Signature: _____ Date: _____
Teen Signature: _____ Date: _____

Figure 9.4. Eva Perry Regional Library TAB Information/Application Form (*Cont.*)

Here, There, and Everywhere: Effective Ways to Promote Teen Participation Opportunities

Once you have a flyer and application form designed, printed, and ready to distribute to the teen clientele in your community, you will need to consider how, where, and when you will promote your teen participation opportunities. For example, when you are doing readers' advisory, helping teens with homework assignments, doing a school visit, or registering teens for library programs, mention what is available to see whether teens might like to pursue what you have to offer. Distribute and post flyers and applications in places where teens congregate or visit, both in your library and other places in your community. If you are in a public library, ask for help from the schools to encourage your teen participation endeavors. If you are in a school library, be sure your teen library activities are treated and promoted like any other school club or group.

Include your teen participation opportunities in printed or online calendars of events, through e-mail blasts to announce library activities, and in press releases that are dispersed to local media. Let local agencies serving teens, including school guidance departments, know that your library is a place where teens may complete volunteer assignments and earn service-learning credits. Obtain the help of your volunteer coordinator or other local volunteer agencies to recruit interested and willing teens.

Set up a Myspace.com or Facebook.com site for your library teens. Better yet, have the teens themselves set up the page and moderate it, with you as an onlooker. Through it, and through word of mouth, encourage your teens to recruit peers, friends, and siblings. Have information accessible on your library's teen Web page. Always have an open door policy at meetings and events for teens who want to check out your participatory opportunities without obligation.

For teens who are already sure they want to volunteer, prepare a more detailed "teen volunteer toolkit" to clarify the role of teen volunteers and serve as a guideline for the tasks at hand. This toolkit should include lists of potential jobs and activities, a description of days and times available for teens to volunteer, a business card or other page with contact information for the adult leader or leaders, and an application form.[15]

Now That You Have Them Signed Up, It's Time for Training

Once you have committed teen participants on board, you will have to move forward in a timely manner to train and schedule them. It is important for teens to know up front what you expect from them and the perimeters of their volunteer assignments. The next chapter will take you through the process of training and keeping teens on an even keel as they embark on their library involvement activities, in whatever forms those might take.

Whether you have individual teen participants or a group, these steps are vital to successfully incorporating their contributions and making them feel comfortable about choosing the library as their volunteer focus. When you finish these steps, you might be delighted with the results, perhaps like the staff at the Summit Library branch of the Pierce County Library System in Tacoma, Washington (www.piercecountylibrary.org). Once an active teen council was established, suddenly teens from the community were regularly using the library and coming to a variety of programs. The teen council volunteers did readers theatre shows, partnered with librarians for an impressive job-shadowing project, coordinated a kite-making craft activity for families, entered data for a thousand children's summer reading surveys—and they even planted a squash garden behind the library for all ages to enjoy after a discussion on Joan Bauer's novel *Squashed*![16]

Remember, the possibilities are boundless when you encourage, support, effectively recruit, plan with, and *carefully train* your teen participants.

ENDNOTES

1. Roger Hart, *Children's Participation: From Tokenism to Citizenship* (UNICEF International Child Development Centre, Florence, Italy, 1992), www.unicef-irc.org/publications/pdf/childrens_participation.pdf (accessed January 5, 2009).

2. Ursula Castrillon, *Girl Scouts Honor Gold Award Young Women of Distinction* (Girl Scouts of America, March 2, 2004), www.girlscouts.org/news/stories/2004/young_women_distinction.asp (accessed November 25, 2008).

3. Giny McConathy, interview with author, January 6, 2009, and e-mail messages to author, January 7, 2009.

4. The Freechild Project, *Challenging Adultism*, 2008), www.freechild.org/adultism.htm (accessed September 20, 2009).

5. Virginia Walter and Natalie Cole, *Teens: The Community Service Solution* (Downey, CA: County of Los Angeles Public Library, 2000), www.colapublib.org/teen/Teen_Manual.pdf (accessed February 19, 2009).

6. Tricia Suellentrop, "Step Right Up," *School Library Journal* 53 (December 2007): 24.

7. Lisa Elliott, e-mail message to author, October 1, 2008.

8. Joann Pompa, e-mail message to author, September 30, 2008.

9. Chirag Bansal, e-mail message to author, September 30, 2008.

10. "Libraries Working with Teens," *Wyoming Library Roundup* (Summer/Fall 2008): 10.

11. Wajeeha Saeed, *Funding Sources for Youth Projects* (Servenet.org, 2007), servenet.org/Toolkit/VolunteerResources/ToolsforGrantees/tabid/224/Default.aspx (accessed September 20, 2009).

12. Youth Service America, *Project Plan-It Toolkit*, n.d., www.ysa.org/planit (accessed September 20, 2009).

13. The Freechild Project, *Funding for Social Change by and with Young People*, 2007, www.freechild.org/funds4progress.htm (accessed December 9, 2008).

14. Learn and Serve America, *How to Apply/About the New eGrants System*, 2009, www.learnandserve.gov/for_organizations/funding/apply.asp (accessed September 20, 2009).

15. Tricia Suellentrop, "Step Right Up," *School Library Journal* 53 (December 2007): 24.

16. Pierce County Library System, *Teen Volunteers Find Fun and Friends at Pierce County Library*, 2008), www.piercecountylibrary.org/about-us/library-quarterly/september-2008/teen-volunteers.htm (accessed September 20, 2009).

10

Teens Learning the Ropes:
Effective Training for Volunteer Activities

No matter what teen participation model you choose to follow, you will have to provide some kind of training. For activities in which multiple teens are involved, training works best when held in groups through which teens who will be working together can get to know one another as they learn how to do the job. It is important to make the training sessions interesting and fun.

Be sure to carefully plan any handouts you will provide for your teens. You might even make a little booklet containing everything they must know about library policies, their job duties, scheduling, and more.

If you are training a small group that will be working closely together, try to find a time when everyone can meet. For example, if you have a few teens who are planning a series of children's puppet plays, they should meet together at one time that is convenient to all. However, if you are training a large group of teens who will be working according to different schedules, you might arrange two or perhaps even three training times. With a large group, it may be extremely difficult to get everyone together at once. By providing choices in training times, you should be able to schedule everyone for at least one session. This might seem like extra work, but it is not. If you hold one session and everyone cannot attend, you will need to arrange make-up sessions anyway. It is better to organize a few staggered sessions up front that you work into your schedule ahead of time, rather then trying to plan make-up sessions after the fact.

Provide various options for training sessions, such as Thursday evening from 7:00 to 8:00 p.m., Saturday afternoon from 2:00 to 3:00 p.m., and Tuesday afternoon from 4:00 to 5:00 p.m. Ask the teens to sign up for the session that is most convenient for them. State a deadline for them to let you know which date and time they are selecting.

Arrange a meeting place that is comfortable for everyone and that allows refreshments to be served. You will want to provide snacks and drinks during your training sessions.

Including a PowerPoint presentation to support your handouts is a helpful approach. The teens will learn better if they have such a visual presentation to go along with their handouts. Show them any special materials with which they will need to be familiar, such as a notebook in which they will record their hours, the cleaning supplies they will be using, or the summer reading records where children and other teens will be keeping track.

HOLDING EFFECTIVE MEETINGS WITH LIBRARY TEEN ADVISORY BOARDS

Teen advisory groups in libraries need regular meetings for planning events and programs, offering feedback, enjoying social interaction, or discussing books. It helps to arrange meetings well in advance and to give each teen a copy of the schedule. Teens appreciate knowing how to plan their time, and parents also need to know when teens are expected to be at the library. Another benefit is that when there is a conflict, teens can let you know in advance when they will be late or absent.

It is a good idea to post a schedule of meetings in more than one place. Hand out copies of the schedule to teens when they attend meetings. Send copies of the schedule to their houses when you distribute permission forms or other items that have to be sent via regular mail. Post the meeting schedule on your library's Web page, preferably in the virtual teen space. You might even add the schedule of meetings for the year to the application form teens fill out when applying for membership. Send e-mail reminders or call teens just before a meeting is going to take place.

Be Sure to Feed Them

Adults might be able to attend meetings and participate in other kinds of group sessions without refreshments, but teens need the extra boost snacks and drinks provide. Whether it is because teens fit their library involvement between the scenes of their busy lives and don't have time to get a bite to eat before heading off to their library participation endeavors; sleep late on Saturday mornings before rushing off to meetings; go to the library to help out right after school; or are often hungry due to growth spurts, they need supplemental nourishment. Consider ways to provide the snacks that will satiate teen appetites and allow them to be more productive whenever meetings, trainings, or other activities take place.

You might be wondering how to pay for all the food and drinks. Perhaps the Friends of the Library group would be willing to pay for the refreshments. Another choice might be to ask local adult volunteer organizations or businesses to provide snacks. You might also want to check with your administrators to see if money for teen participation munchies might be available through the regular library budget. In some libraries, teens take turns signing up to bring treats, but this method has its drawbacks. Sometimes teens forget, are absent unexpectedly, or cannot afford to chip in. In any event, you will want to find ways to have snacks and drinks available for the meetings and events in which your teens take part.

Icebreakers

All fledgling teen groups need to get to know one another and their leader, and even cohesive groups can use a little periodic social boost. Especially when you are working with teens who are very new, unsure of themselves, or uncomfortable in new settings, icebreaker activities allow each of them to feel less stressed and more comfortable. Plan activities that are creative, fun, interactive, and fit the age perimeters of the group with which you are working.

If you already have some teen participants on board, ask them for icebreaker ideas. You might be surprised at the icebreakers some of the teens already know from camp, church, or other activities that they can pass on to your group. If you don't have teens to share ideas with you yet, or you want some more to choose from, here are some teen-tested, all-purpose icebreakers for younger, older, or a combination of teen ages, to get you started:

A Cool Snowball Fight

Give each teen a piece of paper and a pen or pencil. Have the teens write three things about themselves without putting their names on their papers. Each teen will then crush his or her paper into a ball. It is now time for a get-to-know-you "snowball fight!"

Teens cannot begin until you say "go," and they must stop when you say "freeze." When you say "go," give the teens 30 seconds to toss their "snowballs." When you say "freeze," each person should pick up one snowball and find the teen it belongs to by asking questions about what is on the paper.

Allow time for the teens to seek out the person whose snowball they caught, and for the person who caught their snowball to find them. (If time is a concern, an alternative is to ask the teens to write their first names on the top of their papers before throwing their snowballs.) Teens chat with their partners about the information on the sheets and then introduce the teens whose snowballs they "caught" to the rest of the group.[1]

Alphabet Get to Know You

Each member of the group receives a preprinted piece of paper that has the letters A to Z on the left-hand side of the page and a line to write on next to each letter. For each letter, the person has to find out something about someone else in the room. For example, for the letter A, a person could write, "Bob likes Apples or Jen has a broken Arm." The number of responses each teen gets from the other teens depends on the number of people participating, so this would work well for both large and small groups. The object is for the group to meet and learn as much about the other members as possible by asking them questions. If the group is small, finish up by having each person read his or her alphabetical list. To save time with larger groups, the teens could break into smaller groups and share their lists.[2]

Beach Ball Game

This game was brought to my attention a few years ago, when our teens were planning the annual joint Young Adult Advisory Council meeting with the City of Mesa Library's Dobson Ranch Library group and the Main Library group. A committee from the Main Library group, which was serving as hosts for the Dobson group, selected a fun icebreaker called the Beach Ball Game.

For this game, you need an inflatable beach ball or other kind of ball, at least 12 inches in diameter. The ball should be fairly plain, without a lot of illustrations on it. With a dark permanent marker, teens write questions on the inflated ball, such as,

- What is your favorite sport?

- What is the name of your favorite book made into a movie?

- What vegetable do you hate?

- What television show would keep you home instead of going out with friends?

The ball should have at least 10 questions on it, added before the meeting. You may keep the ball for future use once it is prepared.

When your group begins the game, they can do it either sitting or standing in a circle. Teens toss the ball to one another, and they have 20 seconds to answer the question nearest to their right thumb. If they cannot think of an answer, let them choose the next closest question. Keep the game moving! Each teen will share his or her name, grade, or whatever information is decided, and answer the right-thumb question as quickly as possible.

One thing to remember about this amusing icebreaker is to clear the area of any open-top drink containers. The beach ball has an uncanny ability to zero in on them and cause a mess. Be proactive and ensure that all drinks are safely out of sight before starting this game!

Two Truths and a Lie

This classic icebreaker is a good way to conduct introductions in a group of 10 teens or fewer. With larger groups, this game becomes boring and tedious. After telling his or her name, school, or age, each teen tells two truths and one false thing about himself or herself. The rest of the group tries to guess which one of the three things is a lie. The person "confesses" to the lie before the game moves on to the next person. Teens get to laugh as the truths are revealed, and they learn interesting things about each other.

Interviews

This simple icebreaker works well with both small and large groups. For larger groups, use fewer questions.

Hand out index cards and small pieces of paper and pens or pencils. Post the questions on a white board or chalk board. You could also run off a handout with the questions on it, with space to add each response. Ask each teen to interview the person sitting next to him or her for five minutes and to briefly jot down his or her partner's responses. Another approach, which allows more mingling, is to have teens draw papers from a hat on which numbers, words, or pictures have been placed. There should be two of each symbol used. Teens can start off by searching through the group for the person who has the same symbol they have, then proceed with the rest of the interview from that point.

Here are some suggested questions:

- What is your name?

- What school do you go to, and what grade are you in?

- What is your favorite subject in school?

- What is your favorite leisure activity?

- What do you think is the best movie you have seen this year?

- What is one really interesting thing about you no one would guess?

- What book are you currently reading?

After the interviews are finished, each teen introduces his or her interview partner to the group. The note cards or papers will come in handy when they do this!

More Icebreaker Ideas

Amnesty International Canada. *Human Rights Activism for Youth: Icebreakers.* 2009. www.amnesty.ca/youth/youth_action_toolkit/icebreakers.php (accessed September 21, 2009).

Burns, Jim. *Uncommon Games and Icebreakers.* Ventura, CA: Regal, 2008.

Group Games: A Collection of the Best Group Games and Icebreakers! 2008. www.group-games.com (accessed September 21, 2009).

Macgregor, Mariam G. *Teambuilding with Teens: Activities for Leadership, Decision Making, and Group Success.* Minneapolis, MN: Free Spirit, 2007.

Youth Group Games: A User Library of Games and Activities for Youth Groups. n.d. www.youthgroupgames.com.au/games/index.cfm (accessed September 21, 2009).

Ground Rules

Be sure that your library teen participants are on the same page regarding ground rules for behavior. Everyone benefits when behavior issues do not interfere with meetings and participatory activities. It helps to have the teens themselves assist in creating and promoting these rules, perhaps by brainstorming.

What might a list of ground rules look like? Following are some points that could be included on a ground rule list. Help your teens to create the list by giving them one topic to get started.

- Start and finish the meeting on time.

- One person speaks at a time.

- Limit side conversations—save them for before or after the meeting, or during breaks.

- When the "quiet" signal is given, everyone stops talking.

- Raise your hand if you have something to contribute.

- The person with the prop has the floor.

Other Rules and Responsibility

Make sure that the teens you are working with know the overall library rules and what is expected of them when they are involved in and representing the library. If the teens are permitted to use the staff break room, what are the rules are about using it? What hours they are they expected to work, and what procedures should they follow if they have to be absent? If they are involved in a project, what are its perimeters, if any? For instance, our library requires that when the teens do window painting in their teen space, they must restrict their painting to the lower window sections. Painting the very top windows presents a safety hazard because they are too high. Teens need to know these kinds of inherent rules in advance.

Be sure to outline the rules during trainings and provide a handout that describes expectations and guidelines. Explain the rules using positive, upbeat terms rather than negative ones. For example, you might say that teens should remember to use soft voices when working in the library, rather than saying that no loud talking is permitted.

Make sure teens feel comfortable asking you for clarification about anything. Include your complete contact information on any handouts you give them, and make sure they know whom to ask if you are absent.

Instilling Consequences

I think that volunteering at the library is a fantastic experience for our teens. They can help their community and themselves. The majority of our teen volunteers are in the sixth to eighth grades so this is their first job-like experience. They sign up for specific shifts and are required to show up at specific times. There are consequences if they do not do what they say they are going to do. For example, if they have three 'no shows,' which means they signed up for a shift and did not call to say that they could not make it, they cannot sign up for additional shifts.

Working with the younger students in the Tutoring program is especially rewarding for the teens. I think it's great that our teen volunteers are so visible to other teens visiting the library. I think that this lets them see that teens are valued here.[3]

Jennifer Dillon
Youth Services Supervisor
Farmer's Branch Manske Library, Texas

Hand and Vocal Signals That Mean "Quiet"

A technique that works well for many teen meetings and training events is to have a signal that means, "Stop extraneous talking, and let's get back on track." This might become part of your teen participatory ground rules. A teen from our library's IRS group brought an effective method to a meeting, and the rest of the group agreed unanimously to adopt it. It is very simple, but powerful.

When side conversations ensue or there is too much "talking over" the person who has the floor, the person having the floor or another person from the group who wants the noise to cease says loudly, "Three, two, one . . .". As soon as they realize a call for quiet has begun, everyone else joins in, usually on, ". . . , two, one." After "one," everyone CLAPS together. This is an easy way to calm things down and get back on track, and the best part is that everyone smiles while doing it. Keep this technique handy to present to your teens if you need a noise diffuser during meetings.

The Power of Props

Another ground rule component might be a prop of some sort to indicate who may speak. This prop may be anything your teens decide, as long as they agree that the person who is holding it has the floor.

Through the years working with the teens at the City of Mesa Library, we went through a variety of props. One was a model of the starship *Enterprise*, which kept being accidentally dropped, and finally it could not be repaired any longer. Following that was a too-heavy volume of *The Lord of the Rings*, a squeaky plastic gavel that eventually fell apart, and finally an odd plastic blow-up toy character left over from the children's summer reading program, with feet that faced in the wrong direction. The teens dubbed the toy "Mutey," the mutation, and he became the ultimate prop—squeaky, unbreakable, funny, and easy to pass around.

As you can see, teens aim for their props to have an element of humor. That is a great bonus, because there is nothing like instilling humor in teen groups! You want your teens to be serious about their contributions to the library, but at the same time, you want them to have fun. Be sure to add entertaining elements to all meetings and activities with your teens.

Effective Brainstorming

Brainstorming has been mentioned at various times throughout this book as a technique that promotes creativity and produces numerous ideas very quickly. It may be used with teens to name their library group, name their teen space, solve a problem, give feedback, create ground rules, or respond to a question.

It is important to prepare the teens prior to beginning any brainstorming session so that they truly understand the process. Brainstorming is most effective when the teen participants feel comfortable that their ideas and input matter, that they are empowered to make group decisions, and that what they contribute will be respected and utilized.

Here are some guidelines for accomplishing successful brainstorming sessions with the teens who are involved in your library:

- Focus on a topic and related question about which to brainstorm. The question should have many possible answers. Using a white board, chalk board, or easel with pad of paper, write the question where everyone can see it during a group meeting. Examples of questions you might brainstorm are: "What is a good name for the teen space at our new library branch?" "What summer reading activities would teens in our city most enjoy?" "How do we get more teens to use our library?"

- Once the topic and question are established, ask the teens to contribute their ideas. Write their responses where everyone can see them. These should be written in single words or short phrases.

- Explain to the teens that during a brainstorming session they must not comment on each other's ideas until the end, or repeat ideas that have already been contributed.

- Encourage everyone in the group to share ideas, but do not move around the group in a circle or force participants to think of a response. Doing so will inhibit creativity. Let the teens raise their hands and be called upon by you or an appointed teen facilitator from the group as they give their input.

- Let the teens give all the answers. Only make a comment when participants seem stumped and need a general suggestion as inspiration and to prod them forward.

- If a contributing statement seems unclear, ask the teen to clarify his or her thoughts, or paraphrase to make sure that you have effectively captured the idea.

- Write down *every* new suggestion, even the ones that may seem off the wall or unusual. Often, "out of left field" suggestions evolve into the most creative, helpful, or interesting ones.

- Once the stream of ideas wanes, stop the brainstorming. Go through the list and ask for comments. Through group discussion, combine similar ideas and create a "short list."

- Teens may now discuss the ideas from the narrowed-down list and head toward a solution. The group may need to refine the list a few times to get to this point. Be patient and flexible, but be sure to encourage the teens to stay on task toward a final vote. This can be accomplished by a show of hands or by a secret ballot, whichever they prefer.

- There might be multiple answers, depending on the original question. Whatever the teens' final conclusions, be sure to act on their ideas and recommendations as soon as possible.[4]

Have fun during your brainstorming sessions, but make sure teens remember that the ultimate goal is a serious one—to bring ideas to life, to come to good decisions, and to make library services and processes for and with teens run more smoothly and effectively.

Organizing Teen Advisory and Other Library Groups

Discuss with your teens how they would like their teen participatory group to function. Some of the initial brainstorming sessions should focus on organizational issues. Your teens might want to develop a mission statement, vision statement, and maybe even goals and bylaws. Let them decide how flexible or stringent they would like their group to be.

Another issue to decide on is whether or not to have officers or other set roles that the teens will fill. For instance, at the Corona del Sol High School Friends of the Library Club, the teens chose to have a well-established set of officers for their group, including a president, vice president, secretary, treasurer, historian, and publicity manager.[5]

Other groups might want the arrangement to be less formal. For example, teens might like to take turns running meetings or being in charge of projects instead of having a president. In lieu of an official secretary, group members might like to rotate taking minutes of meetings and assisting with other clerical tasks. As much as possible, let your teens decide how they would like to operate and what duties to assign.

A Shining Example: Pima County Library, Arizona

Some of the most effective library teen volunteer programs in the country take place at the Pima County Public Library system in Arizona (www.library.pima.gov/teenzone). Part of the DeWitt Wallace/Reader's Digest Fund's "Public Libraries as Partners in Youth Development" initiative in the late 1990s (www.urbanlibraries.org/showcase/plpyd.html), and an exemplary library system even before it served as a component for this project, it has expanded and improved its offerings to children and teens in a number of areas since then. One of these is in the caliber of its teen library volunteer programs.

Pima County Public Library teen volunteer programs encompass many of the opportunities you have already encountered in this book and especially in this chapter. The following pages describe a few examples of the outstanding materials the Pima County Public Library system uses to promote and run teen volunteering activities (see figures 10.1 through 10.3), shared here with permission from Gina Macaluso, Coordinator of Youth Services. The information may be adapted to any library's teen volunteer program and will provide assistance as you begin or improve a teen volunteer program at your own library.

TRAINING LIBRARY STUDENT AIDES

Teens who help out in their school libraries also need direction and to learn the ropes. At Bowie High School (see chapter 3), Kelly Hoppe has a special training process all student library aides must go through. At the beginning of the year, she shows them a PowerPoint presentation that she created, which explains all the duties required. She then demonstrates how to check books in and out and observes teens doing it several times before allowing them to do it on their own. She also carefully explains the Dewey Decimal system and the way books are organized on the shelves. Her training system is straightforward and easy for students to follow. Here are its major points, organized in an effective fashion, which you might find useful to adapt for your library's training:

- **Mission of Library Aide Program.** To provide educational experiences that lead to real-world job skills and lifelong learning for the participants while improving the quality of library services for students, faculty, and staff.

- **The Rules.**

  - Be polite: This means, be approachable.

  - Treat library users (or patrons) with courtesy and respect. Respect for library user privacy is essential for ensuring happy, satisfied patrons who will return and continue to use the library.

  - If you are assisting someone and another patron approaches you for help, politely tell that person you will be right with him or her or find another aide or the librarian to help.

  - Set a good example for other students by using a quiet voice and good manners.

  - Consider the library a professional workplace.

Pima County Public Library
Teen Volunteer Orientation & Training

- **WELCOME!**

  The Library welcomes you as a volunteer member of the library staff. Thank you for your interest in becoming a teen volunteer. Your time, energy, and talent enable our library to continue providing a high level of service. We hope your association with the library meets your needs as well as ours.

- **POLICIES AND PROCEDURES**

  Volunteers are considered members of the library staff and have the following rights and responsibilities:

  - **Attendance**

  Schedules are planned to give the library coverage needed to provide adequate and efficient library service. Volunteers are depended upon to work the hours they are scheduled. Promptness in coming to work is expected. Please notify the Volunteer Coordinator in the event of absence or tardiness. Please try to give adequate notice of planned absence so that schedules may be rearranged.

  - **Volunteer Name Badges**

  Volunteer name badges are to be worn by all volunteers on duty. Volunteer name badges help library customers distinguish between volunteers and paid staff and also serve to promote the volunteer program.

  - **Dress**

  Volunteers are asked to dress appropriately for working public service. Specific guidelines:
    *Closed-toed shoes are required to protect against injury from dropped books or book carts.
    *Jeans are acceptable, but ragged, frayed or cut-off jeans with holes in them are inappropriate on the job.
    *Please refrain from wearing sweatpants.
    *T-shirts with messages or promotional graphics relating to drugs, alcohol, or sex are prohibited.

  - **Conduct**

  Friendly, efficient service is expected at all times. Since the public sees you as a staff member, you represent the library and its commitment to excellent service.

  Try to be pleasant and courteous to everyone using the library, regardless of their demeanor. If you are not absolutely certain how to answer a customer's question, refer her/him to the staff member at the Information Desk. Questions relating to the location of books and other library materials and reference questions should always be referred to staff at the Information Desk.

  Visits or personal telephone calls are not appropriate in a place of work. If you must contact someone, wait until you are not on duty. Emergencies (sudden illness, for example) or the need to inform your family of an unexpected change in scheduling, are considered library business, and you are welcome to use the library telephones for these purposes.

  Food and drink are not permitted in the library except in the staff areas. Smoking is not allowed anywhere in the library.

- **THANK YOU!!!**

Figure 10.1. Pima County Public Library Teen Volunteer Orientation and Training Flyer

Pima County Public Library

Staff Tips for a Smooth-Running Summer Reading Teen Volunteer Experience

- Be prepared. Have all your handouts, time sheets, booklets, file folders etc. all ready before SRP starts.
- Solicit Teen Volunteers through word-of-mouth from last year's group, through flyers, candy-jar contest, and school visits.
- Discuss EXACTLY what you expect. Be positive and reinforcing. Be open to their ideas. Give individual or group orientations.
- Model behavior for giving out prizes.
- Have a separate SRP table in Children's or near Reference, so teens feel they have their own space.
- Have posted schedule, and also give teens a copy of schedule.
- Have a list of teens things-to-do for teens and librarians.
- Have a "project box" for volunteer teens.
- NEVER (if you can help it!) have more than 2 teens at a time.
- Lots of Thank You's, Praise.
- Emphasize that you can give a written recommendation if they do a good job.
- As much as possible, allow the teen volunteers to take charge of replenishing incentives, counting, letting you know what is low.
- Have incentives on something mobile (like a cart to move to reference).
- Make clear that they refer all reference questions to librarians.
- Have teen volunteers check in with person in charge.
- Introduce individual teen volunteers to library staff, and give them a tour of the library, lunchroom facilities.
- Allow teen volunteers to READ if they don't want to do projects.
- Above all make the teens feel useful, welcome, and appreciated!

Figure 10.2. Pima County Public Library Staff Tips for Summer Reading

PIMA COUNTY PUBLIC LIBRARY
TEEN VOLUNTEER PROGRAM

- ## WHAT WILL I BE DOING AS A TEEN VOLUNTEER?

Examples of teen volunteer activities:

- During the summer months, assist librarians during busy times by handing out and explaining summer reading program materials to children or teens.
- Alphabetize children's books by author and shelve them.
- Straighten up books on shelves and straighten up furnishings in children's room.
- Help with children's programs:
  - Help set up meeting room before programs.
  - Help clean up and organize meeting room after program.
  - Take attendance at the door and count children.
- Gather and arrange books for children's book displays.
- Tape and jacket books.
- Prepare craft materials.

- ## WHAT WILL I GET OUT OF IT?

- An opportunity to learn and practice a variety of job-related skills.
- Satisfaction from knowing that you are helping to promote reading and literacy in your community.
- Something different and interesting to do.
- An opportunity to meet new people.
- A pleasant, air-conditioned working environment during the long, hot summer.
- Volunteer experience, a welcome addition to college, scholarship, and job applications.

- ## WHO IS ELIGIBLE FOR VOLUNTEERING?

- Teens who want to (not because their parents are making them do it)!
- Teens who are self-motivated and reliable.
- Teens who are 14 years old or older.

- ## HOW DO I GET STARTED?

- Fill out the attached application and turn it in to the Information Desk at any participating library branch. The Volunteer Coordinator will contact you.

If you have any questions about the program or application, feel free to call:

NAME:	BRANCH:	PHONE NUMBER:
Sue Parker	Himmel Park Branch Library	791-4397

Himmel Park Branch Library
1035 North Treat Avenue
Tucson, AZ 85716

Figure 10.3. Pima County Public Library Teen Volunteer Program Information Sheet

- **Be productive.**
  - You are "on duty" during the entire class period, and your library duties come first.
  - After completing daily library duties, use down time constructively and wisely while waiting to assist patrons. This means you will not be allowed to play games on the computers or Internet, but you may use this time to study, read, or work on something else.

- **Be positive.**
  - If a patron needs assistance, stop what you are doing and help.
  - Be approachable. The library is a service-oriented institution, and our goal is to provide patrons with the help they need to locate the information they are seeking.

- **Be punctual.**
  - Arrive on time for your duties in the library.
  - Always ask permission before leaving the library for any reason.
  - Consider the library a professional workplace.

- **Be prepared.**
  - Enter the library daily with the attitude of helping the patron.
  - Bring any necessary items you might need to be productive during your down time.
  - If you choose not to sit behind the desk, sit nearby so you can go right over and assist patrons when they walk up to it.

- **Duties of a Library Aide.**
  - While at the circulation desk, help to greet classes and monitor drop-in students. Make sure all drop-ins have a pass.
  - Check the book cart each day at the beginning of the period and reshelve any books. Reshelve magazines.
  - "Read" and straighten shelves. Books should always be in order and neatly arranged, at the front edge of the shelf.
  - Help keep the library neat and orderly by straightening chairs, books, newspapers, and magazines, and picking up any trash.
  - Help with bulletin boards or other library displays.
  - Help with processing new books.
  - Help with equipment as needed.
  - Become familiar with computers and be able to locate a book on the shelf after using the catalog.
  - Know how to load paper into the printers and copy machines.
  - Make copies for students.
  - Become familiar with the online databases plus Internet access in order to assist students who need help.
  - Take care of fines.

- **Things *not* to do:**

    - Operate the laminator without permission.

    - Make copies for students of things that are not related to school assignments. If they need copies of this nature, have them talk to Mrs. Hoppe, because they will be charged 10¢ a page.

    - Leave the library without permission.

    - Delete a friend's fines without permission from Mrs. Hoppe.

    - Let anything leave the library without scanning it. If it is something without a barcode, like a newspaper, just write down the name of the person and what it is he or she is taking, then give the information to Mrs. Hoppe.

    - Allow students to enter the library with food or drinks.

    - Make change from the fine cash box. There is not enough change to do this for all. The change we have must be kept for taking care of patrons who want to pay their fines.

    - Answer the phone in Mrs. Hoppe's office. The phone has an answering machine, so if it rings and Mrs. Hoppe isn't available, just let the machine pick up.

    - Tell anyone, teacher or otherwise, what an individual has checked out. Discuss individual checkouts only with the patron himself or herself. Patron privacy is of the utmost importance. If a teacher wants to know what a particular student has checked out, politely tell him or her to talk to Mrs. Hoppe.[6]

Library Helpers Stick It to Collection Shelving

Teaching library aides of all ages to shelve properly can be a challenge. Students must first understand how libraries are organized in general, and then how their library is organized in particular. They must know the differences between fiction, nonfiction, and a variety of other media. Considering how confused students can be from the "customer" side of the desk, when they are looking for materials, you can imagine how challenging it might seem to a volunteer or aide who is learning the ropes of proper shelving for the first time.

Keeping this in mind, students at the Raytown South Middle School in Missouri (www.raytownschools.org) who serve as library helpers are trained intensively for their first two months of service to shelve books using the Dewey Decimal Classification System. Their library uses a special technique to make learning easier. Wooden paint stick stirrers, spray-painted a variety of colors, one color assigned per aide, are placed in each page-down/spine-up book during shelving. Library media center staff may then check to be sure the books were put in their proper locations. When books are placed properly, praise is offered. When improvement is needed, further instructions may tactfully be given to the "owner" of a particular color stick. This little trick could be useful in any library setting where teens are responsible for shelving materials.

School librarian Betty Sproul says, "The Library Helper's Program gives students a feeling of ownership in their library media center. Students who come to shelve books have the ability to locate their own books and have a marketable skill for future jobs in other libraries. Library Helpers make friends with other students in the building and feel like they fit in and belong to a group of people with like interests."[7]

RETENTION OF TEEN PARTICIPANTS

A vital aspect of working with teen library participants is retaining as many of them as possible for as long as they remain interested and engaged, while keeping an open door policy for prospective new members. As previously discussed, there are many reasons why every teen does not stay involved throughout his or her entire span of teenage years. Some teens sign up when they start in middle school and will still be connected when they head off to college. Others will only be there to pitch in at the library for a limited time. Either way, one of the most important keys in retaining teen volunteers and other participants is special thanks and rewards.

Showing Appreciation for and Recognition of Teen Participants

There are many ways that you can give recognition to your teens. Here are the ways that several of the libraries you have read about in this book offer appreciation and perks to their teens:

- At the Ames Public Library in Iowa, teens have free pizza at TAG meetings. TAG teens get the first shot at new advanced Reading copies and have their opinions honored through the First Reads Club.[8]

- At Bowie High School, aides may eat snacks in the library as long as they do it in the back room away from the circulation desk. They receive small bags of candy and trinkets for Christmas and usually for Halloween or Valentine's Day as well. Each senior aide receives a small graduation gift at the end of the year. Teens may request job or academic references when they are needed.[9]

- At Cedar Valley Middle School library, TAB members get first looks at new books and may check out books without their cards after meetings. Members get snacks at meetings and are treated to an end-of-year ice cream party.[10]

- Corona del Sol Friends of the Library Club members earn a certificate of participation at the end of the school year when they have completed 20 hours of community service.[11]

- The Farmers Branch Manske Library provides several perks. There is a Teen Volunteer Lock-In at the end of every summer that is very popular. To receive an invitation, teens must work for at least 10 hours during the summer and turn in a completed reading log. In addition, teens who do an exceptional job during the summer are nominated by library staff for the All Stars program. A special pizza party is held for them at the end of the summer, at which they receive a special goody bag and during which they may play Rock Band or Dance Dance Revolution and sing Karaoke. Besides that, the Farmers Branch mayor gives each teen volunteer a letter of appreciation that includes the total hours he or she worked during the summer. Teen advisory group members also get pizza and cookies at their meetings.[12]

- At the Ketchikan Public Library, TAG members "get fed regularly." Because they are part of the library, they have a voice, get to participate, and make decisions—which the teens consider perks. They are given small treats on occasion, such as a Christmas stocking of goodies. Those graduating from high school get a few small gifts from their fearless adult leader, who also made simple mementos for each member to commemorate TAG's first anniversary.[13]

- Each teen volunteer at the City of Mesa Library receives a greeting card on his or her birthday. Cards are also sent for holidays and other personal events as appropriate. Throughout the year there are staff potlucks, holiday parties, and a formal luncheon in the spring to honor all volunteers for service, including teens. In addition, teen volunteers get a 20 percent discount at the used bookstore, an extended checkout period for library materials, and a waiver of late fees. Teen advisory group members also receive a membership card and a YAAC T-shirt.[14]

- Teens who serve as Teen Library Advocates at the Pima County Library not only earn $100 for their efforts, but they qualify to attend a library sleepover especially for those who have completed the program.[15]

- Poudre River Public Library District teens who are members of the Interesting Reader Society receive an IRS T-shirt. They also get to go to special events such as the Colorado Teen Literature Conference each April.

- At the Santa Cruz Public Library, the TAC/ACT members may "work off" overdue fines by attending meetings and assisting with programming or events. They also get a first shot at donated books and advanced reading copies after staff review. Local businesses also provide perks, such as free unlimited ride passes to the local boardwalk.[16]

- Members of the Off the Shelf Book Club, and sometimes of the Media Squad, at the Shepherd Junior High library get to come to all author events and personally get to meet the authors. Group photographs signed by the authors are hung on the library's Author Wall. A perk of being on the Media Squad is getting a first chance to check out new books in the library. The library also gives the teens pizza parties at the end of each semester to celebrate a job well done.[17]

- A special ice cream party is held at the South Brunswick Public Library during the last Youth Advisory Council meeting of the year, and includes Teen Special Forces members. In addition, the library hosts a Teen Volunteer and Page Staff Appreciation Luncheon. Each teen who volunteers more than five hours is invited, and there are special giveaways for graduating seniors. Enjoying "the glow of success" is also a perk for the teens.[18]

- The Youth Advisory Council members at the St. Timothy's School library get special lunches, receive advance reading copies of forthcoming books, and get to go on field trips, such as to bookstores.[19]

The Ultimate Reward: Library Lock-ins or Sleepovers

One fun and notable form of recognition that you will have noticed some libraries offering their teens is a "library lock-in" or "library sleepover." These events are usually reserved as rewards for a job well done by teens who serve on library advisory groups or for volunteers who complete a particularly challenging or long-term project. Lock-ins take place overnight while the library is closed, during which time creative and enjoyable activities are scheduled for the teens. Some teens do try to sleep, so provisions for that option have to be included.

Because of the potential liability involved, it is important for libraries that want to offer this type of reward to plan carefully and to ensure that proper permission forms are fully completed by parents or guardians before the activity takes place. Special permission must also be secured to allow access to and to use the library overnight.

Spring Lea Henry's Top Ten Tips for a Successful Lock-in

Spring Lea Henry, a former teen services librarian from Colorado Springs, Colorado, and now the publisher of The Grumpy Dragon press (www.GrumpyDragon.com), which prints books and other works by talented teen authors, has had a great deal of experience doing teen library lock-ins. Here are her top 10 recommendations for conducting a successful lock-in event:

1. Be sure to have scheduled activities for every hour of the night, because some teens will not lie down and go to sleep no matter how much you beg, and unscheduled or unstructured time is when any problems might occur.

2. Conversely, have a separate space for the teens who do want to sleep, and always keep it monitored to prevent those who are wide awake from disturbing them.

3. Make sure to have at least one adult for every five teens.

4. Plan carefully to have plenty of food and drink for the whole night, including some breakfasty items for the morning.

5. Be sure to have a good telephone number for each parent or guardian in case there is a need for a middle-of-the-night pickup.

6. Related to number 5, be sure to have a clear list of rules for the lock-in on the permission form. (See figure 10.4.) Parents and teens BOTH have to sign the contract, which includes phrasing about how they understand that breaking these rules means that mom, dad, or legal guardian *will* get a middle-of-the-night phone call to pick up the teen.

7. Also be sure the teens know that if they try to leave before official pickup in the morning, mom, dad, or legal guardian will get a message saying they left the event.

8. Themed lock-ins are awesome because they provide a connection through all the structured activities. Successful lock-in ideas include an *American Idol* karaoke contest, a themed movie-a-thon, and a computer or other gaming night.

9. The last hour or so before pickup, be sure to involve all the teens in helping to clean up the spaces that were used for the event.

10. Be sure to check off each teen's name from your attendance list as he or she is picked up.[20]

If the list of things to keep in mind for a teen lock-in seems daunting, do not let that discourage you. Plan early, consult with your teens, enlist reliable adults to serve as either paid or volunteer chaperones and assistants, and make sure all the permissions that you need are in order. Your teens will appreciate this unique event as a memorable reward for all the time they spend helping the library. You will, too!

Service Learning Credits and Letters of Recommendation

Be sure your teens know that you are happy to sign their service learning or other community service charts or forms to verify whatever time they spent volunteering in or for the library. The time it takes for you to sign your name and complete the charts or forms is minimal and well worth it for what the teens contribute.

Poudre River Public Library District
IRS Summer's End Lock-In
Friday, August 15th at 8:00 p.m. to Saturday, August 16th at 7 a.m.

In order to participate in the Lock-In, teens and parents/guardians must read this form, complete a permission slip and bring it to the Main Library's or the Harmony Library's Reference/Information Desk on or before the lock-in date of August 15, 2008. You may also return it on the night of the lock-in.

- The Lock-In begins at 8:00 p.m. on Friday (snacks will be available throughout the evening, but please eat dinner before coming to the library).
- The Lock-In ends promptly at 7 a.m. on Saturday. Please drop off/pick up your teen promptly at the front entrance of the Main Library, Poudre River Public Library District, at 201 Peterson Street. A staff member will be stationed at the front door to greet teens on Friday evening.

Parent and Teen Information

- The Lock-In will take place at the Poudre River Public Library District's Main Library branch, located at 201 Peterson.
- There will be organized games and activities.
- No teen will be allowed to leave the library between 8 p.m. on Friday and 7 a.m. on Saturday. Teens may arrive later on Friday if they have made prior arrangements with Sue-Ellen.
- An area for sleeping will be provided for anyone wishing to do so. Sleeping bags, blankets, and pillows will not be provided—teens must bring their own.
- If a teen breaks any of the rules listed below in the code of behavior agreement, the parent/guardian will be called to pick the teen up.
- Sue-Ellen Jones is the library staff person in overall charge of the Lock-In. Sue-Ellen's cell phone number in case of emergencies is (970) 555-4116. Diane Tuccillo's cell phone is (970)-555-9926. Sue-Ellen will be the official chaperone for the lock-in.

Code of Behavior Agreement
Rules of behavior expected for all Teens:

- Teens must stay in designated areas of the library (they may not go into staff work areas, the staff room, etc.)
- Teens agree to follow the directions of library staff.
- No one is permitted to leave the library building at any time during the lock-in unless their parents arrange to pick them up early or library staff contact parents to pick the teen up.
- Teens must respect library property.
- Absolutely no drugs or alcohol are permitted.
- Weapons of any kind will not be permitted in the library.

The Poudre River Public Library District will make reasonable accommodations for access to its services, program, and activities and will make special communications arrangements for persons with disabilities. Please call 221-6380 for assistance.

Figure 10.4. Poudre River Public Library District, IRS Lock-in Permission Form

Parent/Guardian and Teen Release Statement
(Please detach this page and return. Keep the first page for your information.)

As parent/legal guardian of _____, I have reviewed the information about the Lock-In at the Poudre River Public Library District's Main Library at 201 Peterson, and give permission for _____ to be involved in the Lock-In activities.

I/We understand that teens involved in the Lock-In will be dropped off at the library's front entrance at 8:00 p.m. on Friday, August 15, 2008 and will be picked up at the library's front entrance no later than 7 a.m. on Saturday, August 16, 2008. I/We have reviewed the rules of the Lock-In and understand that I/We will be called at any hour of the evening to take our teenager home if the teen is unable to comply with the code of behavior agreement.

I/We agree to make no claims against the Poudre River Public Library District. I/We understand that all reasonable safety precautions will be taken at all times by the chaperones of the Poudre River Public Library District's Lock-In during the night's events and activities. I/We agree not to hold the Poudre River Public Library District, its trustees, chaperones, employees, and volunteer staff for damages, losses, or injuries incurred by the subject of this form, including any claims for negligence.

Parent Guardian/Signature _____ Date _____

IRS Member's Signature _____ Date _____

Person to call in case of emergency _____ Telephone Number _____

Alternate emergency contact _____ Telephone Number _____

****

Note: You do not have to sign the following Photo Release in order to attend the Lock-In.

Photo Release: I hereby consent that photographs of my teen taken at the Library Lock-In may be used by the Poudre River Public Library District in library publicity, newspaper articles, and audiovisual presentations; furthermore, I hereby consent that such photographs and the plates from which they are made shall be their property, and they shall have the right to duplicate, reproduce, and make other uses of such photographs and plates as they may desire free and clear of any claims whatsoever on my part.

Parent/Guardian Signature _____ Date _____

Figure 10.4. Poudre River Public Library District, IRS Lock-in Permission Form (*Cont.*)

Another way that you can pay your teens back for their library involvement is by letting them know you may provide letters of recommendation for them based on the actual time and effort they spent helping the library. These letters are usually requested for college admissions, scholarship applications, other volunteer applications (such as for a local hospital), and sometimes employment. At times, the request might be for a letter (on letterhead). At other times, teens will ask you to complete a form with check-off boxes about their capabilities and work performance. In addition, you might be asked to provide a verbal reference via a phone call. Remember that minutes and attendance sheets from meetings and trainings, and any notes you have made, will help you a great deal when you need to generate these personal references. Keep them handy.

Be honest about each teen's contributions when evaluating his or her record of time spent in library activities. Tell how long you have know a teen and how long he or she has been involved in the library; explain the activities in which he or she took part; and give some feedback about the teen's skills, talents, reliability, and interpersonal relationships as you have observed them. Remain as objective as you can, and be tactful about any shortcomings a teen might have.

Some recommendations will have to be sent to a specific person through the regular mail. Teens may also ask you for a letter that you seal in an envelope, initial on the back, and give to the teen to turn in with his or her other paperwork. Before completing a recommendation, be clear as to the format required and how it needs to be handled. You do not want to spend the time providing a reference only to discover it was not accepted because you did not follow proper procedures. This is one of the perks teens get for their library participation, so make sure to follow through as requested.

Culminating Thoughts about Rewards and Recognition for Teens

The number and variety of perks vary greatly from library to library, with some libraries offering numerous ongoing perks and others only offering community service credit. Think about how you would like to reward your teen participants, and find out what your library is able to do for them. Even if your library can only afford something small, extending thanks and presenting teens with an award or certificate of appreciation should be a minimum (see figure 10.5, p. 222).

Of course, do remember that "basking in the glow of success" is always a perk for teens!

A FINAL THOUGHT: *YOUR* REWARDS

For all the time and effort you put into figuring out (1) what kinds of teen participation will be a good fit for your library; (2) who will be just the right person or persons to serve as teen leaders; (3) how to recruit teens for the cause; and (4) ways to effectively direct teens through worthwhile and productive activities, you will get your just deserts. You will be rewarded abundantly, as much your teens will be rewarded.

You will draw teens to the library who might never have known it was there. You will get teens who already come to the library to become a more integral part of it. The image of youth services in your library will be improved as the teens you actively recruit ultimately get involved and exhibit their dedication. Your library will be better connected to the community. Best of all, you will be encouraging teens to be the readers, leaders, and library users of the future.

Thanks for volunteering!

We appreciate all of your hard work!

Teen Lock-In

Teens who have volunteered for at least 10 hours and completed a reading log will be invited to the library Lock-In on Friday, August 8.

Volunteer All Stars

Library staff will nominate exceptional teen volunteers for the All Stars list. You'll be invited to the All Stars Pizza Party and you'll win a prize!

Letter from the Mayor

At the end of the summer you'll receive a letter from the mayor thanking you for your service to the community.

Remember...volunteer experience looks GREAT on job, scholarship & college apps tions!

Figure 10.5. Farmer's Branch Library Teen Volunteer Appreciation Flyer

ENDNOTES

1. Carly Sween and Penelope Cook, *Ten More New Icebreakers: Cool Introductions* (Education World, 1996–2009), www.educationworld.com/a_lesson/lesson/lesson271.shtml (accessed September 21, 2009).

2. Youth Group Ice Breaker Games, *Alphabet Get to Know You*, 2006–2009), teens.lovetoknow.com/Youth_Group_Icebreaker_Games (accessed September 21, 2009).

3. Jennifer Dillon, e-mail message to author, August 13, 2008.

4. Amnesty International Canada, Brainstorming (Human Rights Activism for Youth, 2009), www.amnesty.ca/youth/youth_action_toolkit/brainstorming.php (accessed September 21, 2009).

5. Joann Pompa, e-mail message to author, March 23, 2007.

6. Kelly Hoppe, "BHS Library Aide Program" (PowerPoint presentation, Bowie High School, Bowie, Texas, n.d.).

7. Betty Sproul, "Implementing a Library Helper Program Is Easy, Economical, and Energizing," *Library Media Connection* 24 (April–May 2006): 44.

8. Tracy Briseño, e-mail message to author, July 28, 2008.

9. Kelly Hoppe, e-mail message to author, July 6, 2008.

10. Kate DiPronio, e-mail message to author, May 8, 2008.

11. Joann Pompa, e-mail message to author, March 27, 2007.

12. Jennifer Dillon, e-mail message to author, August 13, 2008.

13. Kelly Johnson, e-mail message to author, May 18, 2008.

14. Kathee Herbstreit, e-mail message to author, January 11, 2008.

15. Pima County Public Library Teen Zone, *Teen Library Advocates* (Pima County Public Library, 2009), www.library.pima.gov/teenzone/getinvolved (accessed September 21, 2009).

16. Sandi Imperio, e-mail message to author, October 4, 2008.

17. Melanie Limbert-Callahan, e-mail message to author, February 21, 2008.

18. Saleena Davidson, e-mail message to author, July 29, 2008.

19. Ernie Cox, e-mail message to author, September 29, 2008.

20. Spring Lea Henry, e-mail message to author, February 12, 2009.

11

Focus on Feedback:
Assessing Your Library's Youth
Participation

When you offer teens the opportunity to contribute to the library via their participation, how do you know if what the teens are doing is successful? How do you know what should continue and what needs improvement? How do you learn about new ideas based on what the teens have already accomplished? The answers to these and other relevant questions are encompassed in one last element that is crucial to effective library youth participation: assessment.

Youth participation assessment differs from *youth participatory evaluation*, discussed in chapter 8. Remember, youth participatory *evaluation* allows teens to share their ideas and to provide input on library-oriented programs, projects, and focus groups for the purpose of development or improvement. It encourages teens to speak out at conferences and to serve on library boards with adults, and gives them a voice in building effective library service for all young adults.

On the other hand, youth participation *assessment* gauges the quality and quantity of teens' actual involvement. It examines the success of the activities, events, programs, and projects in which teens are actively engaged in their libraries. It also allows supervisors or advisors to evaluate the volunteer work performance of individual teens. These assessments help you encourage improvements in teens' work, offer rewards and praise when warranted, and make adjustments as needed. They also give you (and library administrators) statistics and other feedback to justify the existence of teen participation and documentation for providing academic and job references for teens.

Such assessments can be challenging because of the nature of the beast. Advocates may have difficulty "proving" that youth participation works and produces benefits, and that it should not been viewed as a frill. Administrative policy decisions about programs and

225

activities often require "hard evidence" to justify them, and the gains that result from youth participation can be tricky to measure. That is because elements such as development in maturity, responsibility, self-confidence, and empowerment among teen participants are also valid considerations. Although we can provide quantifiable information about active teen involvement, the qualitative part is as applicable—perhaps even more so—and balance is called for in any library youth participation assessment.[1]

With the many problems today's libraries face regarding financial issues, staffing, and even organizational survival, you might be thinking that there is not enough time to spend doing evaluations. However, particularly because of these things, it is more important than ever to plan and prepare evaluations for your teen participation activities. To do so within the perimeters of any time constraints you are experiencing, it is important to keep your evaluations simple, yet to the point. The suggestions included in this chapter will help you do that.

EVALUATION OF TEEN PARTICIPATORY ACTIVITIES

Because all volunteer projects have a "tendency to become entrenched and justify their own existence" and "may perpetuate themselves long after they have outlived their usefulness," a system of regular review should be part of every volunteer activity, whether it is in a library or elsewhere. Most often, when a project has been recognized as a success there is difficulty recognizing its need to be restructured or even phased out completely. It is irresponsible to continue a project just because of its positive results years before if those results are no longer achieved. It is just as irresponsible to cancel a program or project that is successful without doing everything possible to continue funding, staffing, and other support.[2]

Teen volunteer projects are no exception. The key to effective evaluation is anticipating change, whether positive or negative. In planning and developing your library's teen participatory program, always keep in mind that change is probably your most important commodity. The activities of your teens are directed toward change within the structure of your library and community, and it stands to reason that the organization of your teen program will itself be subject to change. Plan to adapt to change from the very beginning of your teen participatory projects.[3]

Suppose your library has been working with teens to produce a printed book review newsletter. You have had funding for printing costs, and the teens have been working hard to write reviews and to edit, produce, and distribute the newsletter. The newsletter even earned the prestigious Mayor's Award for outstanding youth project in your community.

In the last year, you have noticed that most of the printed copies of the newsletter have not been taken from the distribution points in schools and local teen agencies. You find yourself recycling more copies than are being read. The teens who are working on the project say that hardly anyone seems to be reading the printed newsletters in their school library anymore—they would rather read things online. The reaction of the teen participants to this apparent lack of interest by their peers is a corresponding lack of enthusiasm on their part. The project has become a chore, and you have to constantly prompt the teens to write their reviews and attend the newsletter preparation meetings. What happened? How can you fix it?

Or consider the opposite scenario: Maybe the newsletter is such an outstanding success that copies are disappearing much more quickly than anyone anticipated. You only have funding for a certain number of copies per year, but that quantity does not meet the demand. A grant to increase the number of copies and their frequency would help. How do you justify the additional staff time and money that the project will take to increase production? What rationales do you present in a grant application to increase funding for the project?

In either case, an honest assessment will give you answers and offer direction. It will help you realize strong points, determine what has changed, and figure out how to discontinue, intensify, or improve the project depending on the assessment results. Perhaps it is time to move the project to an online format, or for the teens to use their peer reader advisory skills in another manner. Perhaps it is time to expand and enhance newsletter production and distribution. You may decipher what is going on and where to aim the project by conducting a well-planned evaluation that includes not only participation statistics, but also cost figures and teen feedback.

A Basic Plan for an Assessment

Whether you are preparing to evaluate the overall picture of or individual programs within your teen participation activities, you will need a plan to create your evaluation. (See figure 11.1, p. 228.) It helps to decide on a course of action in advance. The following basic steps may help you develop an evaluation plan that reflects a clear image of your youth participation endeavors:

- State the reason(s) you are evaluating your teen volunteer activities. Is it because your administrators call for an annual report? Is it a requirement for a grant? Is it simply to give your youth services staff and teen participants some direction?

- Name the primary audience(s) for whom you are doing your evaluation.

- List the most important goals of your teen participation program or individual activities. You might zero in on one or two specific goals to examine more thoroughly.

- Describe how you will determine if the goals have been or are being reached.

- Decide on an evaluation plan and describe the assessment tools and measures you will use to figure out the progress and results of the goals.

- Keep statistics as well as notes as the teen participation activities progress.[4]

Analyzing Your Goals

When you are listing and evaluating your youth participation goals, responses to the following questions might serve as a guideline:

- Is the project making satisfactory progress toward its goals, and what indicates success?

- If the goals are not being attained, can they be defined in more realistic terms?

- Are "technical difficulties" inhibiting the project? For example, are computer capabilities suitable for the teen redesign of the Web page? Is there enough funding and supplies to see the project through?

- Do the teen participants carry out their assignments? Do they follow rules and instructions? Is their attendance dependable?

- Is there effective cooperation among your teen volunteers, the staff, and any other community members or participants?

- Has the project given you new perceptions and direction in considering new or improved ways for using teen volunteers? Are there new goals you would like to attain?

- Does the project contribute to the overall mission of your library? Is it helping to meet the needs of your library and community?

- Does the project contribute to positive youth development and resiliency?[5]

Teen Participation: From Planning to Evaluation

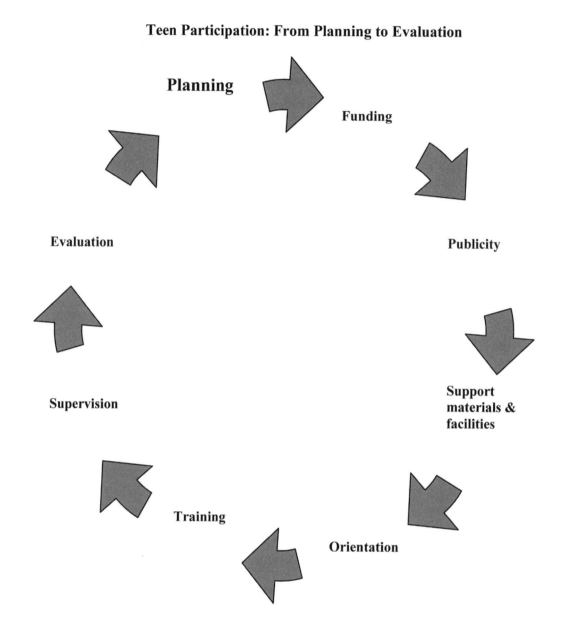

The youth participation activity process always returns to the **planning** stage. As evaluation leads to restructuring, the planning process begins again, and it is important to review each component to see that it is working according to the plan. If your teens are actively involved and their participation endeavors are vital, you might go through this cycle several times in the course of a year. Remember that the **evaluation** part of the process is important, and that plans must be altered and restructured as needed. **A project, activity, or event that serves its purpose will always be dynamic, flexible, and responsive to changing conditions.**

Figure 11.1. Teen Participation: From Planning to Evaluation Diagram. Adapted from *A Manual for Students Volunteering*, published by the National Student Volunteer Program, Volunteers in Service to America ACTION, Washington, DC, 1971.

Youth Participation Output Measures

Providing statistics to substantiate the results of your goals is essential. You might be wondering what the best figures to supply are, and how they might be used. A number of choices can aid you in putting together an evaluation that effectively reflects the quantitative elements of your teen participatory offerings.

One concrete way you can provide statistics on how the teens in your community are contributing to your library is by analyzing the *young adult participation rate*. All teen and tween participants who volunteer their services to assist with decision-making or service-delivery activities should be counted. This includes teens who are court referrals, even if their participation might not seem voluntary. In actuality, teens who are referred by the courts usually have a say in where they will complete their community service, and therefore, those who select the library should be counted.

In organizations that use adult volunteers, the contributors are generally viewed as an *input*, or *resource*, instead of an "output." Conversely, when the advancement of positive societal roles as part of healthy young adult social and emotional development comes into play, we can plausibly regard teen library involvement as an *output* of library service to teens. As we have seen, true youth advocates embrace teen library participation opportunities as instrumental to an effective plan of library service for this age group.[6] To substantiate this assertion, it is always beneficial to evaluate results—to justify activities, make changes or improvements where necessary, and acknowledge successes.

Determining the Teen Participation Rate and Other Figures

Figuring out the library participation rate or other involvement rates of teens in a school or community is fairly simple, and these data should be included in reports you prepare for your administrators or library board. Following are some basic procedures to decipher the rates:

- Keep track of all middle- through high-school-age library volunteers who participate in programming, help with operations, provide feedback, or assist in decision making.

- For a public library, compare the annual total to the number of teens living in your community or district.

- For a school library, compare volunteer figures with the entire school enrollment, with the number of teens involved in other school activities, or with student library participation levels at other schools in your community.

- Your school district's community research department may be able to assist you with current enrollment and youth population figures.

- To determine the percentage of teen participation, divide the annual number of teen participants by the total teen population of your service area.

- You may break down the figures further by tallying how many teens participated in each volunteer activity, or perhaps determine the average number of teens in relation to the frequency.

- Determine the economic significance of the teen volunteer hours by multiplying them by the current minimum wage or your library's lowest hourly pay rate.

- The first year's results will give you baseline measures, and subsequent results will indicate an increase, decrease, or stabilization of teen participation at your library. You may use this information to justify or alter teen library involvement, especially when combined with further evaluative measures, or to gauge the quality of teen supervision. You might also use it for other comparisons, such as to weigh the teen rate against the adult volunteer rate or to assist in calculating a community-wide teen participation rate.[7]

Evaluating Attendance and Outreach Resulting from Library Teen Participation

An attention-grabbing statistic you might seek is how many teens in your community or school were reached due to the efforts of the teens who are involved in your library. In addition to keeping tabs on how many teens actively contribute to the functioning of programs, activities, and events for fellow teens, indicate attendance and other figures for targeted teens who directly connect to the library because of teen volunteer contributions.

To illustrate, if you have 10 teens who assist with gaming programs, and the programs draw in 100 other teens to the library each month, for your community that might be an impressive track record. If you have 5 teens who create an annual literary magazine, and all 500 copies are snapped up by their peers each year, those 5 teens have proportionately reached 100 times their number. If you have 15 teens who represent the library at a street fair, and they paint the faces of 50 children and read stories to 100, those figures probably reflect time and effort well spent on your part and the teens' part.

When reporting the results of your library teen participation efforts, keep in mind that it can be exceedingly supportive to include any effects that library teen participation efforts have on youth or other elements of the community.

Gathering Data

For statistics to be available, careful records of youth participants must be regularly kept (see figure 11.2). One person should be designated to do this. Depending on the library, it could be a library assistant or even a volunteer coordinator. Each library staff member would keep the statistics on his or her teens and then turn them in to the person appointed to serve as the data clearinghouse. For example, if there is a youth services librarian in charge of teen volunteers, another person in charge of a teen advisory group, and still another working with teen computer assistants, they might each turn in the monthly statistics of participation to a volunteer coordinator who is collecting and tallying all the information for the year.[8]

Statistics may be kept in paper format, in Word documents, or on Excel spreadsheets. Use whatever system your library staff is most comfortable with. Experiment with using graphs and charts when completing your reports—maybe even in PowerPoint presentations—to make the statistics clearer and to increase their impact.

Soliciting Teen Responses

When you evaluate teen library participatory activities, make sure teen reactions are an instrumental part of your report. Remember, you *do not want teens to associate giving their feedback with school-like testing*! You want to ask for and get their responses about volunteer experiences, including their ideas for improvement, in a manner that allows them to feel comfortable and honest when they are telling you what they think.

Explain to your teens that you need to write an evaluation of their activities. Ask them how they might want to share feedback. Do they each want to write a paragraph or two describing their feelings, reactions, and recommendations? Do they want to discuss their thoughts at a meeting at which you will take notes? Are they willing to complete individual evaluation forms? If evaluation forms are an option, a Library Youth Participation Survey form that you can adapt is included in this chapter (see figure 11.3, p. 232).

Whatever teens are able to contribute to your assessment, be sure that you take their comments and recommendations to heart and do not accept them in a vacuum. Follow up by including their comments and ideas in your written assessment. This is an important step. When teens help to make the decisions about their library involvement, including how their participatory activities are evaluated, it goes hand in hand with their buy-in of the results.

Individual Youth Participation Record

Name: _____

Address: _____

Telephone number: _____

Birth date: _____ School: _____

Library Participation Activities

Date	Activity	Total Hours

Figure 11.2. Individual Youth Participation Record. Used with permission of Charles R. McClure, *Planning and Role Setting for Public Libraries: A Manual of Options and Procedures.* Chicago: American Library Association, 1987.

Library Youth Participation Survey

Your name (optional): _____ Grade: _____

Library branch: _____ Date: _____

Name of library supervisor or advisor: _____

Library volunteer program(s) in which you are involved: _____

_____

Please rate the following sentences about your overall volunteer experience by checking the appropriate boxes:

	Always	Usually	Sometimes	Never
1. I enjoy my library volunteer work.	☐	☐	☐	☐
2. I would tell other teens to volunteer.	☐	☐	☐	☐
3. My volunteer work is fun.	☐	☐	☐	☐
4. I get along well with my supervisor.	☐	☐	☐	☐
5. I think that adults respect me.	☐	☐	☐	☐
6. The volunteer work I do is important.	☐	☐	☐	☐
7. I am learning new skills.	☐	☐	☐	☐
8. I am learning things that could help me in the future.	☐	☐	☐	☐
9. I have a lot of responsibility when I volunteer.	☐	☐	☐	☐
10. My work is appreciated.	☐	☐	☐	☐
11. I want to do a good job.	☐	☐	☐	☐
12. I am helping my library and my community to improve.	☐	☐	☐	☐

Additional ideas and comments (use reverse side if needed): _____

_____

Figure 11.3. Library Youth Participation Survey. Adapted with permission from David A. Payne, "The Volunteer Survey," in *Evaluating Service-Learning Activities & Programs*. Scarecrow Press, 2000, p. 145.

Writing Your Assessment

When it is time to complete the evaluation, gather the information your have collected, tally figures as needed, sort written documentation, and put everything together in your final report. Every report will differ, depending on for whom it is written, its purpose, and administrative requirements. In general, a final report will include the following parts:

- a description of the youth participation program or activities being evaluated

- a list of the program goals and objectives

- a description of the evaluation methods used, including copies of any sample instruments

- the results of the evaluation, including statistics, quotes, cost figures, and other supporting documentation. These might be excerpts from newspaper articles about your teen activities, letters from members of the community, photographs, or other verification.

- analysis and recommendations based on the evaluation results[9]

Once your assessment is complete, share the findings with those in your intended audience and anyone else who might be interested. You might ask for feedback from those who are affected by the final results and recommendations, including your teens.

Be sure to use your assessments each year as foundations for making proposals, supporting new decisions, and making adjustments to subsequent youth participation programs and activities.[10] If you recognize that your youth participation rate needs improvement, review chapters 9 and 10 in this book to be sure you are approaching, monitoring, rewarding, and publicizing your teen volunteer opportunities in an effective manner.

Assessing Individual Teens

There are a number of reasons why you want to evaluate the *individual* teen participants in your library. You will need a record of each teen's activities, abilities, and accomplishments so that you are able to serve as a reputable academic or employment reference at a later date. You might need to complete paperwork for service learning, court-appointed reports, or a club's community service requirements. You might have a great number of teens interested in participating and want to be sure that those with the best track records are selected for opportunities requiring leadership skills and more responsibility.

On the other hand, keeping tabs on teens who are not meeting their volunteer agreements can supply documentation to help them improve. Plan to meet with such teens for one-on-one, objective consultations based on your records, to address any problems that have surfaced. Perhaps the task to which a particular teen has been assigned is not a good match, or the teen has an immaturity issue that is causing disruptions. Maybe another organization that needs teen volunteers might be a better placement. In these cases, it is necessary to keep careful evaluations on each teen's involvement, and to meet *privately* with teens who need advice or coaching. Give such teens a chance to improve through a written, agreed-upon course of action, and continue documentation.

In rare cases, advisors of teen volunteers must dismiss a youth from service. It is best to be prepared for this step with facts and figures that confirm the continuing problem so that you can discuss the dismissal by focusing specifically on *behavior*, not the teen *as a person*.

Keep the overall teen volunteer evaluation process simple, without long and involved evaluation forms. Figure 11.4 (p. 234) is a sample of a basic, easy-to-use form that you can adapt to your needs. You might consider completing a form for each teen who spends time actively participating in your library, adding notes and other documentation as appropriate.

Volunteer Evaluation Form

Name of volunteer: _____ Date: _____

Volunteer duties or tasks, or other participatory activities:

_____

_____

How many hours has this teen contributed to the library for each volunteer activity?:

_____

	Superior	Above Average	Average	Below Average	Don't Know
Ability to work with other volunteers	☐	☐	☐	☐	☐
Ability to work with your library staff	☐	☐	☐	☐	☐
Dependability	☐	☐	☐	☐	☐
Leadership qualities	☐	☐	☐	☐	☐
Resourcefulness	☐	☐	☐	☐	☐
General effectiveness	☐	☐	☐	☐	☐

General reactions of other teen volunteers, library staff, and the public to this volunteer:

_____

_____

Additional comments (continue on other side if needed):

_____

_____

_____

Would you be willing to write a reference for this teen volunteer?   YES ☐   NO ☐

List seven positive work performance attributes of this teen volunteer:

_____

_____

Figure 11.4. Volunteer Evaluation Form. Adapted from "Sample Volunteer Evaluation Form," in *A Manual for Students: Volunteering*, National Student Volunteer Program, Volunteers in Service to America (Washington, DC: ACTION, 1971), appendix B.

Encourage Teens to Write about Their Positive Experiences

One important way for teens to reflect upon their library participatory experiences is for them to write about them. Throughout this book, you have found personal impressions from teens who have been involved in library youth participation in various ways. Encourage your teen writers to express themselves by documenting their experiences in similar ways.

Professional journals that focus on teen issues in libraries sometimes provide opportunities for teens to contribute their ideas and reactions by offering columns that publish teens' work. Both *Voice of Youth Advocates* (*VOYA*), which has a column called "Notes from the Teenage Underground," and *Young Adult Library Services* (*YALS*), which includes a column called "Teen Perspectives," do this.

To illustrate, recall Alyssa Ratledge's *VOYA* article (mentioned in chapter 8), in which she described her positive experience serving as a full-fledged member of an adult library board. Likewise, Renee Roberts, who was a high school freshman at the time, shared feedback in *YALS* on the outstanding opportunities she encountered while serving on the Abington Community Library's Teen Literature Committee (ACL-TLC). In her article, she deftly described how the ACL-TLC provided reading activities for children through a Pirate Day, Victorian teas, and even a camp-out, plus Game Nights and book discussions for her peers: "The ACL-TLC has encouraged me to get more involved in my community and to think of ways to benefit those who live around me. I enjoy planning activities and then watching as children and teens come to the library and are surprised by what the library offers inside the hallowed doors."[11]

Published teen observations such as Alyssa's and Renee's not only provide excellent publicity for their libraries and share valuable perspectives that other teens may emulate, but *they can play an important part in assessing teen library participation*. There are other places where teens might contribute their written reactions about their volunteer experiences. How about the local newspaper? It might provide an opportunity for a teen to write an article, or even a column, about what goes on for teens in the library and what good books are there. School newspapers are another place where teens might try their hand at writing about their library volunteer experiences. In addition, if you have a teen library Web page or blog, your teens could post articles about their library participation experiences there.

One excellent arena for teens to share their viewpoints is in a Friends of the Library newsletter. Most libraries have Friends groups, and often it is the Friends who provide funding for teen projects and events. You might encourage a teen to write an article about the way Friends funding enhanced a teen volunteer experience or drew other teens to the library.

Friends of the Library members delight in hearing about teens in the community and how they are connecting to the library. Keep in mind this often overlooked outlet for teens to publish stories about their experiences. At the same time, if there are other businesses or agencies in your community that have helped fund teen library activities, your teens might similarly write a piece for their newsletters, if they have them.

These kinds of articles provide feedback for you and publicity and goodwill for your library, and give teens a chance to see their work in print. They may also supplement and reinforce any reports about teen services in your library when you submit them to your administrators, giving a perspective to your analytical assessments that can make the reports come alive.

In essence, when teens write articles about their library participatory experiences, the articles themselves become another facet of positive teen involvement.

IN CONCLUSION:
AN ACTIVE TEEN PARTICIPANT SUMS IT ALL UP

Lisa Yosevitz from the South Brunswick Public Library shared a heartfelt explanation for her library involvement. She encapsulates the personal, positive outcomes of her own library contributions and also reflects on many of the constructive aspects of teen participation that we have explored in this book:

> I started out as a puppeteer in 6th grade, then joined the Young Adult Council, helped plan and run the Summer Reading Festival, and helped at other events for all ages and interests with whatever was needed, such as arts and crafts, games, food, set up, or clean up. During the year, I became a Homework Buddies tutor, and started serving on the Teen Executive Board.
>
> Why did I want to do these things? Why not? The library is a place that gave me so much. Saleena and the other staff are always listening to us and giving us what we need and want, as far as the budget will extend. Why wouldn't I want to be active and join in making the library better and more fun? The library gave us a wonderful opportunity to gain leadership skills and make lasting friendships with our peers outside of school.
>
> Everything I did at the library was gratifying. Sometimes, I would see right away that it worked, like helping a child with homework and seeing him or her finally getting it. Sometimes an idea would take awhile, like the Friday Night Teen Lock-In that we finally got permission for after a few years of asking! Do you know we were allowed to decorate our Teen Room? I think that helps to us feel ownership and pride—and that the library values us![12]

As you consider Lisa's positive expression about her library participatory experiences and think back to the many other teen examples and ways to involve teens that you encountered while reading this book, remember how important it is to affirm teen library contributions.

Today's teens are our libraries' future. A 2008 *Library Journal* article stated, "If we don't get them in as kids and keep them as teens, we likely won't see them later in life. Kudos to librarians embracing service to teens."[13]

We have to do more than that, though. We need to make sure to not only embrace service to teens, but to ensure that teens have *a say, a place, and an active role* in how those library services are provided for and with them. When we give teens positive youth participatory opportunities in our libraries, we are building the next generation of readers, library users, and library supporters. We are helping to develop positive, self-assured youth who will be the adults living in, working in, and leading our communities—and our very libraries. These concepts bear repeating—and remembering.

That, in a nutshell, is what library youth participation is all about, and why it is so important to put it into practice.

ENDNOTES

1. Patricia B. Campbell, *Evaluating Youth Participation: A Guide for Program Operators* (New York: National Commission on Resources for Youth, 1982), ii–iii.

2. National Student Volunteer Program, *A Manual for Students: Volunteering* (Washington, DC: ACTION, 1971), 32.

3. National Student Volunteer Program, *Manual for Students*, 33.

4. Mark Batenburg and Denise Clark Pope, *The Evaluation Handbook: Practical Tools for Evaluating Service Learning Programs* (San Mateo, CA: Service Learning 2000 Center, 1997), 5–6.

5. National Student Volunteer Program, *Manual for Students*, 69.

6. Charles R. McClure, *Planning and Role Setting for Public Libraries: A Manual of Options and Procedures* (Chicago: American Library Association, 1987), 77.

7. McClure, *Planning and Role Setting*, 77–78.

8. McClure, *Planning and Role Setting*, 77–78.

9. Campbell, *Evaluating Youth Participation*, 10.

10. Batenburg and Pope, *Evaluation Handbook*, 6.

11. Renee Roberts, "Involving the Youth in the Local Library," *Young Adult Library Services* 3 (Spring 2005): 20–21.

12. Lisa Yosevitz, e-mail message to author, August 23, 2008.

13. Michael Casey and Michael Stephens, "The Transparent Library: Embracing Service to Teens," *Library Journal* 133 (May 15, 2008), www.libraryjournal.com/article/CA6556178.html (accessed September 21, 2009).

APPENDIX:
ORGANIZATIONS THAT FOSTER YOUTH PARTICIPATION

America's Promise—The Alliance for Youth
  909 N. Washington St., Suite 400
  Alexandria, VA 22314-1556
  703-684-4500
  www.americaspromise.org

American Library Association, American
Association of School Librarians (AASL)
  50 East Huron St.
  Chicago, IL 60611
  800-545-2433
  www.pla.org/ala/aasl/aaslindex.cfm

American Library Association, Young Adult
Library Services Association (YALSA)
  50 East Huron St.
  Chicago, IL 60611
  800-545-2433
  www.ala.org/ala/yalsa/yalsa.cfm

American Youth Policy Forum (AYPF)
  1836 Jefferson Place NW
  Washington, DC 20036
  202-775-9731
  www.aypf.org

At the Table: Innovation Center for
Community and Youth Development
  6930 Carroll Ave., Suite 502
  Takoma Park, MD 20912
  www.atthetable.org

Community Partnerships with Youth, Inc.
  6744 Falcon Ridge Court
  Indianapolis, IN 46278
  317-875-5756
  www.cpyinc.org

Energize, Inc.
  5450 Wissahickon Ave.
  Philadelphia, PA 19144
  215-438-8342
  www.energizeinc.com/index.html

Forum for Youth Investment
  7064 Eastern Ave., NW
  Washington, DC 20011
  202-207-3333
  www.forumfyi.org

The Freechild Project
  711 State Ave. East, 3rd Floor
  Olympia, WA 98506
  360-753-2686
  www.freechild.org/index.htm

Global PACT International
  12 Lenox Place
  Maplewood, NJ 07040
  732-579-8500
  www.globalpact.org/

Learn & Serve America: A Program of the Corporation for National and Community Service

1201 New York Ave., NW
Washington, DC 20525
202-606-5000
http://www.nationalservice.org/Default.asp

National Service-Learning Clearinghouse

ETR Associates
4 Carbonero Way
Scotts Valley, CA 95066
1-866-245-7378
831-438-4060
www.servicelearning.org

National Clearinghouse on Families & Youth

PO Box 13505
Silver Spring, MD 20911
301-608-8098
http://ncfy.acf.hhs.gov

National Collaboration for Youth

1319 F St., NW, Suite 402
Washington, DC 20004
1-877-NYDIC-4-U
www.connectforkids.org/node/3236

National Youth Development Information Center (NYDIC)

A Project of the National Collaboration for Youth
1319 F St., NW, Suite 402
Washington, DC 20004
Phone: (202) 347-2080
www.nydic.org

National Youth Leadership Center

1667 Snelling Ave. N, Suite D300
St. Paul, MN 55108
651-631-3672
www.nylc.org

Search Institute

The Banks Building
615 First Ave. NE, Suite 125
Minneapolis, MN 55413
612-376-8955
www.search-institute.org/

Youth Partnerships

United Nations Population Fund
220 East 42nd St.
New York, NY 10017
212-297-5000
www.unfpa.org/adolescents/initiatives.htm

Youth Activism Project

PO Box E
Kensington, MD 20895
1-800-KID-POWER
301-929-8808
www.youthactivism.com

Youth On Board

58 Day St.
Somerville, MD 02144
617-741-1242
www.youthonboard.org

Youth Service America

1101 15th St., Suite 200
Washington, DC 20005
202-296-2992
www.ysa.org

SELECTED BIBLIOGRAPHY

Alessio, Amy. *Excellence in Library Services for Young Adults.* 5th ed. Chicago: Young Adult Library Services Association, 2008.

Alessio, Amy J., and Kimberly A. Patton. *A Year of Programs for Teens.* Chicago: American Library Association, 2007.

Asis, Susan. "Types of Youth Participation Programs in Public Libraries: An Annotated Webliography." *Young Adult Library Services* 40 (Summer 2006): 26–30.

Batenburg, Mark, and Denise Clark Pope. *The Evaluation Handbook: Practical Tools for Evaluating Service Learning Programs.* San Mateo, CA: Service Learning 2000 Center, 1997.

Benson, Peter L. *All Kids Are Our Kids: What Communities Must Do to Raise Caring and Responsible Children and Adolescents.* 2nd ed. San Francisco: Jossey-Bass, 2006.

Bolan, Kimberly. *Teen Spaces: The Step-by-Step Library Makeover.* 2nd ed. Chicago: American Library Association, 2009.

Braun, Linda W. *Technically Involved: Technology-Based Youth Participation Activities for Your Library.* Chicago: American Library Association, 2003.

Brautigam, Patsy. "Developmental Assets and Libraries: Helping to Construct the Successful Teen." *Voice of Youth Advocates* 31 (June 2008): 124–25.

Campaign for America's Libraries. *Speaking Up for Library Services to Teens: A Guide to Advocacy.* Young Adult Library Services Association, 2007, www.ala.org/ala/mgrps/divs/yalsa/advocacy_final.pdf (accessed September 21, 2009).

Campbell, Patricia B. Evaluating *Youth Participation: A Guide for Program Operators.* New York: National Commission on Resources for Youth, 1982.

Carlson, Chris. "What's Happening with Programming on the Teacher Librarian Front." *Voice of Youth Advocates* 31 (April 2008): 32–33.

Checkoway, Barry N., and Lorraine M. Gutiérrez, eds. *Youth Participation and Community Change*. New York: Haworth, 2006.

Doyle, Miranda. *101+ Great Ideas for Teen Library Web Sites*. New York: Neal-Schuman, 2007.

Dresang, Eliza T., et al. *Dynamic Youth Services through Outcome-Based Planning and Evaluation*. Chicago: American Library Association, 2006.

Feinstein, Sheryl. "The Teenage Brain: Under Construction." *Voice of Youth Advocates* 31 (June 2008): 122–23.

Flores, Kim Sabo. *Youth Participatory Evaluation: Strategies for Engaging Young People*. San Francisco: Wiley, 2008.

Gillespie, Kellie. *Teen Volunteer Services in Libraries: A VOYA Guide*. Lanham, MD: Scarecrow, 2004.

Gnehm, Kurstin Finch, ed. *Youth Development and Public Libraries: Tools for Success*. Evanston, IL: Urban Libraries Council, 2002.

Hart, Roger. "Children's Participation: From Tokenism to Citizenship." Florence, Italy: UNICEF International Child Development Centre, 1992, www.unicef-irc.org/publications/pdf/childrens_participation.pdf (accessed January 5, 2009).

Henderson, Nan, ed. *Resiliency in Action: Practical Ideas for Overcoming Risks and Building Strengths*. Ojai, CA: Resiliency in Action, 2007.

Herald, Diane Tixier, and Diane P. Monnier. "The Beasts Have Arrived: The Blooming of Youth Participation in the Young Adult Library Services Association (YALSA)." *Voice of Youth Advocates* 30 (June 2007): 116–19.

Honnold, RoseMary. *Get Connected: Tech Programs for Teens*. New York: Neal-Schuman, 2007.

———. "Get Teens Active @ Your Library®!," *Young Adult Library Services* 4 (Summer 2006): 18–19.

Institute for Educational Leadership. *Some Things DO Make a Difference for Youth: A Compendium of Evaluations of Youth Programs and Practices*. Washington, DC: American Youth Policy Forum, 1997.

Institute of Museum and Library Services. *Nine to Nineteen: Youth in Museums and Libraries: A Practitioner's Guide*. IMLS Office of Policy, Planning, Research and Communications, April 2008, www.imls.gov/pdf/YouthGuide.pdf (accessed September 21, 2009).

Irby, Merita, et al. *Youth Action: Youth Participating in Communities, Communities Supporting Youth*. Community & Youth Development Series, Volume 6. Takoma Park, MD: The Forum for Youth Investment, International Youth Foundation, 2001, www.cpn.org/topics/youth/cyd/pdfs/Youth_Action.pdf (accessed September 21, 2009).

Jones, Jami. *The Power of the Media Specialist to Improve Academic Achievement and Strengthen At-Risk Students*. Columbus, OH: Linworth, 2007.

Jones, Patrick, Michele Gorman, and Tricia Suellentrop. *Connecting Young Adults and Libraries: A How-to-Do-It Manual*. 3rd ed. New York: Neal-Schuman, 2004.

Kaye, Cathryn Berger. *The Complete Guide to Service Learning: Proven, Practical Ways to Engage Students in Civic Responsibility, Academic Curriculum, and Social Action*. Minneapolis, MN: Free Spirit, 2004.

Kunzel, Bonnie, and Constance Hardesty. *The Teen-Centered Book Club: Readers into Leaders.* Westport, CT: Libraries Unlimited, 2006.

Lerch, Maureen T., and Janet Welch. *Serving Homeschooled Teens and Their Parents.* Westport, CT.: Libraries Unlimited, 2004.

Lerner, Richard M. *Liberty: Thriving and Civic Engagement Among America's Youth.* Thousand Oaks, CA: Sage Publications, 2004.

Lerner, Richard M., and Peter L. Benson, eds. *Developmental Assets and Asset-Building Communities.* New York: Kluwer Academic/Plenum Publishers, 2003.

Lesko, Wendy Schaetzel. *Youth Infusion: Intergenerational Advocacy Toolkit.* Kensington, MD: Activism 2000 Project, 2001.

Lesko, Wendy Schaetzel, and Emanuel Tsourounis II. *Youth! The 26% Solution.* Kensington, MD: Activism 2000 Project, 1998.

Macaluso, Judy. "We Empower Teens @ Ocean County Library." *Voice of Youth Advocates* 29 (August 2006): 214–18.

Martin, Shanetta, Karen Pittman, et al. *Building Effective Youth Councils: A Practical Guide to Engaging Youth in Policy Making.* Washington, DC: The Forum for Youth Investment, Impact Strategies, 2007, www.noys.org/Developing_Youth_Councils.pdf (accessed September 21, 2009).

McClure, Charles R. "Applying the Planning and Role Setting Process to Library Services for Young Adults." In *Planning and Role Setting for Public Libraries: A Manual of Options and Procedures*, 7–37. Chicago: American Library Association, 1987.

National Clearinghouse on Families & Youth. *Putting Positive Youth Participation into Practice: A Resource Guide.* Family and Youth Services Bureau, February 2007, ncfy.acf. hhs.gov/publications/pdf/PosYouthDevel.pdf (accessed September 21, 2009).

Neiburger, Eli, and Matt Gullett. "Out of the Basement: The Social Side of Gaming." *Young Adult Library Services* 5 (Winter 2007): 34–38.

Nichols, Mary Anne, and C. Allen Nichols. *Young Adults and Public Libraries: A Handbook of Materials and Services.* Westport, CT: Greenwood Press, 1998.

O'Dell, Katie. *Library Materials and Services for Teen Girls.* Westport, CT: Greenwood, 2002.

Payne, David A. *Evaluating Service-Learning Activities and Programs.* Lanham, MD: Scarecrow, 2000.

Pearson, Yvonne, Kristin Johnstad, and James Conway. *More Than Just a Place to Go: How Developmental Assets Can Strengthen Your Youth Program.* Minneapolis, MN: Search Institute, 2004.

Pierce, Jennifer Burek. *Sex, Brains, and Video Games: A Librarian's Guide to Teens in the Twenty-First Century.* Chicago: American Library Association, 2008.

Strauch, Barbara. *The Primal Teen: What the New Discoveries about the Teenage Brain Tell Us about Our Kids.* New York: Doubleday, 2003.

Tuccillo, Diane P. *Library Teen Advisory Groups: A VOYA Guide.* Lanham, MD: Scarecrow, 2005.

———. "Standing Room Only." *School Library Journal* 53 (March 2007): 46–48.

———. "Successful Teen Advisory Groups: Teen Driven . . . with Guidance and a Helping Hand." *Voice of Youth Advocates e-VOYA* (December 2005), pdfs.voya.com/VO/YA2/VOYA200512SuccessfulTeens.pdf (accessed September 17, 2009).

Vandermark, Sondra. "Using Teen Patrons As a Resource in Planning Young Adult Library Space in Public Libraries." In *Planning the Modern Public Library Building*, ed. Gerard B. McCabe and James Robert Kennedy. Westport, CT: Libraries Unlimited, 2003.

Walsh, David. *Why Do They Act That Way?: A Survival Guide to the Adolescent Brain for You and Your Teen.* New York: Free Press, 2004.

Walter, Virginia, and Natalie Cole. *Teens: The Community Service Solution.* Downey, CA: County of Los Angeles Public Library, 2000, www.colapublib.org/teen/Teen_Manual.pdf (accessed August 10, 2008).

Walter, Virginia A., and Elaine Meyers. *Teens & Libraries: Getting It Right.* Chicago: American Library Association, 2003.

Welch, Rollie James. *Guy-Friendly YA Library: Serving Male Teens.* Westport, CT: Libraries Unlimited, 2007.

Youth Voice Toolbox. The Freechild Project, 2008, www.freechild.org/YouthVoice/index.htm (accessed September 21, 2009).

INDEX

Note: Page numbers for flyers, posters, forms, and photographs are in *italics*.

ABOUT THE AUTHOR

Diane P. Tuccillo started working with teens as a high school English teacher and earned her MLS degree from Rutgers University in 1980. She was the Young Adult Coordinator at the City of Mesa Library in Arizona for almost 25 years, and is the author of *Library Teen Advisory Groups: A VOYA Guide* (2005).

Tuccillo is active in professional organizations at the local, state, and national levels, which includes serving as the 2005 ALAN President; has served on YALSA's 2005 Printz Award and the 2009 Morris Award committees; and has had continuous involvement in YALSA's Teens' Top Ten/YA Galley Project. She has done presentations and conducted workshops on books, reading, and especially youth participation in libraries. Tuccillo's articles and book reviews have been published extensively in professional journals, among them *Voice of Youth Advocates*, for which she serves on the editorial advisory board, and *School Library Journal*. In addition, she authors and edits "The Library Connection" column for *The ALAN Review*.

Tuccillo was the recipient of the first Rising Moon Outstanding Youth Services Librarian Award from the Arizona Library Association in 1998 and the winner of YALSA's 2004 Sagebrush Award for a notable program promoting teen literature. She has taught in-person and virtual library courses for several universities.

Currently, Tuccillo is Teen Services Librarian at the Harmony Library branch of the Poudre River Public Library District in Fort Collins, Colorado, where, among other great things, she is fortunate to work with an amazing group of teenagers who belong to the library's Interesting Reader Society.